MARXISM AND EDUCATION

This series assumes the on-going relevance of Marx's contributions to critical social analysis and aims to encourage continuation of the development of the legacy of Marxist traditions in and for education. The remit for the substantive focus of scholarship and analysis appearing in the series extends from the global to the local in relation to dynamics of capitalism and encompasses historical and contemporary developments in political economy of education as well as forms of critique and resistances to capitalist social relations. The series announces a new beginning and proceeds in a spirit of openness and dialogue within and between Marxism and education, and between Marxism and its various critics. The essential feature of the work of the series is that Marxism and Marxist frameworks are to be taken seriously, not as formulaic knowledge and unassailable methodology but critically, as inspirational resources for renewal of research and understanding, and as support for action in and upon structures and processes of education and their relations to society. The series is dedicated to the realization of positive human potentialities as education and thus, with Marx, to our education as educators.

Series Editor: *Anthony Green*

Renewing Dialogues in Marxism and Education: Openings
Edited by Anthony Green, Glenn Rikowski, and Helen Raduntz

Critical Race Theory and Education: A Marxist Response
Mike Cole

Revolutionizing Pedagogy: Education for Social Justice Within and Beyond Global Neo-Liberalism
Edited by Sheila Macrine, Peter McLaren, and Dave Hill

Marxism and Education beyond Identity: Sexuality and Schooling
Faith Agostinone-Wilson

Blair's Educational Legacy: Thirteen Years of New Labour
Edited by Anthony Green

Racism and Education in the U.K. and the U.S.: Towards a Socialist Alternative
Mike Cole

Marxism and Education: Renewing the Dialogue, Pedagogy, and Culture
Edited by Peter E. Jones

Educating from Marx: Race, Gender, and Learning
Edited by Shahrzad Mojab and Sara Carpenter

Education and the Reproduction of Capital: Neoliberal Knowledge and Counterstrategies
Edited by Ravi Kumar

Social Change and Education in Greece: A Study in Class Struggle Dynamics
Spyros Themelis

Education and Social Change in Latin America
Edited by Sara C. Motta and Mike Cole

Mass Education, Global, Capital, and the World: The Theoretical Lenses of István Mészáros and Immanuel Wallerstein
Tom G. Griffiths and Robert Imre

Mass Education, Global Capital, and the World

The Theoretical Lenses of István Mészáros and Immanuel Wallerstein

Tom G. Griffiths and Robert Imre

Mass Education, Global Capital, and the World
Copyright © Tom G. Griffiths and Robert Imre, 2013.

Softcover reprint of the hardcover 1st edition 2013 978-1-137-01481-8
All rights reserved.

First published in 2013 by
PALGRAVE MACMILLAN®
in the United States—a division of St. Martin's Press LLC,
175 Fifth Avenue, New York, NY 10010.

Where this book is distributed in the UK, Europe and the rest of the world, this is by Palgrave Macmillan, a division of Macmillan Publishers Limited, registered in England, company number 785998, of Houndmills, Basingstoke, Hampshire RG21 6XS.

Palgrave Macmillan is the global academic imprint of the above companies and has companies and representatives throughout the world.

Palgrave® and Macmillan® are registered trademarks in the United States, the United Kingdom, Europe and other countries.

ISBN 978-1-349-43693-4   ISBN 978-1-137-01482-5 (eBook)
DOI 10.1057/9781137014825

Library of Congress Cataloging-in-Publication Data is available from the Library of Congress.

A catalogue record of the book is available from the British Library.

Design by Newgen Knowledge Works (P) Ltd., Chennai, India.

First edition: December 2013

10 9 8 7 6 5 4 3 2 1

For two Williams: the memory of my father Bill and vitality of our son Guillermo

For Zsuzsa, Bibi and Rezi

Contents

Series Editor's Preface ix
Anthony Green

Acknowledgments xxix

Chapter 1
Wallerstein and Mészáros: Scholars for the
Twenty-First Century 1

Chapter 2
Wallerstein's World-Systems Analysis 11

Chapter 3
Mass Education and Human Capital in the
Capitalist World-System 41

Chapter 4
Educating Critical Citizens for an Alternative World-System 67

Chapter 5
Mass Labor: Reviving the Concept of Community and
Collectivity 99

Chapter 6
Work in the Post-Industrial World 119

Chapter 7
Global Capital: From the Polanyi Thesis to
World-Systems and beyond Capital 143

Chapter 8
Conclusion 159

Notes	167
Bibliography	171
Index	185

Series Editor's Preface

István Mészáros and Immanuel Wallerstein: Mass Education, Global Capital, and World-Systems Analysis

This volume is a first for the Marxism and Education Series in three distinct respects. One, its focus is specifically devoted to theoretical and methodological, abstractive, and analytical concerns rather than directly substantive descriptive contemporary and 'historical' aspects of and for critical practices. It is thus deliberately taking focused, abstracted overview and commentary as its agenda, though of course it provides many items of substantive reported analysis deployed to carry the knowledge in descriptive anchoring points.

Two, as a monograph, it focuses on the work of two contemporary 'Marxist' scholar activists, Immanuel Wallerstein and István Mészáros, and respective research movements, World Systems Theory, and Budapest School Humanist Marxism, which are not generally considered together, nor are they typically associated with problematics in radical education.

Three, in terms of recognizable objects in conventional education practices, the book is a kind of 'textbook.' Thus, while it does something quite original, the unique conjoining in reconsideration of the work of these eminent scholar activists, it does so as a practical *recontextualisation* to constitute an educational resource rather than as origination. Its aim is bringing these authors' work to the attention of a new potential readership. In this sense, the book is a device or pretext largely for initiation, scholarly reproductive ground-clearing prior to more creative production, rather than the scientific/critical/philosophical purposes of posing and *making new knowledge* by committed collaborative scholar activists.[1]

Overall, then, this work is self-consciously an "introduction," effectively formed as informative, for description and demonstration rather than for proposing a transformative synthesis through argument in its own right. Nevertheless, it is a text to be engaged with, constituted, and built anew in 'writerly' forms of creative engagement and developed from as an 'elementary', framing of some foundational elements of material practices.[2]

There is no denying that such elements have a variety of critical energy sources, not the least of which is realizing arguments indicative of meta-level resonances and methodological forms where there are massive issues at stake intimated at—as well as directly aired—here. The task of this preface is not to preempt the volume's specific *contents* but to highlight some of this book's *significant contexts* and thus locate it in relation to the series—recontextualizing the recontextualization, if you like.

Finally, where Marx wrote about education, his treatment was somewhat fragmentary; nevertheless it was actively constructivist and 'critical' with respect to pedagogy and institutionalized forms as well as providing intimations of future possibilities, as seen from his mid-nineteenth century contexts.[3] While he did not develop a theory of education, as such, nor is this at issue here, his work as general theory and methodology is the necessary pre-text in the context of practices.

The series intends to maintain the open-ended legacy of Marxism and the struggles for socialist transformation in non-sectarian mode, thereby constantly regenerating a radical 'educational' resource. The overarching theme is *pedagogy of critique* viewed through the organizing contexts of *recognizing ourselves in struggle*. It is useful to remind ourselves that this series is concerned with Marxism and education, not declaring definitive assessment on the work of Marx, nor addressing his writings or activist practices as if they could possibly contain the last word, or in idealist mode, the essentialist key or the secret of history. It is impossible to frame such final judgements, though searching for them in Marx and the Marxist traditions is inspirational practice indeed.

Marx's legacy is in providing tools in conceptual, theoretical, and modeling frameworks for transformative practices, scholarly activism in critical representation and direct material, highly contextualized engagement as contributions to progressive struggles in an emergent critical 'totality' in process. It is open in form, unfinished textuality to be re-made, extended in innumerable ways, and thereby demonstrating undogmatic methodological protocols requiring ever-active interpretation for 'application,' and references for action in our here and now.

Marx, as reported by Engels, appears to have used the famously intriguing remark, "I am not a Marxist," opening extensive possibilities for Marx-*ism* as an organic movement of critical practice to be made and remade in action, simultaneously including various symbolic and rhetorical forms, as it has been, of course for good and ill, since the mid-nineteenth century[4] (6). Dogmatism is out of the question; pursuing and practicing Marxism as *education in and through contingent and contextualized struggle is the ever-renewing order of any day*. As Huxley put it,

> If we are to achieve progress, we must learn to uncrystalize our dogmas (1947). In full form, this is realism and demands that dialectics is our fate, the human condition for irresolvable final resolution to the conundrum of uncertainty, questioning everything but sustained with open materialist expectation of progress.

There are four framing elements: (1) Educating the educators, (2) Interesting times, or the present conjuncture, (3) Articulating historical materialism in/as critical realist practices, (4) What is to be done in the face of neo-liberal strategies of class struggle from above? Each of these contexts can only be addressed superficially, suggesting some pertinent themes to stimulate analysis which may be critical of and, more ambitiously, possibly critical to progressive practices in relation to the intriguing textual resources that follow in Tom Griffiths and Rob Imre's presentation.

As will become clear, I draw liberally upon some of the methodological themes in *critical realism*. Roy Bhaskar's work, which has now become *dialectical critical realism*, was emergent in major part through his engagement with Marx and Marxism and has influenced my perspectives and appreciation of the historical materialism and the struggle for democratic socialism since the early 1980s.[5]

Educating the Educators

This theme is time-honored for well over 150 years, productively constituting Marxism *on* education, and dialectically instantiating Marxism *as* education, and even longer still, given that Marx's originating formulation is responding as much to Plato as to Feuerbach.

Thus, Marx announced the provocative Third Thesis on Feuerbach (Marx:1845):

> The materialist doctrine concerning the changing of circumstances and upbringing forgets that men change circumstances and that it is essential to *educate the educator* himself. This doctrine must, therefore, divide society into two parts, one of which is superior to society. The coincidence of the changing of circumstances and of human activity or self-changing can be conceived and rationally understood only as *revolutionary practice*. [Emphasis added]

What Marx is getting at here—and it is the life-source of the Marxism and Education Series—is that no one will be educating the educators, other than the educators themselves, namely *our*-selves in the contexts of struggling for radical progressive transformation of all levels of social reality. Revolutionary dialectics necessitate self-discovery, in and for itself, in transformative social movement and collective practices of mass action. Objectivity and subjectivity flowing in mutuality of practices located within constraining conditions, circumstances to be changed by working *within*, *with*, and *against* the very circumstances into which we are thrown. Transcending extant social forms, addressing the circumstances and pre-requisites of struggle, inevitably involves changing ourselves as a part of the circumstances of our social relations if we are to identify and make analytical topics of the structural conditions for those struggles, patterns of constraints as well as opportunities for movement. However this complex consideration may be interpreted and actively adopted in practice, it entails identity in individuality and most importantly in forming social collectivity in commonality, and, dialectically, as both topics and resources of, in, and for these struggles.

'I' and 'we' are both problematic and necessarily part of the circumstances, and indeed, we are *always already* in struggle: the shimmering dialectics as critical practices of restraint, renewal, and vitality. Deploying metaphorical assistance of conventional educational terminology for critically alternative conceptions and practices for the moment, we can mark the agenda of boundaries for transgression in varieties of socio-historical curriculum, pedagogy, and/or andragogy,[6] constituting necessary conditions for radical assessment, 'certification' and 'credentialization,' awarding ourselves 'grades,' namely social recognition of our *knowing what we know*. That is to say, at stake here is assessing reflexively in practices of our claims to knowledge of *where, what*, and *who* we are within critical awareness of our historical conditions of existence. Progressively, this refers to the fitness of that *knowing* for conditional practices that are intended to be both materially effective, as well as *doing* 'good' on the open horizon of humanity's materiality of time/space possibilities. Thus, knowing *what our doing does*, and *what our knowing knows* are issues already high on the agenda for coming to terms with the constitutive *depth* and *multi-dimensional layering* of social reality and our practices of understanding and representing social reality while actively participating in and partially constituting it.

These considerations are vital to constituting social critique. Thus, zooming in for a moment in potential radical *situationist* activist mode:[7] the slogan "Eat the rich" is a useful "educative" text for seriously playful practice which provokes possibilities of critical pedagogy at every level (including moral, ethical, political, economic, aesthetic, etc.) in relation to production, consumption, and forming identity in relation to negativities, *things to be put right* in our present conditions of existence. As 'educative' inquiry, then: *How* do we cook them? *How* do we eat them? *What sauces might we embellish them with*? *How* do we combine to forge the appropriate culinary tools for preparing the rich for our feast? And, tellingly as a reflexive pedagogic tool, therefore, *Who* exactly are 'the rich'? This could be important when we identify them while foraging in and/or cultivating our improving eco-system, especially if we pose the obvious mirror question: *Are we the rich*?

As practical *conscientization*, this echoes and extends Freirian normative work, and with Gramsci, potentially counter-hegemonic organic intellectual labor for critical pedagogy, not simply as abstracted 'science' or 'philosophy,' but practical epistemology necessitating complex reflexivity to address human *being in objectivity, subjectivity, and uncertainty*.

Foundations are to be made and shifted in the making. This is practical *ontology*, too, constituting the *real* while instantiating it in *being of the totality of practices*, realizing pedagogy of critique. It is transitive *life-world* work in social phenomenological terms, as well.[8] Delicately pulling the stray thread for the productive problematic, *Who are the rich*? as it manifests itself in our 'experiences,' is potentially productive to our understanding systems of social relations, materials for immanent critiquing constraints in systematicity that are constitutive of potentially radical knowledge, and realizing critical appreciation from within our systems of social relations. Such analysis frames our powers and capacities, while recognizing responsibility for our 'selves' *within* and *without*, the vast arrays of properties of structured and structuring social relations operating in social 'depth.'

In other words, the problem is 'educational,' autodidactically addressing *systems* of social relations as patterned in chaotic moments of complex emergence taking *form* and thereby congealing, consolidating as potential 'fact' in structuration for *alienation* to be overcome. It constitutes dialectics of *reification*, too, as processual and patterned in reproductive negativities of objectification in both critical reality of social phenomenology of/in 'experience' and with respect to emergent opportunities in 'constraining' realities. Alternatively put, this is about identifying social facts with potential for emancipation, for making communities, not commodities.

Interesting Times

So far as Marxism is concerned, capitalism is the ever-present generative source of its own invention, its renewable topic for state policy formation, and its ever-present critical resource, the life blood for practices of resistance, opposition, and radical mobilization. Thus, so long as there is capitalism, there will be Marxism: analyzing, describing, and generating critique in the face of political economy's immanent capacity for structural crisis and self-crippling injustices and irrationality—constraints on the development of ingenuity for humane possibilities for realizing good and beautiful social forms.

In these terms, the present crisis is systemic in contradictory forms and as deeply, if not more deeply, penetrating mass society in 'modernity' than any in living memory, certainly since the 1930s. While this situation is even more sharply reinforcing the already existing social inequalities locally, regionally, nationally, and globally, it constitutes in Marxist terms a form of the already structural necessity of 'class war from above' on behalf of corporate capital, to realize global plutocratic hegemony. Among many forms, this is conducted through 'civilized' and 'civilizing' practices of effectively blaming the victims. The dominant system of social relations in production of creditable value thus socially constitutes the systemic 'losers,' the 'downsiders,' by expropriating their individual and collective value, realizing multiple modes of differentiation for alienation to reinforce economic powers of appropriation top-down and thereby increasing the potential for their exploitation as commodified individual and collective human energy; this is done, moreover, with the 'upsiders' acquiescence constituted in the well-formed, educated 'majority.'

Dominant modes of government present the current crisis situation as a temporary 'technical'problem of adjustments to *system imbalance*. The Marxist critical response is to explain it as the chronic immanent characteristic of the system of social relations, rendering the capital's own technical vocabulary into an ideology of irrational domination that is stratifying moral and ethical responsibilities in a meta-vocabulary of fatality, TINA ("there is no alternative"), current austerity, and sharpening social inequalities. Thus, 'Stay calm, the recession is only temporary,' is the 'expert' elite assessment. In the meantime, a generation of millions of citizens—potential labor power in capitalist mode—remains outside its conventions of productive commodified potential to produce and is displaced into non-existence, rendered redundant while the degradation of the global eco-system is only slightly slowed, if at all, by this very downturn in industrial production and domestic consumption.

The system is not only in technical imbalance but teetering on the edge of financial and democratic institutional disarticulation and collapse. Global plutocracy is thus emergent in contradiction, as ever more deeply consolidating class *for and in itself*, capitalizing further on financial and economic shock (Klein: 2007) while separate and separating in accumulation of unearned, unaccountable credit, reinvigorating financial capitalization for its empowerment through privatizing the historically emergent global commons.

What then is at stake here? The hegemonic rhetorical forms currently seem to suggest that socialism for the rich requires capitalism for the rest in order to ensure everyone's freedom against the threat of a variety of potential barbarisms. The magical multi-dynamic paraphernalia of fetishistic powers gripping tightly in greed and fear of loss of control instantiates and holds to account liberal rationalizations of 'freedoms' on the one hand, and benign necessity of 'lesser' evils—the fatalist pragmatics of utilitarian satisfaction in 'This is as good as it can be'—on the other. This is so, not least while the dominant system self-presents, too, as practicing the possibility of just selection by 'merit' as the realistic condition of liberty and liberalism's promise for modernity, namely institutionalizing 'education' as *the* functional allocation system articulating spheres of *reproduction* in connecting 'family' forms and the spheres of economic *production*.

All of this is in play while inequalities of income and wealth are clearly increasing at all levels, nationally and internationally. The keystones of Marxism are in demonstrating how this operates systematically, both as transitive cultural forms and as material realities. It does so through *immanent structural* critique complementary to *ideology critique*,⁹ thus undoing the very frames in language and culture, the rhetorics and representational tropes of systemic 'capital,' empowerment, and the critique of political economy. As ideology critique, it aims to expose the lies of liberalism, showing genesis and effects of real structures of opportunities to 'freely choose' repressive self control, for instance, or by identifying acquiescence in the face of alternative indignation and resistance at the deepening and spread of precarity. Thus, we demonstrate how liberal socio-cultural mechanisms of control are effectively deployed in alluring promises of modernizing material hope, and democracy through spreading wealth as opportunities for 'more.'

Pedagogy of critique aims to put to the test social relations of state and civil society—the political forms, relations in production and economy as critique of political economy, and necessarily critical reflexivity in empowering/disempowering cultural forms for mobilizing alternative progressive powers. Today's class exercise, then: Tell all this to the many and various people and practices on the streets across Brazil or Egypt…or to the 'beneficiaries' of new illegal migrant legislation/tightening borders for US sovereignty[10] and so on, by listening in solidarity to their own pedagogic protocols, teaching and learning in action.

Dear reader, when you engage with this text, you will, of course, have far more to consider as curriculum items in topicality for critical social movement in your own *here and now* than when these words were written in July 2013. Such are some of the vagaries of radical critical praxis mediated through corporate publishing in contemporary hard copy book form!

In these 'interesting times,' critical analysis means to work with and through the problematics that recognize positive social change cannot be done 'from above' because upside/downside is itself the material time/space constituting the distributional dividing line of struggle in society; the progressive anti-capital will-to-power is a stratified problematic which must be addressed and is necessarily at stake to be understood *at*, and connected *to* each 'level' of the social. Moreover, this calls for generative collective auto-didacticism from below of a very intensive, very high, and fully grounded order. This work is itself, as meta-work in struggle, part of the very fabric of that struggle which divides society into these 'two parts': *educators* and the *to-be-educated* by demonstrating what lies behind and below the constitutive surfaces of the dominant life-world.

It is dialectical work, too, as will be suggested next in a little more detail, for activist- educating the educators requires shifting the above/below 'line,' while demonstrating from below what the line is and showing its inhuman/inhumane effects and inevitable irrationality for both oppressors and oppressed. The targets are structures of oppression, generalizing commodification of everything in and through structures of ownership, distribution, and exchange-as-capitalization and the repressive illiberal consequences of 'liberal' practices.

Historical Materialism in/as Critical Realist Practices

Rousseau (1762) remarks in *The Social Contract* " Every time I see a mansion being built in the capital, I fancy I can see the whole countryside covered with hovels," and while prefiguring so much—from the French Revolution through to urban and rural transformation into the twenty-first century—we might even more broadly acknowledge that dialectical interconnectedness and complex causalities abound in social reality; furthermore, there are innumerable empirical routes to radical political economy directly and indirectly associated with 'education.' For instance, through the scrutiny of urban gentrification and urban/rural relational structures, or its detailed specifications of current school/university building and funding programs, both in context of education and social class formation, and so on, with endless critical possibilities. What we 'see,' immersed in our life-world 'data' of what we "experience," is always a possible pretext for practicing depth ontology: self-critical practices for constructing system-critical representational work while articulating an alternatively expansive critical epistemology. It involves re-seeing in articulation with 'depth' across several dimensions concerning what is systematic in *emergence*, and *structural* to our social relations as patterns of opportunities and constraints. This is both social and/or 'material' and itself 'thrown,' in existentialist terminology, in relation to transitive forms, that is, prior representations.[11] The keynote legacy of Enlightenment scientific and ethical thinking for Marxism and its own productive legacies are in methodological realism, and in openness and tireless rigour. This is also so in alliance with existential uncertainty and an anti-authoritarian commitment to refusing either swift resorting to any specific 'authority,' or to imposed 'consensus' for viable factuality.

This is all to be realized in open practices and ongoing benefits of empirical analysis, always intransigently opposed to empiricist and idealist methodologies.[12] Beliefs, that is, the unquestionable, are methodologically irrelevant. As assumptions, however, they are of course important to recognize in conducting empirical research, and are to be identified, described, and made ever-dialogically open to revision in the light of the community of empirical science practices. Science, art, and life-world are thus in continuous moral and ethical renewal, restless in normative productive critique.

In these terms, the central object for Marxism and education is the capitalist mode of production and its transformative potential to be recognized as *real*, not in existence because it is imagined to be so as constituted in 'experience.' It is complex and multiform *as real*. It can only be represented in abstracted form because the historically extant 'now' is far more complex than the historical case studies any critical investigator is forced to construct in disciplined investigative imagination, as Marx knew only too well in his historical, let alone his journalistic, outputs. It is constituted in descriptive modeling to reassemble and thus *resemble* 'reality' more or less accurately as trends, at best, and in empirical detail as complex partial 'case-study' wholes, including fuzziness with respect to boundaries of relative autonomy of elements in the contextualizing totality of one or other of the constituent parts.

Analytical autonomy is rendered problematic, not misrecognized as a methodological absolute, and such relativity is generally the main topic of investigation to the extent that the inquiries are concerned with emergent systems in patterns of constraining relations. It can have many specifications that are never absolutely settled as truth in positive knowledge of relational forms and mechanisms.

So, autonomy is not relative to the knowledge forms of its representational media but requires maintaining constant openness and criticality about forms of measurement and representational procedures for understanding relational forms *as* and *of* the real. This scientific and communicative ethic is vital to providing meta-forms (background considerations) for Marxism as historical materialist practices in realist critical knowledge modes, not the least of which is educating the educators, for instance.

With realism,[13] we recognize that what we know is always attempting to address 'objects' different from and not true by virtue of being logically constituted in our ways of knowing them, the epistemological fallacy of relativism. That is to say, as openly dialogical work, such investigative practices are about focusing on things other than simply recycling themselves in thought, hypostatized in logical forms of representation. There are always issues, questions, puzzles, and uncertainties to energize the domain of knowledge as empirical science even, or perhaps especially so, at the levels by which they approach cosmology and paradoxes in abstracted theory of everything. Perfect knowledge is impossible from the intimate to the infinite.

However—and here is the rub, for so much that is central to this way of practicing knowledge production as critical realism in historical materialist mode[14] reality is bi-modal—it has both intransitive and transitive forms and dimensions. It is constituted, too, in *both/and*, not just *either/or* in this respect. Thus, synthesis requires analysis, and analysis requires synthesis. Reality of social and cultural forms is at any moment of time/place identifiable forms, any historical nodal point, an emergent of objectivity in subjectivity, and subjective appropriation of the objective, subjective objectification.

The transitive real is the emergent life-world of cultural discursive forms, and is 'real' in that it is instantiated in the social mind, with an infinite collection of nodal 'individual' variants (both personal and collective) in historical practices mediated in language, and its ontological prerequisite for epistemology as *real* cultural practices. This, in turn, is what makes for the possibility of productive 'scientific' communication through *questioning everything*, rigorous 'testing' of both assumptions and 'observations' in a public or 'commons' of critical practices. There are no 'foundations.'

This is also what makes for the possibility of critical 'artistic' communications in realism too, and the ever problematic traversing of the boundaries between these, apparently 'alternative' practical lifeworlds.[15] As *commons* in this context, language forms are at best always available to address both 'sides,' and there is both the possibility of repair as well as re-jigging by openly introducing 'novel' assumptions or recontextualization to create critical moments for inquiry and potential explanation.[16]

Clearly, the latter model of knowledge practices is an abstracted 'idealization' and the reality of scientific practices, especially where they relate to power, policy and material support for their own conditions of existence, as well as competitive career-making, can and do fall short for much of these practices. Bias is thus an ever-present possibility. And most importantly *differends*—irresolvable moments in the boundaries which are at stake—can occur, constituting irreconcilable explanatory modes applicable to the 'same' information as it is recast as data in alternative analyses (Lyotard: 1988).

Importantly too, in *artistic practices* of modernity and engaging with borders to be crossed as pedagogy of critique, *ambiguity* and ambivalence are the stock-in-trade in modes of *critical realism* as forms of explanatory 'description' and potentially capturing senses of the *real-as-surreal*. They 'capitalize,' too, as educative practices, on the already known of the becoming-educated, making forms of pedagogy never simply 'transmission,' but always dialoguing and opening, however apparently closed the contexts and direction of transmission between 'teacher' and 'pupil.'

Thus it is only *apparently* paradoxical in critical materialist terms that the educator always has to be educated by the novice in order to do educating, and on the other hand, 'teachers' already know more than they suspect they know and also 'learn' so much in the process of "teaching' about what they 'know.' This is especially so when it comes to 'education' in collective, indeed in 'mass' contexts, too, in and for progressive social movements where *leadership* is an ever-present critical democratic focus of attention, a resource ever-problematic in individual and collective terms.

What becomes of 'experience' is recognized within the construction of collectivities based on wider causal processes but cannot reliably do a closing theory of history, because human action is always possible to generate disruptive alternatives to any specific nodal system based on relatively accurate reflexive analysis of structures. However, this can never be achieved with total accuracy. Reliability and validity in knowledge is always at risk of falling under the more or less decisive influence of major unknowns both in the inaccuracy of there being unknown unknowns, and in contingencies in the dynamics of unforeseeable emergent structures.

The point of analytical Marxist games theory, for instance, is that where it tries to deal with the 'social,' it tends to obscurantism by depiction of paradoxical impossibilities of resolution or into banalities of common senses, and more generally as it has only a narrow space of applicability which is abstracted and 'experimentally' unreal in itself. This is emergent on its forms of methodological individualism, not so different from the possessive individualism of neo-classical economic theory, trading an a-historicism for an anti-historicism.

On this account, critical materialist work defends an emergentist methodology[17] that can be best expressed by taking seriously the idiomatic 'common sense' that the 'whole is greater than the sum of its parts' in dialog with representations which often make it difficult to 'see the wood for the trees.' For radical pedagogy of social critique then, dialogical closure for critical mobilization is likely to be chronically postponed and disrupted, frequently disrupted, too, by emergent sectarian splitting.

The purpose of such methodological theorizing as productive meta-theory,is to generate an analytical tool set by which we understand the duality of agency and structure. As the argument goes, people interact to create social structures that are then irreducible to the individuals involved; that is, *social structures are the emergent products of human interaction* and vice versa. The objective in empirical praxis for this approach is to demonstrate that the maxim is honored in *productive critical work* rather than obfuscation in *disguised circularity*, reproducing but not 'resolving' the problem, though very possibly doing so in intriguing and engaging ways. The aim must be shifting into explanatory power by progressively moving beyond circularity and restatement of the problematic.

The prize in knowledge is in an effective argument and explanatory description to show the plausible direction of causal processes and describe the mechanism(s) in play *whereby the structures move*. Put in other, more lyrical, terms derived from Marx for this occasion, it is about *composing the music by which the circumstances will dance to their own tune*.[18]

The critical conditions of our own transitivity are rarely simply chosen in full 'awareness' when making 'new' knowledge because in critical praxis we are always already within that which we *want* to change, and that which we *need* to change is always already within us. As dialectics, this is to be worked out at many 'levels' to be addressed in ever more realistically complex fashion, indeed across multiple dimensions of the real as our emergent history of making and being made. Thus, human beings make history but not in conditions of their own making (Marx:1852), that is, dialectics of methodological dualism underpins explanatory work accounting for duality of specific historical structures in structuration.[19] The latter cannot 'reduce' social reality to experience, or intentionality, but it is contingent on emergent properties in both directions in and through collective and individual practices.

Herein lies both challenge and support for aspects of Humanist Marxism, for instance, accepting the ethical irreducibility of the human individual, but thereby notably opening up to liberal sensibilities, while accepting that structuration disrupts this, too. Moreover, the *topic* for policy, morality, and ethics, as well as *the necessary knowledge resource* for generating really useful knowledge, requires maintaining in focus 'educating the educators' here, our meta-theoretical resource as praxis in pedagogy of critique.

Human practices are never 'free' in any absolute terms; the freedom of the will to act is both individually and collectively constrained. Thus, such circumstances provide both topics and resources for normative science *and* ethics. Actions are always about praxis, always dynamic, always in struggle, and always uncertain of outcomes. This is so because perfectly consensual 'democracy' is impossible though an effectively energizing myth, and perfectly totalitarian dictatorship is also virtually impossible across any time/space though a recycled founding myth of 'democratic' alternatives. Complex forms of these 'realities' tend to involve middle ranges of conventionally majoritarian liberal democratic/social democratic socio-political theory and methodology though polarization is ever possible, as is evident in the present conjuncture, especially of the authoritarian racist and neo-fascist politics on the move, and in dehumanizing bureaucratic alienated practices always possible in the regulation and distribution of 'services' and 'rights,' too. Our job is to realize this in the struggle for socialism.

These methodological considerations are background, vital for generating 'data' for critical research and formulating activist policy, and inevitably throw up dilemmas and issues for self-educating pedagogy of critique for radical movements. Occupy, for instance, with its democratic, 'anarchist' consensualism, tends to hamper its own collective organization and strength in 'movement.'

A concomitant theme is that, as with much of neo-Marxism, this kind of theorizing challenges unitary 'workerist' models of class formation for generating real power in production relations, and is thus highly problematic for socialist movement where trade unions are weakened by state forms, legislation for labor regulation, underpinning continuing, etc. If this is elevated into an alternative socialist philosophical ethics, such as by abstracting Rawls' second principle alone, it is likely to be self-defeating, too.[20]

The point is to be realistic and critical, and to recognize immense complexity while acknowledging that capital is continuing in the ascendant now and looking very likely to continue to do so for in our present foreseeable future. The struggle is not reducible to ethics, as such, though without ethical and moral energy, it is without purpose or direction; it is *hope*-less, too. Such themes indicate primary, if ambiguous, strength of ethical aspects of humanist Marxism, perhaps, along with its capacity for embracing complexity and historical specificity of the here and now complementing agnosticism on class essentiality in struggle.

What Is to Be Done?

Classically to quote Marx conjoining immanent and ideology critique (Marx: 1967) for 'class' struggles, capital is *thing-like* and is 'objective,' but it is not simply that. It is necessary therefore to approach capital as "a definite social relation between men, that assumes, in their eyes, the fantastic form of a relation between things." The 'thing'-like and the 'fantastical' appearances are of constant importance in the life-world of radical practices and require investigation to be articulated through both deconstructive and complementary empirical research practices for the politics of remaking the life-world of materialist critiques. This continues to be pertinent and effectively problematic in articulating world-systems and in humanist Marxist senses, and, most significantly here, in generating practical knowledge for acting on their progressive relations. Such themes stand as the central motifs, pretexts for this text concerning *What is to be done?* and for reflexive re-contextualization for generalizing progressive practice of possible democratic socialism, realizing progressive post-capitalist relations of social production and reproduction.

This is always already normative work, too, and is so because alienation cuts in both directions, reifying while it fetishizes in property relations, turning social relational forms into one meaning, a thing to be owned by an individual (both personal and corporative) into another 'thing,' a characteristic essentially constitutive of the individual as virtual property, or as a *non-thing* reflective of the endless potentiality for the global human condition of negativity in capital. Or have bourgeois social forms of state/civil society progressively moved on, defanging the menaces of the market into restrainable, regulable entities to realize benign powers of state capitalism, or indeed, of possibilities for the 'market of socialism'?

Educating the educators maintains a critical focus on these issues in the popular transformative curriculum for socialism, methodologically most especially so in contra-empiricist depth ontology in critical pedagogy for ongoingly realizing the opportunities and constraints in that baseline social agenda, our pre-figurative objectification of the patterns of social relations for reproducing our social relations, as de-reified entities. These may be represented in critique, exposing the 'hidden' depths, mechanisms of repression lurking below surfaces to be explained and realized in the critical practices for exposing such dis/empowerments.

The teacherly labor processes invoked are of course dialectical, too, in social and cultural contexts, and dialogical in ethical forms of recognizing both 'expertise' and capacity in rational good sense, while renewing senses of ever-open questioning of any authority's potential for congealing possibilities in misrecognizing 'isms' and fallibilities in its practices. These practices constitute irreducible methods of truths, dogma for our fate in rote learning for repressive political economy ever displaced from expressing critique.

Finally, broad 'lessons' for the practical educative issues in *What is to be done?* can only be recognized in reflexive practices with respect to identifying progressive historical outcomes. Alternative conditions of possibility are almost always available to address the expression of human needs, to reverse fatalism in acquiescence or submission to direct force in master/slave relations. These are potentialities recognizable as absences, for instance in species of necessary invisibility sliding across the points of tension in *being and nothingness*, and in the *solitudes*,[21] all as yet to be critically *realized as expressions of critique in thought, words and actions*. Art, philosophy, and science are all potentially available in combination, as for instance (amongst innumerable other personalities and genres), in the work of Sartre and Garcia-Marquez indicated here and above.

By Way of Summary and Conclusion

This book provides innumerable vital topics, resources in activist scholarship, and pointers to potentially mapping practical routes for transcending neo-liberal hegemony in relation to addressing theory and practices of class in Marxism (as well as in Marx, where much remained open for his never-to-be-completed future consideration); the ever-rejuvenating debates concerning variable political practices around *social democracy versus socialism*; identifying the routes to possible democratic communist social relations *on a mass scale*; addressing what can be learned from history so far, *if anything*; radically renewing around anarchism and the primacy of political forms, namely, the 'problem' of state powers and routes for socialism following the 'demise' of twentieth century 'Marxist' regimes in Eastern Europe and the USSR; considering current enthusiasm for Latin America's "pink tide"[22] in relation to world systems and humanist Marxist analyses and their possible rearticulations; learning lessons for the real and realistic sources of non-violent democratic powers in the context of apparent contradictions between democracy and economy, especially in the face of technical versus democratic state 'solutions' to both capitalism's deep crises (the austerity salvation) and the inhumanity of reified categorizing of human individuals apparent to humanist Marxism strictures realized in so-far-existing socialisms. Moreover, how can progressive actions be achieved without lapsing into abstractive methodological individualism in either direction, namely repeating history as tragedy or possibly as farce in the absence of a viable Fifth International?[23]

The histories of twentieth century socialisms provide much to ponder. Overall, taking forward the complex potentials in social and historical emergence in openness constitutes a challenging agenda, given the present fragility of radical leftism. The tools we have are the here and now, our life-worlds of social mind—transitive while institutionalized in 'common sense ,' and in multi-layered cultural forms of the habits of practice in joy, frustration, anger, and terror, too, as understanding and energizing creativity in cooperation and respect for individuation while glimpsing their emergence in historical time/place contingencies.

Systemic totality is ever more evident. In the Marxist 'traditional' legacy for radical praxis, capitalism and its state forms must wither, and the problems of democratic socialism en route to communism must emerge and become 'superior' in new forms of social relations of production, distribution, and exchanges and require taking on all the problems consequent of these new social forms for progressive practices in formation.

In summary then, this preface has suggested a wide and loosely integrated collection of issues, any or all of which complement and contextualize the themes of this book for the Marxism and Education Series and perhaps provide an epistemological agenda, plus realist ontological methodological pointers. The normative ethics of "From each according to their abilities, to each according to their needs" and its companion in dialectical mode, "The well-being of the one necessitates and requires the well-being of all," in combination articulate individuality in collectivity *across* and *within* social and economic production and its relations with distribution of credits and benefits. In these respects, the problematic *real* of social reality is 'fundamentally' relational, too, as emergent and constituted in depth, as layered structures, each 'layer' itself structured in depth as well (in the processes of its emergence in its contexts of being) at any particular stratum or perhaps more appropriately, specific dimension in multi-dimensional time/spaces of humanized nature.

So this book is a context for questioning, grounding reflexivity, and posing issues in dialoguing and action for progress. It is not a resource for locating certainty, nor authority in narrative direction and destination, nor should it be. Its generative value arises to the extent it is open, while seriously and responsibly groping agnostically in these terms so far as 'destiny' is concerned. All this is vital work and necessary contributions to the popular 'university' of good sense for generating and mobilizing topics and resources for Marxist pedagogy of critique.

In holistic terms, this educational resource is everywhere and in everything, therefore potentially available in the ongoing universal instantiation of progressive educational 'spirit.' As Marx famously put it, "Philosophers have contemplated the world, the point however is to change it" (Marx: 1845). In this context, massive expansions in modern communications technology provide opportunities in all manner of web sites, the blogosphere, social media, numerous Marxist universities, and endless free-access on-line journals, etc. But most especially there are the ever-renewed sites of economic struggles in production, on the streets and in the fields, forests, plains, and jungles as well as endless real and virtual times and places to be 'occupied' and redefined as circumstances for instantiating critique and transformative making of our times and places, humanizing nature.

Thus, while new communications technologies provide extraordinary opportunities for democratization through progressive exposure, as does whistle-blowing, they are also sites of surveillance, of course, enabling and repairing repressive state capitalist forms on both national and emergent global scales. These are contexts and contents for the arts and sciences of demonstrating tensions in commodification, alienation, and control, contradictions and potentials for progressive transformation, and transcendence, if not the transcendental. All this stands progressively in contradistinction to reified theory of inevitability in historical direction, congealing hope into technicist immobilizing complacency, and blunting critical reflexivity. Capitalism itself continuously provides contexts of renewal for such creative destruction, which must include itself in thought and action, too.

As with every manuscript, indeed any educative moment, this book is a rich'menu-script'; and in line with the spirit of the Marxism and Education Series, provides numerous contexts for educating the educators, and a vehicle to do so in addressing the widest of possible horizons. It is a valuable contribution and model for future secondary and tertiary critical scholarship to play its effective part for the Marxism and Education Series in relation to the task of articulating reconsiderations of Marxism in contemporary struggles for twenty-first century democratic socialism.

Let's allow Marx and Engels some last regenerative words for our reconsideration as they reflected on their lifetimes in struggle:

> So far as we are concerned, after our whole past only one way is open to us. For nearly 40 years we have raised to prominence the idea of

the class struggle as the immediate driving force of history, and particularly the class struggle between bourgeois and the proletariat as the great lever of the modern social revolution; hence, we can hardly go along with people who want to strike this class struggle from the movement. At the founding of the International, we expressly formulated the battle cry: The emancipation of the working class must be the work of the working class itself. (Marx and Engels: 1879)

...for their 'moment,' and for ours, too.

ANTHONY GREEN, July 2013

Acknowledgments

There are always too many people who sit behind an endeavor like this to acknowledge, so we begin with an open-ended acknowledgement to all involved in the ideas, the thinking, and the reading and debates that directly and indirectly brought us to this point.

As one of the authors, I, Tom Griffiths, am indebted to colleagues in the CIEGUN (Comparative and International Education Group University of Newcastle) writing group who responded to drafts of a couple of chapters, and to our Faculty of Education and Arts for its Research Programme scheme which has supported CIEGUN's work, and which provided a fellowship to free some time to work on this project.

I must of course acknowledge the impact of Wallerstein's work on my own teaching, research, and activism, dating back to my doctoral study of Cuba's revolutionary education from a world-systems perspective that began almost twenty years ago. As is apparent in this volume, this incisive analysis continues to inspire and excite this politically engaged academic. I would also like to acknowledge the love (and patience) of my compañera Euridice, with whom I sat on a *La Habana* beach reading *The Agonies of Liberalism: What Hope Progress?* among other essays, a long time ago, and who has endured my obsession with world-systems analysis ever since. And Guillermo, the great light of our life, the hopes and dreams of a better world contained here are for you, and for us together, now and in the interesting times ahead of us.

Chapter 1

Wallerstein and Mészáros: Scholars for the Twenty-First Century

That the world confronts a series of contemporary crises—whether focused in the political, social, cultural, or economic realms—is surely a given. Žižek (2010, 86–87) has suggested that we have moved into a situation of "permanent economic emergency" that is becoming "a constant, a way of life" with the ever-present threat of "far more savage austerity measures, cuts in benefits, diminishing health and education services and more precarious employment." Perhaps this has always been the case, or at least it has been the case for decades or centuries, depending on the criteria used to make such characterisations.

Similarly we see a wide, and seemingly endless, array of responses to these global crises. At the time of writing, these include mass mobilizations and protests in Turkey that, according to some reports from the ground, are transcending long-established divisions between ethnic and religious groups, and those associated with different Leftist political currents and parties, toward some sort of anti-systemic movement.[1] Not long ago, the global "Occupy" movement, with variants like *los indignados* in Spain, advanced similar goals.

Of course the list of such movements is long, and in recent years is coupled with dramatic effects such as those witnessed in Tunisia, Libya, and Egypt, and other significant protests grouped under the banner of the Arab Spring. This volume does not set out to provide a review of these movements, and nor will it offer any sort of systematic evaluation of their impact. Such work is important for all those with an interest in interpreting their causes, processes, trajectories, and wider implications, but it is not the object of our analysis here. Rather, we cite these high profile examples as indicative of a general climate, which of course varies dramatically across geographical and political contexts; it can be read as qualitatively different from historical cycles (expansion and recession) and so, may be interpreted as constituting something new and distinctive.

We begin from this very broad perspective, which has been a premise of the work of the two scholars whose work we are considering and seeking to apply to educational thinking. In what follows, we set out their substantial arguments in favor of such a view, each argument elaborating the case that global capitalism, or the 'capitalist world-system,' in Wallerstein's nomenclature, is approaching and/or has reached a set of absolute limits whose resolution requires an alternative, noncapitalist, socioeconomic, and political framework.

As in any case of scholarship, one question confronting the authors is how far back in the line of reasoning one needs to go to justify, or at least to substantiate, the arguments being presented. One of the authors has clearly adopted a partisan use of Wallerstein's work (e.g., Griffiths: 2009a; 2011a, Griffiths and Knezevic: 2009), and so views this project explicitly as a way to further disseminate Wallerstein's work, to debate its merits, and to consider its utility in comparative and international educational research. Wallerstein's argument that we are engaged in a period of systemic transition from a capitalist to an uncertain replacement system is thus elaborated in some detail, as an explicit intervention advocating this reading of social reality.

This book's approach is to both introduce new readers to his world-systems analysis and to set the ground for its application to educational questions. Moreover, it is done in the interest of presenting to the reader a comprehensive framework for navigating and acting in contemporary conditions. As we note throughout the volume, Wallerstein's perspective puts forward a reading of contemporary and historical social reality, and more limited strategizing for the future, the latter consistently done in highly qualified terms with respect to the uncertainty of future developments, and in the spirit of generating broad alliances. A result is provisional or conditional programatic claims that might constitute a qualitatively different anti-systemic movement.

Similarly, Mészáros' approach is also critical of current perspectives on the global system. For Mészáros, the grounding for current problems exists in the inception of the industrial revolution and the eventuating global totality of that change. This historical process, and indeed the global nature of that process, is the core of his analysis throughout his work. For Mészáros, the main change in the capitalist system as a proper global structure is not even that it is 'capitalist' in the sense of a 'free market' that controls the relations of production, but that capital itself—that is to say, an overarching financial structure—creates and limits our world. This is the hegemony of capital for Mészáros.

Our underlying argument here is that by virtue of the nature and substance of their work over four or five decades, the time for renewed consideration of their work is ripe. If we accept that the globe faces dilemmas that are, in some respects, unprecedented, the most obvious candidate being global warming and the risks of irreversible climatic damage, then the work of Wallerstein and Mészáros makes a vital contribution to our understanding of contemporary conditions, and on this basis, to considering how to respond to these conditions within our particular fields of work. In this sense, we concur with Wallerstein's (1999b) assertion that world-systems analysis' time has come, noting that what once constituted his most controversial claims are now frequently accepted as givens, as part of the landscape in which we operate.

For example, and crucially for this volume, he argues that the anti-systemic character of socialist political parties and movements morphed, in historical practice, to a particular political strategy and pathway for achieving national economic growth and development within the constraints of the world-economy. From the perspective of 2013 such a position seems quite mild or mainstream.

Similarly, for Mészáros, the development of political parties guarantees the continuation of capitalism and its attenuated problematics. For some decades, the debate between 'reform' and 'revolution' was a main discussion among socialists in various parts of the world. For Mészáros, this issue represented his break with the Budapest School in that he sought to remain firmly in the structural Marxist camp, whereas the Budapest School sought a reformist agenda. Mészáros believed that only one way remained to do away with the exploitative nature of capitalism: to achieve a political solution of self-government. Thus, reforms to political and economic systems that sought to redistribute surplus value could never be enough unless the actual labor performed by people was democratized. This is made more complex by the fact that we are talking about 'reform Marxism' in realized (or so-called real-existing) socialism, rather than what eventually became the 'third way' blending of socialism and capitalism within advanced liberal democracies. The challenge for Mészáros was to remain Marxist, decry Stalinism, and continue to share the humanist Marxism of the Budapest School.

The relevance of these scholars to contemporary times is evident in the attention given to them and their work in some key parts of the contemporary world. For example, the late president of the Bolivarian Republic of Venezuela, Hugo Chávez, as one of the high-profile leaders of the movement to develop and enact a model of 'twenty-first century socialism' in Venezuela and the region, designated Mézsáros the 'socialist pathfinder' of our times.[2] Some of Mészáros' work was translated into Spanish and distributed at nominal cost, or in the case of *Social Structure and the Forms of Consciousness*, published and distributed free of charge by the presidential office.

While less prominent, Wallerstein's work has also been translated into Spanish and disseminated widely in Venezuela, at nominal cost, in recognition of the utility of his analysis for the twenty-first century socialism project (e.g., Wallerstein: 2007; 2008). We mention this not to enter ongoing debate about the Venezuelan case, though here again one of the authors is actively engaged (e.g., Griffiths; 2010a; 2010b), but to highlight the relevance of Wallerstein's and Mészáros' work to those at the cutting edge of elaborating systemic alternatives to capitalism for this century.

One distinguishing aspect of these scholars' work is its big picture, or macro, approach to the analysis and understanding of social phenomena. Wallerstein explicitly acknowledges and advocates the need for such an approach, this being at the core of the project he labels the "historical social sciences" and its accompanying alternative ways of viewing time and space in terms of historical cycles, structures, and transformational possibilities (Wallerstein: 1997a; 1998b). The claim here is that the social sciences, tied to nomethetic or idiographic epistemologies, have tended to center on notions of eternal or episodic timespace respectively, which are inadequate to the task of understanding social reality. The very project of world-systems analysis, however, aims to generate viable and, where possible, widely agreed upon interpretations or understandings of social reality from a macro and historical perspective.

Mészáros' approach has, from a different perspective, questioned the development of this reality in his two-volume work, *Social Structure and Forms of Consciousness* (Mészáros: 2010a; 2011). In this tour-de-force of the social sciences, Mészáros sought to unpack the historical development of what is considered to be the modern epistemological position on human beings and how societies historically developed. His challenge to a number of fundamental truth-claims was precisely to pinpoint how unity and universality, among other things, remain a set of contested ideas in our understanding of the world.

Another characteristic of these scholars' work is its multi- or interdisciplinary nature, defying simple categorizations that might seek to contain or limit its scope. Wallerstein's four volume series, *The Modern World-System*, for example, is reminiscent of other major historical works like Eric Hobsbawm's four-volume, *The Age of Revolution / Capital / Empire / Extremes*, or Braudel's three volumes on *Civilization and Capitalism*.

Wallerstein's historical work involves a particular world-systems historiography, shaping the selection and use of source materials, and the reasoning behind the conclusions drawn from the analysis of them, just as Hobsbawm's more orthodox Marxism shaped his earlier work. But Wallerstein's work is perhaps better known in the disciplines of political science and sociology, which is indicative of the breadth or scope of his analysis. His own explicit project to reshape, or 'unthink' the social sciences, and his characterization of world-systems analysis as the historical social sciences, also connects directly with contemporary trends in academia toward such multi-disciplinary research projects. The work consciously and deliberately seeks to challenge established ways of structuring knowledge in favor of a holistic and unidisciplinary approach to the "study of totalities" (Wallerstein: 1999c, 196).

Mészáros' scholarship shares this broad quality for two principal reasons: first, his work is deeply embedded in the original problems of Enlightenment philosophy in questioning all that we know, and second, his work remains in the structural Marxist camp in that he is examining humanity as a whole, not constituent parts divided along disciplinary lines. As such, his holistic view of the problems of contemporary humanity resist the simple classifications of disciplinary approaches found in the established social sciences.

In this volume, we bring the macro and holistic approaches of Wallerstein and Mészáros to bear on the long-standing, big policy question of work, and of education as preparation for work, under the conditions of capitalism. The influence of human capital theory on the official and primary purposes of national education systems is profound, and despite its apparent failure even in its own terms over many decades, this logic persists across the globe. The sort of metaperspective that Wallerstein and Mészáros have developed provides some key explanatory purchase for such a global educational policy across time and geographical/political/socio-cultural space. Our consideration of such educational phenomena through their analytical lenses puts the focus, on the one hand, on macro level considerations of the inherent needs and contradictions of capitalism/the capitalist world economy. Among these are its drive to maximize profits and the accumulation of capital—including efforts to minimize taxation and wage costs—to externalize production and particularly environmental costs, and, if necessary, to relocate capital and production within the world-economy to achieve these ends. This level of analysis generates particular insights into the question of education as preparation for work; such insights move beyond existing literature in the comparative education field.

For example, comparative researchers have thoroughly tracked and critiqued the application of human capital theory in education, and its manifestation in policies of regional and international institutions (e.g., Dale and Robertson: 2009; Klees et al.: 2012). Typically, however, this work continues to be locked into an orthodox developmentalist paradigm, in the sense that it advances an ameliorative program of greater equity and meritocracy to better distribute the development rewards. This is not to downplay the rigorous critiques of current policy failings, particularly the ways in which neoliberal educational policies work directly to exacerbate social inequalities, but to shed light on the contributions that Wallerstein's and Mészáros's perspectives bring. Their demand that we unthink the basic development assumptions under conditions of global capitalism fundamentally changes the way we approach policies like education for human capital formation.

If what Wallerstein describes as the promises of liberalism are simply unachievable for the majority under current political and economic arrangements—and popular acknowledgement of this is growing—then our attention shifts to the construction of replacement paradigms aligned to non-capitalist alternatives and to a definitive critique of policy defining education as preparation for work.

Questioning and rethinking the basic purposes of education systems is a common feature of educational research, including that of advancing greater equity through a fairer and more meritocratic distribution of educational credentials that are converted into occupational and social and economic outcomes. Here we might find, for example, a range of critiques of the reproductive function of mass education under the banner of preparation for work, highlighting its role in both sorting students for unequal futures, and to some degree legitimizing these unequal outcomes by virtue of the distribution of supposedly meritocratically earned educational credentials.

This is a long-standing field of research. The critique, however, is focused on the functional role of educational institutions in wider social inequalities and how it might be reformed in more meritocratic directions. Wallerstein and Mészáros turn this on its head by provoking a focus on the very nature of the social inequality under capitalism, its structural and historical dimensions, and the capacity for education systems to contribute to imagining and constructing non-capitalist futures. This challenge connects with the long-standing tradition of critical pedagogy which promotes educators' actions to lift students' critical consciousness of both the inequalities and injustices of social life, and the roles of education in these. We take this up in detail in chapter 4, which makes an argument for a 'critical world-systems education.'

The limited use of Mészáros' and Wallerstein's scholarship within critical educational research is puzzling, given the depth and scope of their work elaborating the argument that we are in a historical moment of systemic crisis and transition, and a moment in which our capacity to exert our collective human agency, thereby influencing the nature and direction of this historic change, is heightened. As we have argued elsewhere (e.g., Griffiths and Knezevic: 2010), a strong case can be made for there being significant alignment between much comparative scholarship exploring the global dimensions of educational policy creation and dissemination, and Wallerstein's world-systems analysis which decisively decenters the nation-state as the basic unit of analysis. Moreover, for educators and scholars with an interest in making sense of the complexities and uncertainties of twenty-first century social life—as part of some broad normative project to generate greater levels of equality, justice, and democracy—there is much that we can take from Wallerstein's and Mészáros' analyses.

Chapter Outline

Chapter 2 of this volume provides a thorough review of Wallerstein's world-systems analysis, with a view to succinctly establishing the major thrusts and principles of this work. For readers with limited engagement with Wallerstein's work, this chapter establishes the foundations of his approach. For all readers, this chapter illustrates the extent to which Wallerstein's world-systems analysis is about education, through its focus on knowledge and reconstructing the social sciences, and its explicit political project of harnessing this reconstruction to the creation of substantively rational alternatives to capitalism.

Chapter 3 develops a detailed account of human capital theory from a Wallersteinean perspective. It argues that the inability of the capitalist world-system to deliver the associated promise of national economic development for all makes human capital theory inspired policies particularly weak or fragile, despite their apparent resilience over time. The need to unthink such policies, in light of the broader analysis, is said to generate intellectual space and opportunities for alternative ideas of development or progress, and for the role of education in such goals to thrive.

Chapter 4 is more ambitious in scope, seeking to demonstrate a significant degree of alignment between Wallerstein's work and the legacy of critical pedagogy, and on this basis to imagine elements of a 'critical world-systems education' that could advance a project of mass participation in the transition from capitalist to an uncertain replacement world-system. In this sense, the chapter draws inspiration from Cho's (2013, 166) recent volume, one of the very few works about critical pedagogy that draws significantly on Wallerstein's ideas, and his emphasis on critical pedagogy's "search for the 'language of possibility.'" We are well aware of chapter 4's limitations, but underpinning the sketch of what could be, is an argument for the need for such thinking, action, and praxis to "continue to explore counter-hegemonic education" (Cho: 2013, 167).

In many ways, Mészáros has sought to maintain a 'traditional' view of collective action, in that people with a specific class interest still have the capacity to act in their own interests for the good of the collective. In chapter 5 we examine this view of collective action that is grounded in the philosophical anthropology of early Marx. Mészáros discusses human communities and human collectivities as having a 'natural propensity' for collective activity as well as having a universally understood desire to develop trade. Mészáros' analysis is philosophically grounded in Marx's early work and is combined with a Gramscian view of hegemony as well as Polanyi's idea of the destruction of the commons in England.

Bringing back the idea of collective action as positive and able to develop further, we examine how this might be a productive way forward by looking at alternative models of schooling based on a collectivist orientation. A fundamental shift in understanding education and schools is necessary; rather than focus on a set of examination results or 'achievements,' the idea posited here is to allow creativity to function according to the needs of an individual's creativity. The world at large is the educational program, rather than a preconceived set of curriculum content or facts to digest and be tested on.

In chapter 6, we discuss Mészáros' analysis of the contemporary capitalist system as one in which he emphasizes how the utility-maximizing thesis has worked to destroy the marketplace. Rather than create efficiency, or the 'best price/best value' for produced goods, having convinced individuals to act in their own narrow interests in order to maximize their well-being, this personal utility has created a set of difficulties in the post-industrial world. These difficulties have exacerbated the traditional Marxist view of human alienation and taken it to a much higher level. Mészáros claims that work in the contemporary world needs to be thought through in a different way, and asserts that mass education and mass society can provide avenues for that working through. Here we challenge the idea that schooling and work are linked. This challenge is brought about in a number of ways, including normative questions about what we ought to deliver in schools, practical examination of what has worked in schools in terms of teaching content, and ideological ways of considering what sorts of theoretical groundings make sense for students facing this human alienation.

Karl Polanyi's work *The Great Transformation* analyzed the way in which the inception of the industrial revolution changed social life in Great Britain. Polanyi demonstrated how the economy was an aspect of social and productive life that was embedded in societies around the world, and in chapter 7, we discuss this relationship with Mészáros' work. Polanyi claimed that this was a universal truth, and while this may well be contested, the idea that a process of disembedding this economic sphere from human activity had great traction in the post-World War II global economic reconstruction, and Mészáros uses this as a way to analyze the contemporary world structure. Polanyi's approach was based on the 'enclosure' phenomonen, or what later became known as the 'tragedy of the commons,' in which modern productive life could no longer maintain the idea that resources could be used 'in common' without ownership attached to them. This major innovation in thinking about the political and social place of economic activity needs highlighting here and will show how both Mészáros and Wallerstein develop their critiques in a similar fashion.

In chapter 8, we identify some of the major, provisional, conclusions coming from this review and analysis of Wallerstein's and Mézsáros' work. These conclusions seek to inform current and future educational research and its attention to the structural crises of capitalism in the twenty-first century.

Chapter 2

Wallerstein's World-Systems Analysis

> *But obtaining power within a sovereign state that is constrained by an interstate system based on a functioning division of labor has not meant, probably could not have meant, the ability to opt out of the capitalist world-economy. It has meant instead the ability to achieve some limited reallocation of world surplus, in short, the power to bring about reforms, without necessarily undermining the system as such.*
> (Wallerstein: 2001a, 166)

Introduction

Almost four decades ago, the first edition of Volume I of Immanuel Wallerstein's *The Modern World-System* was published (Wallerstein: 1974a). In 2011, new editions of volumes I, II, and III were published, along with the long-anticipated fourth volume, *The Modern 1789–1914*. A fifth and sixth volume are scheduled, if the author can "last it out" to cover the "long twentieth century," which will include treatment of the underlying premise of Wallerstein's extensive corpus of work—the structural crisis of the capitalist world-economy (Wallerstein: 2011b, xvii). World-systems analysis (WSA) has from the outset developed a macro- level account of social reality, offering an explanatory framework centered on the historical establishment and development of the capitalist world-economy, and its current and future trajectories. On the question of grand narratives, Wallerstein (2011a, xxiii) remains steadfast in presenting WSA as an "alternative master narrative...[to]...the orthodox Marxist and modernization master narratives," asserting, "We refused to throw out the baby with the bathwater."[1]

As with any substantial corpus of theorizing, there are multiple ways of approaching its synthesis and presentation which can produce dilemmas, even in a volume like this that devotes a series of chapters to Wallerstein's work. The scope of his work is well demonstrated in the contents of the recently published *Handbook of World-Systems Research* (Babones and Chase-Dunn: 2012), while the absence of direct applications of his theorizing to educational studies and research highlight the importance of this volume.

What selections do we make from the corpus of his work, extending over 40 years, included in more than 45 authored or co-authored books, more than 20 edited or co-edited volumes, and hundreds of scholarly articles?[2] How should we organize and present the body of work, given its ambitious scope as an overarching historical metanarrative, an activist knowledge movement seeking to unthink and recast established structures of knowledge within the social sciences, and as a political movement seeking to influence the transition of our current world-system? Further complicating these issues, Wallerstein has explicitly rejected descriptions of a world-systems theory, insisting a decade ago that WSA was "not a theory or a mode of theorizing, but a perspective and a critique of other perspectives" (Wallerstein: 1999c).

Our purpose in this chapter is to provide a contemporary review of the major identifiable components of Wallerstein's theorizing, mindful of his defining approach that insists on "seeing all parts of the world-system as parts of a 'world,' the parts being impossible to understand or analyze separately" (Wallerstein: 1999c, 195). This world-system as a world, and one that has extended its coverage to incorporate the entire geographical world, is a capitalist world-system, centered on a single capitalist world-economy, within which multiple polities operate through an elaborated interstate system. Of central importance in this volume is his work's extensive treatment of the contemporary crises of capitalism as a world-system, and the argument that we are in a process of transition towards an alternative, but uncertain, replacement world-system. Hence, this chapter seeks also to clearly and comprehensively establish this central argument of Wallerstein as the basis for understanding his work and exploring the ensuing implications for educational thinking, research, and action. To this end, we have structured the chapter across five major sections: (1) A single capitalist world-economy with multiple polities; (2) A dominant geoculture of the capitalist world-system; (3) The world-system in crisis and transition; (4) A knowledge movement; and (5) Politically engaged, activist, intellectual work.

A Single Capitalist World-Economy/Multiple Polities

As we noted in the introductory chapter of this volume, a foundational feature of Wallerstein's world-systems analysis is the insistence that a defining feature of capitalism as an historical system was its international character involving market trade in a world-economy. In broad terms, Wallerstein (1979) describes two types of world-systems—world-empires with a single political system, and world-economies with multiple political systems. The defining characteristic of the latter, which despite the nomenclature does not necessarily include the entire geographical world, is the division of labor, whereby areas that form part of the world-system are dependent on the economic exchange of staples with other areas of the system, to satisfy local/national needs. This characteristic distinguishes a world-economy both from a world-empire, with a single political authority exercised over multiple national economies, or simply from a system in which independent national economies engage in international trade with each other. Part of the argument here is that, historically, world-economies involving a division of labor across multiple politics and cultures have been unstable and tended to evolve into world empires, and hence that the capitalist world-economy has been distinctive in this sense.

In brief, Wallerstein's (1974a, 37) historical analysis argued that the particular conditions of the crisis of feudalism in the fourteenth century, described as a "conjuncture of secular trends, an immediate cyclical crisis, and climatological decline," underpinned the emergence of a capitalist world-economy for the first time. He locates the emergence of the European world-economy, based on a capitalist mode of production and exchange of staples, in the "long sixteenth century," spanning from 1450 to 1640. This push towards a capitalist world-economy was based in the accompanying geographical expansion of agricultural production, driven both by the nobility seeking to restore income levels and by increased activity of merchants trading in staple goods. The geographical expansion incorporated areas with varied methods of labor control, with differential levels of social and economic 'development,' and with varying degrees of strength of formal state machineries. Nevertheless, the incorporation of areas into the world-economy's division of labor was thus set in motion.

The nature of trade between areas or zones of the world is an integral feature of what world-systems analysis identifies as a world-economy, with trade in necessities or staples, rather than luxury goods, as the critical factor that qualitatively changed the nature of trade, and with it the nature of the relationship between trading areas. This trade in essential goods thus both defined incorporation in the world-economy, and provided the impetus for an accompanying division of labor across areas included within the world-economy. The changed emphasis in trade between nations was accompanied by the strengthening of nation's state machinery, or "economic decision-making entities" in participating areas of the world-economy, with the relative scope and strength of this machinery posited as a critical factor in determining an area's location within the world-economy's division of labor (Wallerstein: 1989, 132), and so in determining the relative share of available global surplus value (see below). The seemingly inexorable push for increased consumption of staples, in turn, fuelled the geographical expansion of the capitalist world-economy.

The incorporation of areas formerly external to the capitalist world-economy necessarily centered then on trade with other areas, moving toward greater levels of interdependent trade in staples. Wallerstein (1989, 137) added that in the process of incorporation, the import of goods (rather than receipt of bullion for exports) increased in the incorporated area, while a local bourgeoisie developed to manage the changed nature and scale of this inter-dependent trade.

Detailed analysis of the incorporation of the Indian subcontinent, the Ottoman and Russian empires, and West Africa from 1750 to 1850, for example, are provided in Chapter 3 of Volume III of *The Modern World-System* (Wallerstein: 1989). In that work, he emphasized that this process of the geographical expansion of the capitalist world-economy, incorporating new areas, was not driven by the initiative of those in power within the formerly external areas, but rather by "the need of the world-economy to expand its boundaries, a need which was itself the outcome of pressures internal to the world-economy" (129). These internal pressures of the system relate to the logic of the capitalist world-economy to maximize the extraction of surplus value, as profits, that underpin the systemic logic of the endless accumulation of capital.

The logic of Wallerstein's argument here is clear: As a world-system, the flow of surplus from peripheral to core areas required the further geographical expansion of the world-economy, so as to incorporate more of the available labor into production chains that in turn supported and, in effect, realized this flow of surplus and capital accumulation.

Multiple Polities/Forms of Labor Control

This distinctive feature of the capitalist world-economy meant that economic decisions within incorporated areas were oriented toward participation within the world-economy. Political decisions of areas and units within the world-economy, however, while influenced and informed by involvement in the world-economy, were also oriented toward smaller structures and units of legal control, whether states, city-states, or empires (Wallerstein: 1974a, 67). In *Historical Capitalism with Capitalist Civilization,* Wallerstein (1998a) stressed the importance of this arrangement for the effective functioning, expansion, and development of the capitalist world-system. He argued that the apparent separation between the economic and political arenas—that is to say between a world-system level division of labor with integrated production processes and commodity chains operating to support the endless accumulation of capital; and ostensibly separate and independent states with sovereign responsibility for political decisions within their boundaries—worked to hide the unequal exchange between areas which transferred part of the total surplus or profit being produced from one area to another.

The issue of multiple political systems is particularly relevant to contemporary analyses of the capitalist world-economy, and the particular account of historical socialism and socialist political movements within the world-economy that Wallerstein's world-systems analysis has provided. As we explore in more detail in chapter 4, this question is crucial to any discussion of anti-capitalist/anti-systemic political action or praxis, and accompanying educational endeavors to support that praxis. Some 25 years after the collapse of historical socialism, however, the world-systems account of socialist states as a functional part of the capitalist world-economy, and Marxism-Leninism within these states as "a mercantilist strategy of 'catching up' and 'surpassing' rival states" (Wallerstein: 1984, 89), is less controversial than when first elaborated by Wallerstein and others in the 1970s and 1980s (for a good example, see Chase-Dunn: 1982).

Indeed, Wallerstein's (1979) early writing presented the Russian Revolution as part of the consolidation of the capitalist world-economy in the twentieth century, rather than a rupture or de-linking from it, marking the beginning of an alternative, socialist world-system. Griffiths has applied this theorizing to the Cuban case (Griffiths: 2005; 2009), making the case that world-systems analysis provides a comprehensive explanatory account of Cuba's educational frameworks and policies since the Cuban Revolution of 1959.

In making this sort of alternative interpretation of historical socialism, Wallerstein acknowledged the progressive political role played by socialist revolutionary movements historically, and their anti-systemic origins, which meant they had some success in both undermining the legitimacy of capitalism and its inequalities, and in bringing greater levels of equality within their boundaries. In *Utopistics*, for example, while citing the dystopic possibilities of utopian projects, and acknowledging their historical use as "justifications for terrible wrongs," he added that such revolutions also generated "the sudden intrusion of hope (even great hope) that all (or at least much) can be really transformed, and transformed quickly, in the direction of greater human equality and democratization" (Wallerstein: 1998c, 1 and 7).

We explore this issue in greater depth in chapter 4, in the context of arguing for the need for new anti-systemic movements for contemporary conditions, and for critical educators and education systems to facilitate their development with a view to influencing the post-capitalist transition. The crucial point to be made here, however, is that the historical socialist states provided an alternative political model and structure to deliver rapid, or catch-up, national economic development, and to bring some states into the semi-periphery of the world-economy, in a way that aligned with the modernist/developmentalist logic of all nation-states moving through the same sequence of identifiable stages of development.

The idea of multiple forms of labor within multiple political and cultural contexts, being accommodated within the capitalist world-economy, is central to Wallerstein's understanding and definition of historical capitalism, its emergence, expansion, and development. This is well highlighted in his treatment of the different modes of labor control, including slavery, feudalism, wage labor, and self-employment. Wallerstein argued that these modes of labor control, and the associated relations of production, should not be exclusively associated with particular types of economic systems, but rather understood as particular modes of labor control under particular historical conditions within particular political systems and associated with particular types of productive activities (Wallerstein: 1974a, 87–92). Crucially, he concluded that all have operated at different times and in different areas under particular conditions within a single capitalist world-economy.

This approach defines capitalism in a way that gives priority to the logic of the endless accumulation of capital, and so to the generation and flow of surplus value within the world-economy, rather than particular social relations of production needing to be in place within all areas that are part of the world-economy. For example, a country or area may continue to rely on slavery as a primary means of controlling labor and extracting surplus value, but it can still be a part of the capitalist world-economy (Wallerstein: 1979). This approach allowed Wallerstein to argue that a so-called "second serfdom" in sixteenth century Eastern Europe was in fact qualitatively distinct from the feudalism of medieval Europe, and amounted to "coerced cash-crop labor" as one of multiple forms of labor control in a capitalist, and not feudal, world-economy.

> The world-economy has one form or the other. Once it is capitalist, relationships that bear certain formal resemblances to feudal relationships are necessarily redefined in terms of the governing principles of a capitalist system. (Wallerstein: 1974a, 92)

For Wallerstein this coerced cash-crop labor emerged then as a new or redefined form of social organization producing staples for a world-economy, driven by the market logic of the capitalist world-economy.

Our concern here is not to re-enter debates with orthodox Marxists focused on the social relations of industrial production and extraction of surplus value from labor in these modes of productive activity as the only true form of capitalist production, and so the criteria that must be used to locate its historical emergence. In terms of the larger project of examining crises of contemporary capitalism and possibilities for more democratic and egalitarian alternatives at a world-system level, we agree with scholars like de Sousa Santos (2008) who characterize these as non-productive debates. As Wallerstein (2004b) has argued, the orthodox Marxist position critiques world-systems analysis "for what it explicitly proclaims as its perspective."

For the purposes of this volume, and the attempted application of Wallerstein's world-systems analysis to the field of comparative educational research generally, and critical educational praxis in particular, we are putting forward his approach to such questions. It is precisely world-systems analysis' holistic approach to the study of social reality, evident here, that characterizes Wallerstein's particular intellectual contribution and that we seek to highlight in this volume.

Core, Semi-periphery, and Periphery in the Capitalist World-Economy

The differential (hierarchical) location of zones or areas within the single capitalist world-economy into core, semi-peripheral, and peripheral zones and relationships is, for Wallerstein, an additional defining feature of the capitalist world-economy. As indicated above, a particular strength of the capitalist world-system is its incorporation of multiple cultures and political systems, working for example against pushes towards world-empire and facilitating the operation of a system in which

> ...the economic factors operate within an arena larger than that which any political entity can totally control. This gives capitalists a freedom of maneuver that is structurally based. It has made possible the constant economic expansion of the world-system, albeit a very skewed distribution of its rewards (Wallerstein: 1974b, 348).

This structural feature of the capitalist world-economy is similarly seen in the foundations of the world-system, in which core zones were initially created by virtue of slight comparative advantages over other areas with respect to a series of social and geographical factors, including things like rates of land cultivation and production, and the development and strength of towns (Wallerstein: 1974b, 96–98). The crucial and related factor was the relative strength of the so-called economic decision-making entities, and ultimately the development, effectiveness, and strength of state structures to facilitate the share of surplus from the developing capitalist world-economy flowing into the area or zone.

To illustrate this point, Wallerstein contrasted the decline of Spain with the rise of Amsterdam in the long sixteenth century, citing the over-extension of the Spanish empire, and the "relatively low level of productivity and thinness of bureaucratic framework faced with an expanding economy based on scattered medium-size enterprise" (Wallerstein: 1974b, 185) to explain why Spain did not become the first hegemonic state, or even a core zone, of the nascent capitalist world-economy. For Wallerstein, strong state structures were central to determining a zone's initial structural advantage and location, and any subsequent relocation in the world-economy. The focus here is on state structures capable of controlling imports, of maintaining a favorable balance of trade, or of supporting the development of an industrial base; in short, state structures that are able to build the state machinery which would allow dominant and emerging capitalist classes to profit from participation in the world-economy.

How did these state structures combine with the specific social and geographical conditions to produce the sorts of inequalities between areas of the globe, and between modern nation-states, with which we are so familiar? In Chapter 3 of Volume II of *The Modern World-System*, Wallerstein (1980) explored in detail the struggle within the core of the world-economy, between Dutch hegemony and English and French challenges, from 1651 to 1689. This work is illustrative both of his broader theorizing, which questions both orthodox Whig and Marxist historiography, and of the conditions required to achieve core status within the world-economy. He downplayed, for example, agricultural differences between England and France in this period, arguing that "the two areas were more alike than different. They were both expanding their percentage of the world's production of cereals in order to maintain overall profit levels in a time of stagnation" (Wallerstein: 1980, 90). Moreover, he rejected the thesis that a distinctive "French temperament" meant that the French did not invest in industry and develop foreign trade in ways comparable to the English.

Rather, as is characteristic of Wallerstein's historical analysis, he provided a detailed account of a set of conjunctural factors that provided England with an edge in the inter-state rivalry, and so set the conditions for England and not France to rise to hegemonic status within the world-economy. For example, the relative geographical and population size of the two countries meant that the French needed external markets less than England did. This particular social condition combined with the historical fall in sea transport and the British colonial system reinforcing external trade, and saw the English move toward "*de facto* monometalism" in gold (from external trade) compared with silver in France (from internal trade). This in turn strengthened England's connection to an "international gold banking network" (Wallerstein: 1980, 112).

On the question of state structures and strength, Wallerstein questioned the conventional view that France had the stronger "absolutist state," and that this absolutist aristocratic state stifled bourgeois enterprise. The importance of the state within the capitalist world-economy lies in its capacity to "create structures sufficiently strong to defend the interests of one set of owner-producers in the world-economy against other sets of owner-producers as well as, of course, against workers" (Wallerstein: 1980, 114).

Here we see the Marxist view of the state serving the interests of the capitalist class, building structures that facilitate some owner-producers achieving comparative market advantage, and generating increased surplus, for a cost that is less than the ensuing profits. Wallerstein (1980, 113) listed five key measure of state strength in relation to this capacity: (1) Mercantilism to help capital compete in world markets;

2) Military power to influence other states; 3) Financial capacity to engage in these activities without consuming all public finances; 4) An efficient state bureaucracy; and 5) Alignment between political rulers and the interests of owner-producers as a hegemonic bloc.

Here, too, world-systems analysis conceptualizes a broad hegemonic bloc, including groups based on social status (the aristocracy) and social class (the bourgeoisie), which is not to discount the political struggles between these groups but to acknowledge the ambiguous nature of the classifications in the particular historical period. Thus he argued, for example, that the restoration of the English monarchy in 1660 included agreement within the dominant strata that regardless of whether it was led by Parliament or King, the English state would "concentrate on promoting economic development at the expense of the rest of the world-economy" (Wallerstein: 1980, 122).

These distinctions help to illustrate the founding conditions of states' participation in the capitalist world-economy, vying in this particular case to challenge Dutch hegemony, and more generally, directing state activity and building state machinery to improve the relative position of the state within the world-system. However, the emphasis on the state, and its relationship to other local geographic, social, and political conditions impacting on economic activity and development, must be considered in terms of the development and expansion of the capitalist world-system.

World-systems analysis is founded in the critiques of modernization theory and the elaboration of alternative dependency theory that identified systemic structural constraints on the possibilities for economic development in states and countries located within the periphery of the world-economy (see Amin: 1976; Frank, 1966). World-systems analysis thus built on the critique of Rostow's conception of all states passing through similar and sequential stages of national development, and the associated Marxist conceptualization seeing all nation-states on a trajectory from feudalism to capitalism and then socialism and communism (see Wallerstein: 1974b).

This is not to deny the intent or imperative of states everywhere to achieve national development, but an insistence that it is world-systems, as social systems, that move through stages, and that by definition the capitalist world-economy required and requires some areas or states to remain in a state of relative 'underdevelopment' as a structural part of the world-system's operation.

Finally, as elaborated in the following section, a distinctive feature of semi-peripheral areas, or states, is their mercantilist strategy of expanding local production's capture of domestic markets, along the lines of later import-substitution models of development, intended to maximize rates of profit for some domestic activities that transfer surplus to core zones, while increasing external trade in other areas to extract surplus from the periphery: in short, a mercantilist strategy designed to maximize core-like activities and move into the core.

In his foundational work, Wallerstein (1979, 22–23) identified the semi-periphery as one of three key mechanisms that have facilitated political stability, in terms of "systemic survival" of the world-system.[3] The argument here is that the intermediary role played by the semi-periphery mediates levels of absolute polarization across the world-system, and in this way functions to divide what might otherwise be a unified opposition of all non-core sectors. In a similar way to capital in core areas providing a relatively greater share of their accumulated profits to workers in order to contain or buy off systemic opposition within core states, Wallerstein argues that the semi-periphery acted as a pressure valve for the overall system, by virtue of it being tied to nation-states' strategies for national development and relocation within the hierarchy of the world-economy.

Unequal Exchange and Development

Andre Gunder Frank's (1966) essay on the "development of underdevelopment" in Latin America remains as a classic conceptualization of unequal development between states. Its central thesis expressed Wallerstein's (1979, 7) assertion that such underdevelopment was "the result of being involved in the world-economy as a peripheral, raw material-producing area." For Wallerstein, the systemic, unequal development of geographical areas within the capitalist world-economy centered on the process of "unequal exchange" operating through transnational commodity chains "in which the multiple specific production activities are located" (Wallerstein: 1998a). These commodity chains involve a transnational division of labor, with a disproportionate portion of profit or surplus value produced by labor processes along the commodity chain being transferred to the component located in the core. He noted that the extent to which systems of vertical integration have been achieved has varied, from that involving two or more links in the commodity chain, to the chartered companies operating in the sixteenth to eighteenth centuries (Wallerstein: 1998a). Wallerstein (1998a, 30) concluded that some degree of vertical integration has been the "statistical norm of historical capitalism," facilitating the flow of surplus value and disproportionate accumulation of capital from peripheral to core zones.

With international trade in staples a defining feature of the capitalist world-economy, Wallerstein (1998a, 30) stressed how geographical and historical social and political conditions contributed to the early establishment of differential zones, and states' location within these, arguing that their hierarchical positions were "exaggerated, reinforced, and encrusted" within emerging commodity chains under historical capitalism. In short, the process of unequal exchange involves the movement of commodities between zones in a way that operates to transfer part of the total profit, or surplus, from one zone to another. This transfer occurs as commodities that involve differential levels of real input costs, or labor, are exchanged for the same price, with core zones benefiting from the transfer of surplus which is then available for further capital investments that, in turn, increase its relative advantage in further exchange with peripheral zones. What we see here is a conventional, self-reinforcing cycle, in which the concentration of capital in the core further strengthens the political activities that create and develop state structures to maintain advantage, and in real political terms exercise power over peripheral zones to ensure their primary economic activity remains in areas at the peripheral end of commodity chains.

The hierarchical division of economic activities, and the associated flows of global surplus across commodity chains, is therefore intimately connected to the question of the strength and orientation of state structures and machineries, as reviewed above, and so to the hierarchical location of states, or areas within states, across a global core, semi-periphery, and periphery system. Areas with the semi-periphery were described by Wallerstein (1979, 22–34) as those competing with core areas for sales to the periphery, often with the State using mercantilist techniques as a strategy to both avoid falling into the periphery and as an attempt to achieve core status. As the term suggests, semi-peripheral areas involve economic activities along the commodity chains that extract some of the surplus from peripheral areas, and partially contribute to the transfer of surplus to the core areas. That is, they trade "in one mode with the periphery and in the opposite [mode] with the core" (Wallerstein: 1979, 71).

Here Wallerstein (1979) emphasizes that the point is not to attribute particular products and their sale with core, semi-peripheral, or peripheral areas, given that these change over time, but to focus instead on their relative position in the unequal exchange between areas, and so the associated wage and profit rates associated with particular products and their exchange at particular times within the world-economy.

In summary, we can see unequal exchange and development as systemic aspects of Wallerstein's conceptualization of the single capitalist world-economy, with a division of labor across core, semi-peripheral and peripheral zones differentially transferring global surplus to these zones through transnational commodity chains within which the process of unequal exchange is embedded. Wallerstein acknowledges the Marxist thesis of falling rates of profit under capitalism and the accompanying dislocations to particular capitalist firms and productive activities, but from a world-systems perspective this phenomenon adds to an understanding of the global expansion of the world-system as capital seeks lower labor costs to restore profits. Semi-proletarianized households in peripheral and semi-peripheral areas provide the cheaper labor for relocated production, effectively demoting some activities in the commodity chain while maintaining the underlying principles of unequal exchange and surplus transfer across the system.

Crucially, Wallerstein argues that the operation of unequal exchange is hidden in several ways. The prices for traded goods are presented as being negotiated in a neutral world-market, ignoring the historical use of force, including patterns of imperial conquest (Wallerstein: 2006), that established the differential structures and so the parameters within which trade in the capitalist world-economy operates. Here again the apparent separation between a world-economy and multiple (ostensibly sovereign and independent) polities, functions to hide the structural nature of unequal exchange that maintains the "underdevelopment" of particular areas (Wallerstein: 1998a).

An interstate system to which we now turn, and an accompanying shared geoculture of centrist liberalism (see p. 25), provide further justification for, or acceptance of, systemic inequalities through the assumptions of linear trajectories of growth and development for all states.

An Interstate System

Wallerstein argues that the multiple polities incorporated into the capitalist world-economy operate within an interstate system, and that this is as an additional key component for the effective functioning and maintenance of the capitalist world-system. In general terms, what we are talking about here are formalized mechanisms or processes through which the full range of political, economic, and diplomatic relationships between states operate. Boswell and Chase-Dunn (2000, 25) describe the interstate system in terms of a global or world order, with shared understandings of acceptable interstate behavior, extending to "normative rules of international relations," that we might most easily associate with formal treaties and international organizations to which states are signatories. They highlight the capitalist world-system's inclusion of nation-states and territories of former colonial empires in the initial stages of the world economy, in line with the multiple polity thesis.

Referring to the institutionalist branch of world-systems analysis, whose educational variant is discussed in chapters 3 and 4, Boswell and Chase-Dunn (2000, 25) see the interstate system as promoting and developing over time a world polity, with "shared cultural definitions of what is legitimate among states and other global actors...institutionalizing the parameters of what is a goal worth pursuing." The ensuing world polity is both defined by and defines the operation of the interstate system and the logics of the world-system that underpin these. Their interest is in strategies for transforming the capitalist world-system by changing the world polity, something we deal with in detail in chapter 4.

Participation in an interstate system, like participation in the capitalist world-economy, necessarily constrains state sovereignty and independence, while the idea of the sovereign nation-state is simultaneously a central component of the geoculture of centrist liberalism that constituted the shared logic of the system (see below). In Volume II of *The Modern World-System*,Wallerstein (1980, 225) explored Prussia's move from peripheral to semi-peripheral status and why it succeeded in doing so while Sweden did not, citing Prussia's interaction in the interstate system, but integrally linked to its economic activities and associated state machinery to support these, as key to accounting for its upward relocation. In more conventional Marxist terms, Wallerstein (1984, 50) described the interstate system as the "political superstructure of the capitalist world economy," the critical point being that the interstate system, under the capitalist world-economy, has not transformed into a world-empire. The world polity that institutionalists refer to is more closely related to Wallerstein's conceptualization of the dominant geoculture of liberalism, and does not constitute a single political power/member of the system imposing its political structure over the world-system.

This issue is complicated further by the identification of hegemonic states in the capitalist world-economy, beginning with the rise of Amsterdam and the fall of the Spanish Empire in the long sixteenth century, following by the rise of the United Kingdom in the nineteenth century and then the United States in the twentieth century as the dominant or hegemonic power of the world-economy. Hegemony involves dominance of a core power in terms of its production and trade, its control over these, and the financial machinery that underpin them. It was described by Wallerstein (1980, 38) in the following terms:

> It is...more than core status. It may be defined as a situation wherein the products of a given core state are produced so efficiently that they are by and large competitive even in other core states, and therefore the given core state will be the primary beneficiary of a maximally free world market. Obviously to take advantage of this productive superiority, such a state must be strong enough to prevent or minimize the erection of internal and external political barriers to the free flow of the factors of production; and to preserve their advantage, once ensconced, the dominant economic forces find it helpful to encourage certain intellectual and cultural thrusts, movements, and ideologies...

Not surprisingly, hegemonic status is closely linked to state strength, and the associated capacity to deliver and support economic and military dominance.

But even hegemonic power within the interstate system, and the capitalist world-system, does not translate into a single political structure, though some contemporary developments and theorizing of globalization, for example, characterize United States hegemony in terms of neo-imperialism (e.g. Kiely: 2005). Participation in the interstate system reinforces state structures, which in dialectical fashion legitimize and strengthen the interstate system. In this way, the inclusion of former and historical socialist states in the interstate system arguably contained in some ways the alternative dimensions of socialist ideology—the abolition of private ownership of the means of production for example—within the socialist states, while simultaneously reinforcing the capitalist world-system through their inclusion and the depolarizing effect of the socialist states on the system as a whole.

Centrist Liberalism as Geoculture of the Capitalist World-System

In the preface to the recently published Volume IV of *The Modern World-System,* Wallerstein (2011b, xvi) identifies the French Revolution and its "cultural consequences" for the modern world-system as the cornerstone for understanding the "creation of a geoculture for the world-system—that is, a set of ideas, values, and norms that were widely accepted throughout the system and that constrained social action thereafter." While Volume IV provides a detailed account of the rise of the liberal state, the question of a shared geoculture of liberalism providing the cultural underpinnings of the capitalist world-system has been extensively addressed in Wallerstein's scholarship over many years.

This story centers on the historical struggle between the ideological perspectives of conservatism, liberalism, and anti-systemic socialism, which Wallerstein (1995a) described as political outlooks "forged in the wake of [and in response to] the French Revolution." His particular account identifies a major cultural legacy of the French Revolution as the normalizing of regular political and social change, with the will of the sovereign "people" of the nation playing a central role in this change. Thus he argued there were two major, initial responses to the French Revolution: "those who accepted progress as inevitable and desirable and thus 'were globally favorable' to the French Revolution, and, on the other hand, the Counter-Revolution" (Wallerstein: 1995a, 85). The ideologies of socialism and liberalism were clearly on the side of change and progress, while the conservative counter-revolution is characterized as opposition to the coming of modernity.

For Wallerstein, 1848 was a turning point with respect to the preceding convergence between liberals and socialists, with both groups arguably committed to the desirability, if not the inevitability, of social and political change and progress. The failures of the 1848 revolutions contributed to an ideological rift with a distinctly Marxist variant of socialism breaking with liberal reformers in favor of more radical revolutionary action to rapidly seize state power. The events of 1848 also contributed to the later convergence of the three competing ideologies and the triumph of centrist liberalism as the dominant ideology of the world-system, as conservatives responded to events with a program for gradual, moderate reform and efforts to build "more integrated national societies" (Wallerstein: 1995a, 96) to diffuse popular uprisings. This resulted in a sort of liberal-conservative variant of liberalism.

More controversially, but a central and logical outcome of Wallerstein's work, is the argument that the ideology of socialism became in effect a liberal-socialist variant of liberalism, contributing to the emergence of a single, dominant geoculture of liberalism across the capitalist world-system. This is an outcome of all polities' incorporation into the capitalist world-economy and its division of labor, over time, and of the associated political and ideological struggles seen from the longer-term perspective.

At its most provocative, Wallerstein (1995a, 88 and 89) argued that within socialism's "intense opposition to liberalism, one finds as a core component of the demands of all these regimes the same faith in progress via productivity that has been the gospel of the liberals"; and that while Leninism claimed to be violently opposed to liberalism, "it was actually being one of its avatars." In the same volume, he went on to argue that the transformation of socialist ideology and socialists to the liberal-socialist variant was marked in the period from 1917 to the 1960s by "the acceptance of the objective of socialism within one country, defining it as a catching-up industrialization; and the search for national power and advantage within the interstate system," the result being that "both conservatives and socialists accepted the world-scale liberal agenda of self-determination (also called 'national liberation') and economic development (sometimes called 'construction of socialism')" (Wallerstein: 1995a, 103).

The established and shared geoculture of liberalism is elaborated in other work in terms of a shared belief in developmentalism (Wallerstein: 2005). This common geoculture includes multiple components that are accommodated by ostensibly competing ideologies and the multiple polities that are found within the capitalist world-economy. This involves a shared belief in the universal validity of scientific knowledge and technological advances, and their capacity when under the direction of rational policy makers within strong, sovereign, nation-states and their associated state machinery, to deliver linear economic development and progress. The position was succinctly summarized by Wallerstein (1995a, 103)

> The possibility of the (economic) development of all countries came to be a universal faith, shared alike by conservatives, liberals, and Marxists. The formulas each put forward to achieve such development were fiercely debated, but the possibility itself was not. In this sense, the concept of development became a basic element of the geocultural underpinning of the world-system...Both conservatives and socialists accepted the world-scale liberal agenda of self-determination (also called national liberation) and economic development (sometimes called construction of socialism).

While major differences remained with respect to the classic dichotomy of reform versus revolution, for example, Wallerstein sees some degree of convergence here also in the sense that the liberal and socialist variants essentially shared and adopted a "two-step strategy" of first achieving State power (whether via electoral processes or by insurrection and violent revolution), and second, once in power, legislating to transform the State, the nation, the world (see, for example, Wallerstein: 2002a; 2010)). Once in power, the promise from ostensibly anti-systemic socialist parties, and the liberal and more conservative opponents, incorporated a vision of progress and development, and with it increased consumption and improved living standards for all, something that remains today a utopian vision of a brighter future for all to be realized at some point over the horizon (see Wallerstein: 1998c).

The World-System in Crisis and Transition: Absolute Limits, Asymptotes, and Transition

From the outset, Wallerstein's world-systems analysis has elaborated a comprehensive argument about the short-term cycles and longer-term trends of the capitalist world-economy, with each return to "equilibrium" from the cyclical crises of capitalism moving the whole system toward a series of absolute limits, or "asymptotes," as Wallerstein calls them, that cannot be resolved under the logic of capitalism (for the early detailed account, see Wallerstein, 1974b). On one side, this argument rests on the fundamental account of the development of the capitalist world-economy in the sixteenth century and its geographical expansion over time, which as an historical system "has a life: it is born or generated, it lives or proceeds, and its dies or disintegrates" (Wallerstein: 2000b, 150).

Consistent with Wallerstein's position with respect to orthodox Marxist perspectives, the thesis of transition toward an alternative but uncertain world-system is quite distinctive, rejecting accounts of national societies progressively moving through sequential stages of feudalism, capitalism, socialism, and communism. As Mielants (2012, 59) highlighted in his summary of the debates over the nature and temporal location of the transition from feudalism to capitalism, world-systems analysis is in the unusual position of being criticized for being Marxist by liberal and Smithian theorists, while "Orthodox Marxists claim no affiliation with the perspective."

In short, the thesis here is that regular cycles of expansion and contraction are characteristic of the capitalist world-economy, as leading and usually monopolistic industries in core zones fuel growth and accumulate high levels of capital, before increased competition and overproduction lead to declining rates of profit and recession. It is through this regular cycle of expansion and contraction that industries are relocated to other zones of the world-economy, in search of cheaper labor to restore rates of profit, accounting for a series of shifts over time of industrial activity from the core to the semi-periphery and periphery as the core areas invest in new "quasi-monopolies" that drive the next cycle of expansion and capital accumulation.

Perhaps the most emblematic example is textile production, which "circa 1800...was possibly the preeminent core-like production process...[but which]...by 2000...was manifestly one of the least profitable peripheral production processes" (Wallerstein: 2004c, 29). While each cycle restores the world-economy to some sort of equilibrium, Wallerstein's perspective is that the recurring cycles contribute to longer-term secular trends, whereby structural contradictions that are associated with these cycles and characteristic of the capitalist system as a totality are moving toward their absolute limit, or asymptote, and the "disintegration" of the prevailing historical world-system.

Wallerstein's theorizing has identified several dimensions of the systemic crisis, leading to a phase of crisis and transition toward an uncertain alternative. Most crucial is an identified long-term trend of pressures on the systemic imperative to maximize the accumulation of capital. The cyclical and longer-term pressure on profits and capital accumulation has multiple sources. First, Wallerstein's analysis repeatedly cites the orthodox tension faced by capital seeking to reduce wages as a cost of production to boost profits, and to increase rates of consumption and so demand as a strategy to maintain profits, the latter requiring higher wages. This involves a contradictory requirement for low-rates of fully proletarianized labor to support low-wages, and higher rates to increase demand and consumption. The relocation of production to semi-peripheral and peripheral areas involves the move to areas with lower wages supported by semi-proletarianized labor (Wallerstein: 1979), such that "it becomes very clear that geographical expansion of the world-system served to counterbalance the profit-reducing process of increased proletarianization, by incorporating new work-forces destined to be semi-proletarianized" (Wallerstein: 1983, 39).

As Li's (2008) recent analysis of China demonstrates, however, a longer-term trend of the expansion of semi-peripheral countries and rising wages for greater numbers is exacerbating this tension by further squeezing global profits.

A related contradiction said to be approaching its absolute limit is the capacity of capital to relocate to such semi-proletarianized, low-wage areas to restore profit margins. This process has structural and geographical limits. Wallerstein (1998c, 42) highlighted the short-term nature of the solution of relocating capital to low-wage areas by noting that the relative weakness of workers in peripheral areas, which underpins their low-wages in semi-proletarianized structures, is diminishing over time. The argument here is that the relocation of production to these areas adds to the impetus to fully proletarianize labor, which again over the longer-term adds to pressure on profits, particularly as a more widely proletarianized labor force improves its bargaining power for an increased share of surplus value being generated. The case of China is instructive in these terms, and is indicative of an expanded semi-periphery (Li: 2008, 91–110). Crucially, at the global level this key strategy for capital to renew rates of profit and maintain levels of global surplus flowing to core areas/states, which have historically supported higher wages and conditions in the core, is approaching its asymptote.

Relatedly, Wallerstein has regularly singled out the phenomenon of capital seeking to externalize the environmental costs of production, passing these costs on to the state, amounting to a state subsidy of private profits. These costs are elaborated in terms of waste and the renewal of primary resources (Wallerstein: 2005, 1271), with the former most commonly experienced as the cleanup costs that have historically been borne by the public. In a recent review essay, Wallerstein (Wallerstein: 2010, 139) argued the "from the sixteenth century to the 1960s, such externalization of costs had been normal practice, more or less unquestioned by political authorities…[but]…the health consequences and costs have become so high and so close to home as to produce demands for environmental cleanup and control."

The argument here is that there is increasing pressure everywhere for environmental damage to be addressed, driven by greater awareness of this damage and the intensification of environmental crises, particularly the phenomenon of global warming, which threaten the capacity of the globe to sustain human life in the long-term. The contradictory pressures on both the state and capital are intensified as a result—pressure on governments to resolve environmental degradation, through greater taxation and/or by insisting that capital internalize environmental costs, adding to the pressure on profits. The question of renewable and non-renewable primary resources simply adds to these tensions amidst growing pressure on states to create sustainable systems for the management and use of natural resources.

The role of taxation and the state is crucial in these processes, and is exacerbated by growing demands on the state over time, and across the world-system, to ensure the provision of universal health care, education, and personal income and housing security, the costs of which are growing inexorably and are compounded by simultaneous pressures to meet these and other costs alongside pressures to reduce taxation. Wallerstein attributes these broad processes to the success of historical anti-systemic movements in pushing for the expansion of social services, which were in turn arguably absorbed into a wider geoculture of liberalism across the world-system, whereby the promise of such services, and the associated security for all, became a common feature of diverse political parties and systems. As was recently observed, "No government today is exempt from the pressure to maintain a welfare state, even if the levels of provision vary" (Wallerstein: 2010, 140).

What these processes point to is a period of systemic crises, as the various contradictions cannot be resolved under the systemic conditions and requirements of the capitalist world-economy and its imperative to maximize "the *endless* accumulation of capital" (Wallerstein: 2011c, 32). This crisis is manifest in part in what Wallerstein identifies as the collapse of the dominant geoculture of liberalism, whereby the legitimacy of states is called into question as the promises of liberalism fail to materialize, whether under variants of historical socialism or supposedly free-market capitalism, or somewhere in-between. Wallerstein (1994, 15) previously characterized this in terms of "a form of chaos in the system, caused by the exhaustion of the systemic safety-valves...contradictions of the system have come to the point that none of the mechanisms for restoring the normal functioning of the system can work effectively any longer" (Wallerstein: 1994, 15).

In this same paper of almost twenty years ago, Wallerstein (1994) referred to "the Black Period before us" as the ideological shield of liberalism, which had co-opted antisystemic movements had lost its capacity to do so. Key markers of this end of liberalism were identified as the world revolution of 1968, which questioned both US-based capitalism and the Soviet alternative, and the collapse of historical communism thirty years later. For world-systems analysis, 1989 becomes not the triumph of capitalism, but a major blow to the legitimacy of its geoculture at the world-system level. More recently Wallerstein (2011c, 34) has articulated this as a crisis of "US hegemony but also of Soviet 'collusion' with the United States...[and]...the rejection not only of dominant 'centrist liberalism' but also of the fact that the traditional antisystemic movements (the 'Old Left') had essentially become avatars of centrist liberalism (as had mainstream conservative movements)."

This basic argument has been consistent in Wallerstein's work, citing structural and systemic crises of the historical capitalist world-system, and heightened levels of agency in this period of crisis to influence the direction of the transition and so the capacity to shape the replacement world-system. In contrast to earlier orthodox Marxist perspectives, Wallerstein emphasized uncertainty about the outcome of this historical transition. Wallerstein has at times explicitly advocated for a socialist world-system as the alternative replacement system that we ought to construct (Wallerstein: 1979), and perhaps more commonly set normative goals of greater equality, peace, democracy, and justice, but this is political advocacy and activism rather than some expression of teleological certainty. Recent work has characterized this in terms of a binary choice between the spirit of Davos, site of the annual World Economic Forum, and the spirit of Porto Alegre, site of the first World Social Forum, which amounts to an historical struggle over the nature of the future world.

> We can choose collectively a new system that essentially resembles the present one: hierarchical, exploitative and polarizing. There are many forms this could take, and some could be harsher than the capitalist world-system in which we have been living. Alternatively we can choose a radically different system, one that has never previously existed—a system that is relatively democratic and relatively egalitarian. (Wallerstein: 2010, 140–41)

In chapter 4, we return to this question in some depth, by putting the argued phenomenon of systemic crisis and transition at the center of thinking about educational models and actions that might contribute to a contemporary anti-systemic movement that can realize this sort of vision. For now, we move to the theme of world-systems analysis, a knowledge movement to further elucidate and characterize the approach.

WSA as a Knowledge Movement/Protest Against Established Disciplines

A distinctive feature of Wallerstein's world-systems analysis is its conscious resistance to claims of developing "world-systems theory," arguing that the intellectual project is first and foremost a "knowledge movement" (Wallerstein: 2004b) that is critiquing the (early twentieth century) dominant epistemologies, knowledge structures, and premises of existing social science. Wallerstein (1999c, 192) refers to this critique as "a mode of what I have called 'unthinking social science,'" this being the thematic focus of an earlier volume (see Wallerstein: 1991b).

We have highlighted in the preceding text how a key part of this process of unthinking dominant social science paradigms rests on the critique of modernization theories, including orthodox Marxist variants. This approach extends to the critique of the structures of knowledge disciplines and their associated epistemologies, their terminology and ways of categorizing social reality, as inadequate to the task of understanding the world-system and its historical trajectory. This dimension of Wallerstein's world-systems analysis most directly addresses educational policy and practice, frequently directed at the university education sector and argument to re-conceptualist the social sciences (Wallerstein: 1996). Chapter 4 builds on the overview of this dimension of Wallerstein's work provided here, to explore its application to mass education systems more broadly under the banner of a critical world-systems education.

The foundations of the call to unthink the social sciences social sciences rests in the historical division of knowledge across "the two cultures" of science and the humanities/philosophy, with distinctive nomothetic and idiographic epistemologies. Wallerstein (2006, 52) refers to "the creation and consolidation of the concept of the so-called two cultures, and then within it the triumph of scientific universalism." This "epistemological revolution" is situated within the capitalist world-economy, with the dominance of scientific universalism argued to have been "an essential element in the functioning and legitimation of the political, economic and social structures of the system" (59).

Wallerstein traces how the knowledge disciplines that arise with the construction of nineteenth century social science were split across the two cultures/epistemologies: economics, political science and sociology adopted a nomothetic epistemology seeking to produce generalizable, scientific truths through objective analyses of quantifiable data, whereas history, anthropology and oriental studies moved toward an idiographic epistemology focused on describing in rich detail the complexities of particular events in particular moments of time. Wallerstein (1998b, 76) noted that historians in particular "accepted that there did exist an objective reality outside the investigator, a basic premise of science, and that the investigator should not allow his prejudices to intrude upon his analysis," but initially at least the dominant approach questioned the empirical validity of generalizing from the analysis of historical data.

In addition to the epistemological division, Wallerstein cites other cleavages in the history of the construction of the social sciences, and so the division of knowledge, with implications for the functioning of the capitalist world-system. First, history dealt with the past, while economics, political science, and sociology were concerned with analyzing the present. Second, it was pointed out that understanding of the "nomothetic Western present" was structured around "the liberal distinction of the market (economics), the state (political science), and civil society (sociology)" (Wallerstein: 2003a). Third, there was a cleavage between analysis of "the West" (history, economics, political science, and sociology) and "the rest" (anthropology and Oriental studies) (Wallerstein: 2003a, 454). With world-systems analysis as knowledge movement, "a perspective and critique of other perspectives" (Wallerstein: 1999c, 197), the argument being elaborated here was that the disciplinary and epistemological organization of knowledge in the social sciences has worked against our understanding of contemporary reality.

> The partitioning of knowledge about the social world into these six disciplines was of course not accidental. It reflected the dominant world views of the Western world in the nineteenth century, and most particularly liberalism which became crystallized as the geoculture of the world-system in response to the upheavals occasioned and symbolized by the French Revolution. It was the epoch of a belief in progress, progress towards a more civilized world, progress whose principal impulses were thought to be found in the West, progress towards a world in which differentiation of institutions was considered to be a mainstay of the social system. (Wallerstein: 1998b, 75)

That these cleavages were significantly challenged and re-shaped in the post-World War II period is acknowledged by Wallerstein (Wallerstein: 2003a), who in this and other essays advocates the restructuring of the social sciences as the "historical social sciences." He argues that some claim to science is essential given the premise that the world is real and knowable, however contingent and limited this enterprise may be, while analysis of social reality is inherently and unavoidably historical in the sense that the contexts in which any phenomena under investigation are located are locked in a process of constant change over time.

This reconstruction involves a call for a unidisciplinary conception of knowledge, also referred to in terms of "the social scientization of all knowledge" (Wallerstein: 2006, 70). This call is also based on

Wallerstein's consideration of developments within the natural sciences and mathematics identified as "complexity studies" which, in applying the concept of the "arrow of time" whereby "everything expands inexorably," make a deterministic picture of the universe unviable (Wallerstein: 1997a, 1251). He particularly singles out the work of Ilya Prigogine, citing his critique of Newtonian physics in terms of the limited nature of wholly integrated systems and the argument that most systems involve both deterministic and probabilistic processes (Wallerstein: 1999b, 17). The knowledge movement of world-systems analysis then is charged with overcoming the "false debates" about the "antinomies between universalism and particularism" (Wallerstein: 2004a, 147) by bringing together both the sciences and humanities, and under the banner of the historical social sciences engaging researchers simultaneously in nomothetic and idiographic work.

Aguirre Rojas (2000, 751) described this challenge in terms of moving beyond the "limited projects to defend and promote a 'multi,' 'pluri,' 'trans,' or 'inter' disciplinarity within which, however, the core itself is left untouched regarding the division of social knowledge into 'disciplines.' This is the foundation that should really be challenged and radically demolished."

With respect to the phenomenon of globalization theorizing, Wallerstein has taken a critical position by arguing that phenomena identified as new and distinctive to conditions of globalization are often manifestations of longer-term trends and tensions of the capitalist world-economy. In an essay devoted to the issue, Wallerstein (2000a, 250) noted commonly cited features of globalization—declining sovereignty of states, heightened power of global markets, and with these the reduced capacity for cultures to maintain their distinctive identity. He went on to label this sort of globalization discourse as "a gigantic misreading of current reality—a deception imposed upon us by powerful groups and an even worse one that we have imposed upon ourselves, often despairingly. It is a discourse that leads us to ignore the real issues before us, and to misunderstand the historical crisis within which we find ourselves."

Within the limited literature applying WSA in the comparative education field (for a case study see Griffiths and Knezevic: 2010), Clayton (2004) highlighted the importance of a historical perspective, found to be lacking in much of the early globalization theorizing, as a key way forward. Wallerstein's (2000a, 250) essay makes this argument by pointing towards alternative "time frameworks" to understand the present: the five hundred-plus year history of the capitalist world-economy and its current period of transition, and a cycle of expansion and contraction of the world-economy from 1945, the contraction coinciding with a decline in United States hegemony in the world-system.

Wallerstein does not engage in a detailed analysis and critique of globalization theorizing, but elaborates instead the position and perspectives of world-systems analysis. In so doing he highlights how dimensions of the short-term cycles and longer-term secular trends of the capitalist world-system, in effect, constitute phenomena that others cite as evidence of contemporary globalization. For example, a central reference point for globalization theorizing is the intensified movement of capital across national boundaries, with a decline in the capacity of national states to manage or regulate global or transnational capital. As we have indicated, Wallerstein's work points to the long-standing trends of the relocation of capital seeking lower wages in periods of cyclical downturn, an interstate system which has historically constrained state sovereignty, coupled with the imposition of rules on weaker states within a hierarchical system (Wallerstein: 1983, 57). Similarly, crises in legitimacy are linked to the failure of historical antisystemic movements (whether socialist, social-democratic, or national liberation), once in power, to deliver the promises of liberalism; their incapacity to deliver these promises is set in the structural features of the capitalist world-economy. The ensuing sense of "anti-statism" in turn adds to the crises confronting the world-system, undermining "an essential pillar of The Modern World-System, the states system, a pillar without which the endless accumulation of capital is not possible" (Wallerstein: 1998c, 32).

Part of the project of world-systems analysis, then, is an argument to bring its perspectives to the task of locating and understanding contemporary developments, processes and events associated with globalization. A clear example is the phenomenon of neoliberalism, or neoliberal globalization, which from a world-systems analysis perspective must be understood as a major counter-offensive by capital in an attempt "to roll back remuneration costs, to counter demands for internalization of costs, and of course to reduce levels of taxation" (Wallerstein: 2005, 1272–73).

World-systems analysis provides a lens for understanding such events, but also locates causal status to the cycles and trends of the capitalist world-economy over the longer term as generating the neoliberal counteroffensive. Crucially then, Wallerstein (1998c, 32) argued that "The ideological celebration of so-called globalization is in reality the swan song of our historical system...The era of national development as a plausible goal has ended." As with the selection and interpretation of markers like 1968 and 1989 cited above, we see here the capacity for alternative interpretations through world-systems, and long-term historical and global perspectives.

WSA as Politically Engaged, Activist, Intellectual Work

As a knowledge movement, and critique of other dominant perspectives, Wallerstein's world-systems analysis has consistently and overtly been a normative political project, identifying politically engaged intellectual work as a core component of the whole world-systems and broader academic enterprise. Taking the world-system as the primary unit of analysis means viewing developments within nation-states under investigation through this lens, including their location within the world-economy, their hierarchical positioning, and their efforts to maintain or improve their relative position. It also involves contextualizing improved living conditions within a particular nation-state against increased inequality and immiseration at the global level, with the nation-states and interstate system operating historically to support and legitimize this system via a (fledgling) liberal promise of national development for all.

Wallerstein's scholarship establishes the premise that the capitalist world-system is in crisis and in an extended period of transition toward an uncertain replacement system(s). As we elaborate in chapter 4, the role of academics and educators is said to be shaped by these conditions, with the tasks of engaged academic work centering on the intellectual work of understanding social reality, the moral task of imagining and exploring alternatives, and the political task of acting to realize such alternatives. This is concisely expressed in *Utopistics* as "the serious assessment of historical alternatives, the exercise of our judgment as to the substantive rationality of alternative possible historical systems. It is the sober, rational, and realistic evaluation of human social systems, the constraints on what they can be, and the zones open to human creativity. Not the face of the perfect (and inevitable) future, but the face of an alternative, credibly better, and historically possible (but far from certain) future" (Wallerstein: 1998c, 1–2).

This normative call for politically engaged academic work is further supported, within the premises of world-systems analysis, by the actual moment of transition in which we are historically located. The critical argument here is that such moments are rare, given the long life-cycles of world-systems, and that this imperative to act takes on greater importance given that in these historical moments, "the 'free will' factor will be at its maximum" (Wallerstein: 1998c, 37). Wallerstein (1998b) identifies this period of heightened free will, and hence heightened capacity to influence the direction of the transition, as a rare moment of "transformational TimeSpace," one of five different levels of analysis of time and space.

On the question of structure versus agency, and other similar binary debates, Wallerstein asserted that

> Unlike those who huff and puff about agency, I do not believe that we can transform the world at every instant. We—singly, or even collectively—do not have this power. But we can transform the world sometimes, at the 'right' moment. It is precisely when structures move very far from equilibrium, when they are on the edge of bifurcation, that small pushes in one direction or another can have an enormous impact, and can in fact determine the shape of the replacement historical system that will come into existence. (Wallerstein: 1998b, 81–82)

More recently, this was articulated as "the moment when political agency prevails over structural determinism" (Wallerstein: 2010, 140), referring to the historical choices and potentials facing us in this phase of transition. The crucial characteristic we want to emphasize here is the call for intellectual and academic work to be an active and conscious part of the "struggle for the successor system" (Wallerstein: 2010, 140) that is underway, and the normative call for this work to be based on the principles of seeking to construct a more just, peaceful, equal, and democratic replacement system.

World-Systems Analysis and Education

Chapter 4 of this volume deals in detail with the educational implications of Wallerstein's world-systems theorizing and its potential applications, drawing on literature in the critical pedagogy and comparative and international education fields, and focusing on the roles and capacities of education systems to produce particular types of citizens for the current period of systemic transition. To conclude this chapter, the point we want to foreshadow is the significant extent to which Wallerstein's work is intrinsically and inescapably about education. The whole concept of world-systems analysis as a knowledge movement, critiquing dominant paradigms in the social sciences and advocating an alternative perspective—the historical social sciences—with major disciplinary and epistemological implications, makes little sense unless tackling the question of educational systems and their organization and treatment of knowledge. While frequently focused on university education (Wallerstein: 1996), attention to the construction of knowledge disciplines and disciplinary boundaries, and to their epistemological preferences, is found consistently in his corpus. Wallerstein's world-systems analysis is, we argue, an education project, "setting out on the path of constructing a singular epistemology for all knowledge" and creating "a reinvigorated social sciences, one that is both structural and historical" (Wallerstein: 2003a, 460).

The education project of world-systems analysis is embedded in its intellectual foundations, seeking to build the conceptual language and tools for understanding the capitalist world-system, its current transition, and its potential replacement. The unidisciplinary challenge, questioning the utility of analyzing social reality through three ostensibly distinct and autonomous arenas of the economy, the political, and the social-cultural, challenges how we learn and make sense of the world, and therefore how we might work with and teach others to do the same. This volume seeks to elaborate these challenges for educators on this grounding. As Wallerstein (2003a, 460) concluded

> The adventure of the historical social sciences is still in its infancy. The possibilities of enabling us to make substantively rational choices in an intrinsically uncertain world lie before us and give us cause for hope amidst what are now the gloomy times of a historical transition from our world-system to the next one—a transition that is necessarily occurring in the structures of knowledge as well. Let us at least try seriously to mend our collective ways and to search for more useful paths. Let us make our disciplines less dubious.

Chapter 3

Mass Education and Human Capital in the Capitalist World-System

> *It is simply not true that capitalism as a historical system has represented progress over the various previous historical systems that it destroyed or transformed. Even as I write this, I feel the tremor that accompanies the sense of blasphemy. I fear the wrath of the gods, for I have been moulded in the same ideological forge as all my compeers and have worshipped at the same shrines.* (Wallerstein: 1998a, 98)

This chapter explores the global phenomenon of mass education and its relationship to the associated policy dimension of mass education for human capital development/formation in the capitalist world-economy. This is done here, and in the following chapter, in the spirit of this "sense of blasphemy," seeking to better understand and in turn to challenge the dominance of this accepted paradigm.

This chapter thus reviews the application of human capital theory to mass education, highlighting the key points of alignment with a world-systems analysis perspective. Work in the capitalist world-economy, constrained by its differential distribution of global surplus across core, semi-peripheral, and peripheral areas, is next considered in relation to the capital formation policy agenda. We argue that in the field of comparative education, world-systems analysis provides a more comprehensive explanatory account for the rise of global educational policies such as this, pointing to multiple dimensions and processes of the capitalist world-system and its organization of knowledge to demonstrate how the idea of mass education for human capital formation has maintained its position globally in the face of the failures of liberalism for much of the world.

Mass Education

The worldwide expansion of systems of mass education in the nineteenth and twentieth centuries has been a well-documented phenomenon, driven by multiple forces at multiple levels of scale, and of course taking on particular characteristics within particular temporal and geo-political contexts. This phenomenon was generally preceded by models in which either low-cost and minimal education was provided by charity and church-based organizations, and later by the State, for the designated poor or under-privileged, alongside a high-cost elite education accessed by the privileged/upper classes in accordance with their wealth and capacity to pay (see for example Connell: 1980).

Into the twentieth century, nation-states around the world legislated for the provision of free, frequently secular, public education, to some level, for all citizens/residents of the nation. As is well known, this global trend toward universal education was reflected in Article 26 of the 1948 Universal Declaration of Human Rights which explicitly cast education as a basic human right, proclaimed that it should be free and compulsory at the elementary levels, and should be directed to the twin tasks of developing individuals' potentials and to promoting global understanding, respect for human rights, and peace (United Nations: 1948). Initiatives in the twentieth and early twenty-first centuries to achieve the promise of universal primary education developed under the Education for All (EFA) banner, as part of the Millennium Development Goals (see www.un.org/millenniumgoals), highlight the extent to which even these basic aspirations had not been fulfilled in many parts of the world.

Calls for more education for more of the population came from multiple sources and were supported by a developing global logic, or in world-systems terms, by an overarching geoculture or world cultural framework. In many cases, pressure to expand the provision of education came from social movements in recognition of the benefits of education for individuals' development and well-being. From this perspective, education was seen both as an intrinsic good in and of itself, with the capacity to unleash and develop individuals' talents and capabilities, and as a vehicle for future social and economic well-being. Any review of contemporary educational policy, and indeed broader social policy of governments, NGOs, and multiple social movements, would encounter this view of education as a human right contributing to tangible benefits for individuals. At the same time, pressure to expand the provision of education came from policy makers and economists citing a measurable economic benefit for the nation, presented as the rate of return on the investment by the State in public education. The orthodox logic has been that investments in lower levels of education produce the greatest return on investment (see Klees: 2008c), though more than two decades ago the then-head of the World Bank, James Wolfensohn, acknowledged that the return on investments in higher education had been underestimated (cited in Arnove: 1980, 5).

Vally and Spreen (2012, 178) refer to the rise of human capital theory in the 1960s, the subsequent critique from Marxist and Dependency theorists in the 1970s and 80s tied to a broader critique of modernization and development theory, and the subsequent renewal of human capital theory in the 1990s. The changing fortunes and impact of the theory is one of degree, having never gone away entirely.

As a general policy setting, we argue that human capital logic has consistently played a major role in educational policy over this period, and continues to do so in contemporary contexts, despite much of the critique being shown to have been well-founded. For example, a UNESCO (1971) world survey of education noted a tendency for national policies to put forward a conception of the right to education to guarantee individuals' personal development and their contribution to the development of society (14), with educational planning an integral part of broader planning for national economic growth and social development (22). A World Bank Education Sector paper in 1980 continued to claim that

> Studies have also shown that economic returns on investment in education seem, in most instances, to exceed returns on alternative kinds of investment, and that developing countries obtain higher returns than the developed one's education facilitates the advancement of knowledge in pure and applied fields. (World Bank: 1980, 14)

Human capital logic would have an immediate 'common-sense' appeal, arguing that improving the knowledge and skills of future workers will deliver a more highly skilled and efficient workforce, improved rates of employment and productivity, and in the process reduce poverty by improving the wages and well-being of educated and credentialed individuals. Scholars like Fields (1982) noted the persistent dilemma of determining causation in any correlation between education and measures of economic development, and so the extent to which educational expansion can be said to cause economic growth, and/or to the extent to which the later creates favorable conditions for the former.

This problematic lies at the heart of the Marxist and Dependency theory critiques that highlighted structural causes for economic growth, development, or 'underdevelopment', other than or independent of levels of education. As articulated by Vally and Spreen (2012, 179), "education is perceived as a panacea for problems that have their root causes elsewhere in the wider economy and society." As with other universal policy prescriptions, the fit between expanded mass education and the social and economic needs of particular contexts and countries further complicated the issue (and for a broader treatment see Anderson-Levitt: 2003; see for example Kahn: 1989).

A direct consequence of this dominant logic in education has been to convert educational credentials into a commodity to be exchanged for later employment and wage earning possibilities. Educational credentials thus became the key to upward social mobility, accompanied by a meritocratic promise that they are attained as a result of an individual's ability, interest, and effort, such that the differential social and economic success that the differential credentials are exchanged for can be said to be fair. The meritocratic promise holds a strong appeal for its democratizing logic, ostensibly removing the influence of external (social, cultural, economic) factors on individuals' educational achievement via a true level playing field.

As with human capital theory, the appeal of these ideas extended across capitalist and historical socialist contexts, and given the emphasis on central planning, both were arguably more evident and instrumentally applied in the historical socialist camp. Indeed, the former socialist countries produced more meritocratic outcomes in education, by virtue of the more equalized social and economic conditions seeking to address class, race, and gender-based dimensions of social inequality, coupled with political commitments to provide universal education and equal opportunities for success within educational institutions, based on a common and comprehensive curriculum of varying levels of duration (see for example Bain: 2013; Griffiths and Millei: 2013c). This was apparent, for example, in the case of Cuba, with a high level of educational specialization within the school system, including highly competitive, elite upper-secondary high schools providing an academic track to University (for an overview see Griffiths: 2005; 2009a). Selection under socialism was justified using the same meritocratic promise expressed in capitalist contexts, while the logic of directing mass education toward the most efficient selection and development of human capital was similarly shared across both sides of the ideological divide (see Griffiths and Millei: 2013c).

The logic of human capital theory and the practice of meritocracy have been the subject of ongoing attention in the broad field of comparative and international education (e.g., Tabulawa: 2003), and both continue to attract debate (e.g., Griffiths: 2009b). We can, for example, trace the long-standing critique of meritocracy back to the emergence of the new sociology of knowledge in the 1970s, highlighting the bias and hidden curriculum of ostensibly neutral school education knowledge and pedagogical practices (Apple: 1979; Bowles and Gintis: 1976; Young: 1971). What this work set out to systematically demonstrate was that in contrast to the policy rhetoric, educational attainment and achievement had been (and continue to be) influenced by established social inequalities based on race, gender, culture, and nation. That is to say, educational achievement did not neatly correspond with merit, but rather reflected other dimensions of inequality found in broader society/the world, and that in the process, it functioned to effectively reproduce and reinforce these inequalities via the distribution of educational credentials. Bowles and Gintis' (1976) ground-breaking work made a case for how school curricula and the practices of school organization and teachers' pedagogy, prepared students with the skills and dispositions for distinct, class-based educational and occupational tracks. In the decades that followed, we have seen ongoing debate about the nature and extent of schools' reproduction of social inequalities, incorporating more complex and fine-grained dimensions working against the practice of meritocratic ideals, and systemic interventions in school curriculum, organization, and pedagogical practice designed to alleviate these effects and make schools more meritocratic (e.g., Baker, et al.: 2005). Despite this legacy, and with equity gains made in many cases as a consequence of policy interventions, the impact of non-meritocratic factors on students' educational performance continues as a global phenomenon (Bain: 2013; OECD: 2010).

Wallerstein (2006) has long argued that the structure of knowledge across the two cultures of nomothetic and idiographic epistemology has functioned to effectively position science as outside of and more important than culture, making science "the last domain of justifying the legitimacy of the distribution of power in the modern world." It is not difficult to see then how, at the global scale, the science of meritocracy, providing ostensibly equal opportunities within standardized testing regimes, could (consciously or inadvertently) contribute to the entrenchment and legitimation of an unequal distribution of power, and of social and economic resources, based on factors other than merit. Wallerstein (1998c) argued that while there is general agreement that the principle and policy of meritocracy represents a democratizing pressure, at the same time, "the decks are stacked" (77) in current educational systems in ways which constrain the achievement of meritocratic goals.

Moreover, as Griffiths (2009b) has argued previously, the equity and meritocratic policy agenda is itself limited in the sense that it seeks a more meritocratic distribution of rewards within the constraints of the inevitable inequalities of the capitalist world-economy. Such a goal is undoubtedly worthy in the sense that a more authentic application of meritocratic principles is preferable to persistent inequities that entrench social and economic disadvantage, for lifetimes and indeed for generations, for groups based on dimensions like social class, gender, national, cultural, and linguistic background. In many contexts, however, equity goals have become the major—if not the sole—aspiration of education academics, policy makers, and practitioners, under the banner of a social justice agenda.

The intent here is not to present equity goals and those for more radical transformations of education and society as a simple binary, and so to simply dismiss the equity agenda and its manifestations in policy and practice as incompatible with an anti-systemic transition. Rather, we would describe as false debates by those who demand an absolute choice between one side or the other.

As with the question of structure versus agency, for example, such characterizations are a matter of emphasis, in particular historical conditions. Reforms to improve equity outcomes may not explicitly challenge or seek to address wider social inequalities, but they arguably always contain the potential to contribute to such goals by, for example, highlighting the persistence of systemic inequalities in society, and providing the space for debate about the extent to which these inequalities, even if based on merit, ought to be accepted.

What is evident in recent times, however, is the degree to which the equity agenda has effectively replaced, or subsumed, explicit expressions and practices of more radical, transformative goals. This phenomenon may be a reflection of decades of the neoliberal offensive, putting what may have once been radical and anti-systemic movements on the defensive, to create conditions in which equity gains appear as radical goals that remain out of reach. A major component of the equity agenda in education is to actively develop and distribute the cultural capital required for success within existing educational institutions to identified disadvantaged individuals and groups. However delicately articulated, this agenda acknowledges that the identified individuals and groups' under-achieving is linked to their lack of the required socio-cultural knowledge and dispositions. However, this research is often accompanied by an expressed need to avoid deficit-theorizing and deficit discourses that devalue the alternative cultural capital that some groups bring to the school, and so position individuals within the disadvantaged groups as being inherently deficient and in need of remediation to restore them to the 'norm' (e.g., Mills: 2007).

Not surprisingly, difficulties ensue as we grapple with the multiple tensions and contradictions involved in the pursuit of more equitable outcomes for students. These include the possibility of exacerbating educational and subsequent inequities via the provision of a more 'relevant' or 'meaningful' curriculum for disadvantaged students, which functions to deliver a lower-status credential with all of its subsequent implications; the inherently remedial nature of the enterprise that is likely to be hampered by limited resources for schools and teachers to equip all students with the skills and capabilities for educational success; and the overarching location of the 'problem' within individuals and identified 'equity groups' rather than with the school and other institutions and structures of capitalist society (for some elaboration see Griffiths: 2009b).

This situation is further complicated, we would argue, by the reality that some groups of students are in need of remedial action if they are to succeed within existing systems. Moreover, from a world-systems perspective, we would argue that many students are in need of explicit and systematic interventions if they are to be equipped through education with the knowledge and skills necessary to understand the capitalist world-system, and act in and on that world in ways that might influence the direction of its transition to an uncertain alternative world-system.

To reaffirm, our goal here is not to dismiss equity goals and the policy interventions designed to realize them, but to highlight the need to take account of the complexity of such efforts in our consideration and implementation of them, and in this sense to apply a critical world-systems perspective that retains hold of the longer-term, macro transition.

Work in the Capitalist World-Economy

To explore the question of mass education as preparation for work from a world-systems perspective, we need to begin with the analysis of work in the capitalist world-economy. As we outlined in chapter 2, Wallerstein's approach, by virtue of its focus on the historical development and expansion of the capitalist world-economy, carries a particular understanding of social class. The focus is on workers' involvement and location within the production processes that constitute part of global commodity chains, rather than their proletarian status deriving from involvement in very particular forms of social relations with their direct employers appropriating surplus value from their labor. Wallerstein's perspective gives primacy to whether work contributes to the flow of surplus value, and the accumulation of capital, across the world-economy, without the immediate social relations of production in a particular place necessarily being those of an orthodox proletarianized labor force selling their labor and being entirely reliant on their wages for their subsistence. As we reviewed earlier, for Wallerstein, semi-proletarianized workforces, who sell their labor in formal employment but are forced to also rely on additional activities to supplement the wages received in order to subsist, are a major part of the global working class contributing to capital accumulation across the world-economy.

Wallerstein (1998a) characterized this as an inductive approach to classifying capitalism, arguing for its value over alternatives that take the nation-state as the unit of analysis and require specific social relations in the workplace to be dominant within the nation-state. Instead, he argued that his approach better comprehends what we know of social reality historically and in the present, thus in turn providing a better basis for acting on that reality. His approach includes all people whose work is incorporated into global commodity chains, whether as proletarianized wage-labor, semi-proletarian arrangements, or unpaid labor from which a surplus value is not directly extracted, but which through institutions like household structures, and age- and gender-based divisions of labor, effectively subsidize low-wages paid to workers, and in turn the extraction of surplus value and its flow across the commodity chain. He argued that this reality explains why, at the level of the capitalist world-economy, "the location of wage-workers in semi-proletarian households has been the statistical norm" (Wallerstein: 1998a, 27). Perhaps counterintuitively then, from a more orthodox Marxist position, he argued that the global level of fully proletarianized labor remains partial because this has not been in the interests of capital and capitalism's extraction of surplus value across the world-economy.

As the capitalist world-economy expanded and developed, these types of arrangements for labor varied in levels of concentration across core, semi-peripheral, and peripheral zones of the world-economy. Core areas of the world-economy were able to accumulate sufficient surplus, via global commodity chains and supported by structures of vertical integration, to allow higher rates of fully proletarianized labor with sufficiently high wages for a sufficient sector of the workforce—frequently negotiated via institutionalized labor unions—to achieve active or passive support for the system and contain political discontent that might lead to class-based unrest or revolution. Such arrangements allowed capital to continue to achieve profits in core zones sufficient to support the continued accumulation of capital and expansion of capitalist production.

The argument we want to emphasize here is that the disproportionate extraction of surplus value from the peripheral and semi-peripheral zones, via a wide range of labor arrangements and through global commodity chains and the processes of unequal exchange, have functioned to subsidize the relatively high wages and material standards of living within core zones, this being necessary to maintain the stability of the global system. When considering work in the capitalist world-economy across core, peripheral, and semi-peripheral areas, we need to acknowledge and understand these basic structural requirements for the system's effective functioning, and how they intersect with policy and practices deemed to direct education to the development of human capital.

Recent trends in the world-economy, however, as documented for example by Li (2008) in relation to China, have made a significant contribution to world-systems analysis and the understanding of the contemporary crisis and period of transition. This work points to the rise of China, and in turn other geographical areas of the globe, as a process of semi-peripheral expansion that is adding new pressures on the existing system which are exacerbating longer-term trends, and which the logic of capitalism is unable to resolve. The argument here is that we are witnessing a massive and dramatic increase in fully proletarianized labor in China, with accompanying and intensifying pressures to increase wages and labor's share of accumulated capital within the country, as the nation pushes for core status within the world-economy. In a recent review, Wallerstein (2011c, 36) alluded to this thesis by observing that

> The significant increase in the living standards of segments of the populations of the so-called BRIC countries (Brazil, Russia, India, China, and some others) actually compounds the problems of capital accumulation for capitalists by spreading out the surplus-value and thus

reducing the amounts available for the thin upper crust of the world's populations. The development of the so-called emerging economies actually compounds the strain on existing world resources and thereby also compounds the problem for these countries of effective demand, threatening their ability to maintain their economic growth of the last decade or two.

What distinguishes this process from other historical shifts, and from attempts by nation-states to maintain and/or improve their relative position within the core-periphery hierarchy, is the sheer quantitative scope of the push. This, in turn, is coupled with heightened political consciousness globally in the face of recent crises and instability, and opposition to the orthodox responses of international bodies like the World Bank and International Monetary Fund, further squeezing global profits, and the transfer of surplus to the "thin upper crust" in the core, cited above, to critical levels.

As we have noted, this new phenomenon builds on the existing dilemma for the capitalist world-system of new sites for capital relocation reaching their absolute limit, as long-argued (e.g., Wallerstein: 1979; 1999a), limiting this method of maintaining rates of profit to support capital accumulation. Moreover, Li (2008) argues that the massive expansion of the semi-periphery and accompanying rates of consumption further contribute to global environmental crises, to the point that capitalism as a world-system cannot continue.

World-systems analysis leaves us with this macro perspective of work in the world-economy in transition, for which systems of mass education globally claim to be preparing their members and citizens. In these times of seemingly permanent crisis, uncertainty, insecurity, and intensified technological advances and change, we find nineteenth century factory models of mass education asserting their capacity to prepare workers for the nation to compete successfully in the world-economy. We turn now to the capacity of world-systems analysis to account for this global policy, and to provide distinctive insight into its operation, functions, and future prospects.

Educating Good Workers: World Culture or World-System Analysis

Any examination of an official normative educational policy outcome invokes questions of official purposes of formal mass education, how they are determined and enacted, and how they relate to the wider organization of society and its institutions. With respect to mass education, competing understandings and demands are inevitably found, extending to divisions between more liberal conceptions of a comprehensive education for its own sake, views of education as a social good that contributes to a better society through individuals' full realization of their diverse interests and abilities, instrumental conceptions that view education in narrower functionalist terms—preparing students and citizens for particular roles in society, and, of course, a full range of combinations along such a continuum. We may also find additional and alternative goals along the spectrum, including particular religious/spiritual objectives, specialized secular goals in the arts, sports, or sciences, and in some cases overt political purposes.

The objective of directing mass education to the preparation of workers with the skills, dispositions, and discipline required to deliver national economic growth and development is, we believe, an exemplar of a global educational policy that requires world-systems analysis to account for its content and its dissemination and adoption across multiple polities of the capitalist world-system at varying relative states of social and economic development.

Wallerstein's world-systems analysis incorporates a dynamic view of the relationship between the capitalist world-economy and the accompanying geoculture or cultural framework of the world-system (Griffiths: 2011a; Griffiths and Arnove: 2014; Griffiths and Knezevic: 2010). This framework is shown to have developed historically, with a set of core elements that were broadly shared across the competing ideologies and their political manifestations, and so across diverse nation-states and political systems. Griffiths (2011a) has argued that this geoculture of development holds explanatory power for the ideas and forms of institutions created by the modern nation-state, including national systems of education. Most immediately, world-systems analysis points to the logic of endless and linear economic expansion and growth, and of course capital accumulation, which characterizes the world-system.

The manifestation of this logic in the accompanying cultural framework is thus evident in the projects of all nation-states to pursue and achieve national economic growth and development, and to pursue some sort of competitive edge that might increase their share of global surplus relative to other states. To this end, we argue below that current crises in the world-economy, particularly the failure of the development promise upon which all states have drawn legitimacy, and the exacerbated pressures on states' revenues and expenditures as we have set out above, highlight the fragility of global policies like human capital theory and mass education to prepare workers for national development projects.

We come to the crises and search for alternative purposes in more detail below and in chapter 4. The point we want to make here is that world-systems analysis provides an explanatory framework for the rise of mass education systems and their official efforts to prepare good workers, applying human capital theory, to deliver the national economic development that all nation-states aspire to (see Griffiths and Arnove: 2014). World-systems analysis established the economic imperative driving such a policy globally, as all members of the capitalist world-economy have sought to either maintain or improve their relative position within the core/semi-periphery/periphery hierarchy and their share of available global surplus, through state interventions in the national economy. Just as companies under capitalism are compelled to continuously innovate to hold onto market share and address falling rates of profit, nation-states are required to intervene to deliver these national economic objectives within the constraint of the capitalist world-economy.

Critically, world-systems analysis centered on the impact of the world geoculture, or cultural framework, on the very formation of nation-states and their national policies, projects, and institutions linked to the world-economy. This cultural framework includes a common belief in the capacity of rational policy makers, once in power, to take advantage of the scientific and technological revolutions and dominate the natural environment, to deliver linear national economic growth and development and corresponding material abundance. The cultural framework and the economic demands are clearly inseparable and provide a powerful basis for understanding and explaining the emergence and persistence of global policies like human capital formation through mass education.

World-systems analysis is, we argue, a significant advance on a major and long-standing line of research identified as neo-institutionalist or world culture theory, within the broad field of comparative and international education. World culture theory set out to empirically demonstrate educational policy convergence globally, and to attribute causality to a common world culture with respect to the modern-nation state and its institutions, such as mass schooling. This line of work is sometimes described as a particular type or variant of world-systems research, given the research project's scale, but it is one that clearly and explicitly rejects economic accounts of social phenomena like schooling.

World culture theory practitioners have argued that Wallerstein's analysis is not capable of explaining the levels of convergence in policy found across diverse systems in contexts with diverse political systems and with very different levels of social and economic development (see for example Ramirez: 2003). Thus while Meyer et al. (1997) conceded that it is "plausible to argue that dominant actors directly shape world culture" (167), they insisted that world culture is dynamic in its own right and not simply a reflection of "interaction and power relations among actors" (172).

There are, we argue, major flaws in the world culture theorists' reasoning, which the more comprehensive perspective or world-systems analysis resolves. The foundational work of world culture theorists centered on examining and seeking to account for the global spread of mass education in the nineteenth and twentieth centuries (see for example Boli et al.: 1985; Meyer and Hannan: 1979; Ramirez and Rubinson: 1979). It was the phenomenon of mass schooling that scholars like Ramirez and Rubinson (1979, 79) argued could not be adequately explained by a Marxist functionalist or conflict perspective. They claimed that such accounts focus excessively on the differential power of groups or social classes in society, with the resultant conflict and dominant group interests said to be represented in state institutions like schooling that are constructed (e.g., Boli et al.: 1985). This led some to question why dominant groups in power would bother with designing school systems to help reproduce social and economic structures, if they already held state power and therefore the capacity to simply create and enforce/impose such systems. As articulated by Boli et al. (1985, 152), "If the elites have enough power to build a system of social control through mass education, why do they need the system?"

This reasoning is insufficient to refute a realist, conflict account of social relations, too readily dismissing or ignoring the whole concept of hegemony, by which dominant groups achieve and maintain legitimacy by winning the active or passive consent of non-dominant groups in society (for some elaboration see Griffiths and Arnove: 2014).

World culture theory identifies and seeks to explain the spread of mass education across diverse polities, with accompanying diversity in the levels of economic development and, from a stage theory perspective, varying positions along the pathway to the full development of capitalist relations of production within each nation-state. This is presented as crucial evidence of the inadequacy of a Marxist conflict perspective to explain the simultaneous emergence of mass education across these contexts (see particularly Boli et al.: 1985). According to Meyer et al. (1997, 147), for conflict theorists like Wallerstein, culture is of "only marginal interest...seen as self-serving hegemonic ideology or repressive false consciousness."

In contrast, for world culture theorists, the causal motor is located in a world educational culture. However, in elaborating this alternative account, the articulation of the world culture consistently, and we would argue almost inevitably, involves description of economic aspects of the culture, such that the world culture of producing skilled and disciplined workers emerges as a major line of argument for world culture theorists. They claim a link between education and national economic development, referred to as part of the "world polity's myth of progress" (Ramirez and Boli: 1987, 155), whereby the world culture disseminates the view that "formal education is necessary and beneficial for economic growth, technical innovation, citizen loyalty, and democratic institutions, among other things" (Meyer et al.: 1997, 149).

The world culture perspective appears to ask us to accept this cultural characteristic as a driving force for the expansion of mass schooling, but to do so without attributing any causality to the economics of the economic development idea, and without attributing any importance to the capitalist nature of the economic development that is envisaged in the "myth of progress" (see Griffiths and Arnove, 2014). World-systems analysis clearly argues for the need to do just that, in the process overcoming this shortcoming by elaborating an account from the perspective of the capitalist world-system in its totality, and so by definition requiring us to consider the historical structures and development of the capitalist world-economy, the hierarchical location of nation-states within it, and the cultural framework that has accompanied our current world-system for more than two centuries, in order to begin to understand and explain a global policy like mass education for human capital formation.

To recap, we have indicated that the impact of human capital theory on educational policy and discourse is widespread and long-standing. At a macro-level, world-systems analysis can account for the universal aspect of this policy based on a shared geoculture of liberalism, or developmentalism, driven by conceptions of linear and unending national economic development and growth for all nation-states. This perspective identifies the imperative on all nation-states within the world-economy, whatever their structural location, to seek to maintain and/or improve their structural location and share of global surplus, by a combination of attracting capital for high value-added enterprises and developing labor and conditions for core-like economic activities.

We review the contemporary status and prospects of this global policy below, in the context of significant social and economic crises which are weakening the legitimacy of the accompanying logics of the meritocratic distribution of achievement, work, and reward within the world-economy, these being part of the partial collapse of the legitimacy of liberalism's universal promises of progress, development, and upward individual mobility. It persists, despite the crises and loss of faith in the promises of liberalism, as part of a system in decline, and in the context of the tumultuous elaboration of and movement toward alternatives.

Meritocracy and the Formation of Workers

World-systems analysis elaborates a macro-framework for understanding the relationship between formal educational credentials and their distribution within and between nation-states, and how the adoption of claimed universal values and dispositions promoted by formal education systems are an inherent part of the (universal) national development project. A further and major thrust of Wallerstein's work, with direct implications for this production and distribution of educational credentials and the broader policy goal of education to produce good workers, is focused on other social dimensions like race, ethnicity, or gender and how they have operated under the capitalist world-system to explain and justify socio-economic inequalities.

At the heart of this issue is the long-standing historical tension between conceptions of universal and particular knowledge, including understandings of culture, values, and corresponding understandings of social reality (what is) and how we should change it (what ought to be). As we have illustrated, for example, the tight fit between human capital theory in education and the world-system's geoculture of liberalism involves a dominant and universal cultural framework or geoculture of development for all states. In *Culture as the Ideological Battleground of the Modern World-System*, Wallerstein (1990) argued that the uneven levels of development, and the extreme levels of visible and empirically demonstrable inequality in the world-system, have consistently been justified using particularist conceptions of culture. Thus, we may see conceptions of a culture that seek to distinguish one group from another, or entire nations from each other, under the banner of a "national culture," in ways that invoke a hierarchical distribution of cultural attributes and values, measured against some supposed universal standard deemed to be required for national progress and development.

This process involves what Wallerstein (1990, 51) described as the "paired ideologies of universalism and racism-sexism," whereby the failure to adhere to the proclaimed "universal" values and practices required for national progress and development is used to explain and justify inequalities within and between states. Here again, in sharp contrast to the world culture theory perspective, the world-systems reasoning sees culture as inseparable from the development and operations of the capitalist world-economy, neither wholly determined by it nor wholly creating it, but an inextricable part of it. The basic principle of the construction and understanding of universal and particular cultural values here underpins the long history of imperial invasion and conquest and ongoing military interventions by one state over another (see Wallerstein: 2006). Indeed, political and social movements', or even nation-states' advocacy of alternative understandings of progress and development, and so advocacy of alternative national objectives, are rejected as backward or traditional, while attempts to portray such movements or world-views as something "other than a wilful refusal to be 'modern' is labelled Third-Worldism, or reverse racism or irrationalism" (Wallerstein: 1990, 49).

As with educational studies exploring how so-called disadvantaged groups are constructed in ways that characterize them as lacking something, or in deficit, and to thereby locate the blame for poor performance and failure within the individual (see above), at the world-system level, attempts can be made here to justify the poverty of entire states using a similar logic. The nation-state and its political leaders and/or its people are blamed for their underdevelopment, while denying the reality of a capitalist world-economy in which the liberal promise of endless development and abundant consumption for all, in all states, is a structural impossibility. These processes are crucial to the operation of the capitalist world-economy and its logic of maximizing the endless accumulation of capital, which requires the efficient flow of commodities (capital, labor, goods) within and between states. Mechanisms to identify and allocate the most competent people to their most appropriate occupations follow, including mechanisms like mass education (Wallerstein: 1991a, 32).

As we have observed, the concept of meritocracy and its operation contributes (to varying degrees) to the achievement and maintenance of political stability in the face of inequalities, justifying the unequal distribution of jobs, and with them of socio-economic well being, as a direct reflection of differential levels of 'merit.' Wallerstein (1991a,

32) has also long argued, however, that "the meritocratic system is politically one of the least stable systems," precisely because of the ideologies of universalism and racism-sexism, and the ways in which the latter enters the process to demonstrably illustrate that criteria other than merit underlie the unequal distribution of educational credentials, jobs in particular professions, and socioeconomic well-being.

Among critical scholars in the broad field of education studies, meritocracy has long been presented as a myth (e.g., Griffiths and Ladwig: 2003; Johnston: 2000), given that social and economic dimensions have been shown to correlate consistently over time with differential rates of educational participation and achievement.

This sort of discrimination is underwritten by what amounts to a particular conception of universal values, systems, and processes. It has facilitated capitalism's objectives of maximizing the accumulation of capital and its unequal flow from peripheral and semi-peripheral zones to the core zones of the world-economy. This is achieved by minimizing the costs of production in particular geographical areas of the world-economy, justified by ostensibly meritocratic processes that shift responsibility for low wages and poor conditions to local peoples and their governments. This macro-process encapsulates the tensions between universal and particular knowledge and ideas that are a central feature of world-systems analysis, and that extend to the construction of knowledge within educational institutions globally. In this variant of the ideological battleground that Wallerstein refers to, we see the universal principal of mass education preparing skilled workers and loyal citizens for the nation, and its ideology of meritocracy, as it confronts the anti-universalistic principle of racism-sexism or some other form of particularist discrimination.

Forms of racism are of course multiple and complex, and frequently involve so-called 'minority' groups that themselves assert their difference (under the universal banner of recognition of and respect for diversity). As elaborated in Wallerstein (2003d), the responses of minority or particular groups and interests to universal claims take on multiple forms that may include groups rejecting the exclusive nature of universal claims for their failure to take them into account, putting forward their own particular values/culture/practices as the first and/or better universal, and frequently invoking so-called universal concepts of human rights, development, and well-being to argue for their full application to the particular group experiencing disadvantage, while simultaneously advancing the particular interests of the group in question.

In raising these complexities, we are highly conscious of the argument from Boli et al. (1985), cited above, that if a dominant group in society had the capacity to construct mass educational systems to legitimize inequalities in this way, there would be no need to do so, and more direct forms of coercion and repression could simply be applied. Shifting the lens to the macro-scale, however, we see a long history of social and economic inequality associated with the logic and operations of the capitalist world-economy, and multiple combinations of discrimination aligned with the universal-racist/sexist ideological pairing that, in varying ways and to varying degrees, legitimize social inequalities.

Thus we see dominant ideas presented as universal and beyond reasonable contestation setting the parameters for the construction of mass education systems, including the focus on preparing human capital for universal economic growth and development. These and other constructed universal ideas, in turn, attribute blame for the non-achievement of growth and development to states' non-adherence to the universal norms, while the universal notion of meritocracy similarly attributes blame for differential levels of educational success to individuals and their capacities to succeed within existing universal institutions.

World-systems analysis highlights how some form of discrimination, creating and re-creating new "racial and/or ethno-national-religious groups or communities" that are always ranked hierarchically (Wallerstein: 1991a, 34), has provided a constant non-meritocratic basis to justify inequalities that the capitalist world-system must manage. The creation of essentialized social groups in the process allows even lower levels of pay/reward to be tolerated for segments of the labor force. As we have noted earlier, these can be further subsidized via household structures in which mostly females provide unpaid labor to compensate for the low wages. As Wallerstein (1991a, 35) concluded

> The combination of universalism-meritocracy serving as the basis by which the cadres or middle strata can legitimate the system and racism-sexism serving to structure the majority of the work force works very well. But only to a point, and that for a simple reason—the two ideological patterns of the capitalist world-economy stand in open contradiction to each other. This delicately poised combination threatens always to get out of hand, as various groups start to push the logic of universalism on the one hand and of racism-sexism on the other too far.

Wallerstein (1991a) argued that extreme racism such as fascism has been opposed by capital which, while not objecting to racism in principle, benefits most from an ethnicized and productive labor force; while on the other hand, extreme universalism that advances an authentically meritocratic and egalitarian allocation of credentials and occupations is also resisted by capital, often by opposing (by reference to a universal anti-racist principle) measures to address inequities by labeling them 'reverse-racism.'

The dialectic of universalism and racism-sexism involves the sort of standard notion of inequities associated with social, cultural, and economic dimensions of social life, which have a negative impact on the universal formal policy and aspiration of education systems to deliver truly meritocratic outcomes. As we have noted, the equity agenda itself involves a subtle shift of attention away from the systemic factors underlying social and economic inequality (or disadvantage). Wallerstein's (1990) work helps us to see and understand the process by which identified equity or disadvantage are constructed as having particular values and dispositions at odds with those required for educational success, while such groups' assertion of their particular cultural status can result in their socializing members into "cultural expressions which distinguish them from the dominated groups, and thus into some at least of the values attributed to them by the racist and sexist theories" (47).

This is a classic case of hegemony whereby groups' apparent cultural resistance can function to reinforce their oppression. Such socialization and accompanying cultural expressions, within the framework of a dominant geoculture of development that includes a "universal work ethic" as a centerpiece of modernity (Wallerstein: 1990, 46), reinforce and promote racist/sexist accounts that overtly attribute blame for a lack of success to particular attributes of individuals, social and cultural groups, and entire nations. The result is a combination of differentiation being accounted for by meritocratic and racist/sexist logics.

The logic of blaming entire nations for their relative underdevelopment, attributed to claimed social and cultural attributes of the nation, works to deny the reality that endless and linear economic growth, development, and prosperity is systemically not possible for all nation-states. A consequence, as states confront their relative decline within the hierarchy of the world-economy, is frequently to blame weak or poor leadership. As is common historically, decline may also be attributed to the inclusion of particular/diverse cultures and peoples within the nation, which is said to weaken the state, or alternatively the state is presented as ceding its national culture, values, and sovereignty to some world humanist/cosmopolitan culture.

In the face of three or four decades of the neoliberal offensive to recover profits and capital accumulation, exacerbated by the extreme austerity measures confronting the majority in many countries to effectively pay for the losses of bankers in the global financial crisis (Panitch, et al.: 2010; Stiglitz: 2010), we have seen a rise in the frequency and intensity of these sorts of responses. Perhaps emblematic of the phenomenon is the demonization of refugees in contemporary Australia (for a classic study of this phenomenon a decade ago see Marr and Wilkinson: 2003). As one of the world's wealthiest countries which, due in large part of its export of natural resources to China and other high growth countries and to a short-lived Keynesian response by the Federal government, Australia has not to-date experienced the dramatic effects of the GFC evident elsewhere. Yet, even in wealthy and relatively comfortable Australia, we have recently seen the bipartisan decision to excise the whole of mainland Australia from the country's migration zone, so as to deny asylum seekers the basic right to their claim for asylum being processed on mainland Australia, extending what Marr and Wilkinson (2003) identified as the irrational fear of migrants arriving by boat.

The Australian case appears to align with that found in many parts of the world, where actual or potential future (national economic) decline is blamed on minority groups in general, and refugees in particular, fueling calls to overcome this through the reassertion of some mythical and historical particular cultural past.

Educational Knowledge Structures and Mass Education for Work

At this point, we want to elaborate, from a world-systems perspective, the relationship between the general tendencies or trends in the conceptualization and operation of knowledge disciplines and their corresponding epistemologies, and the global policy paradigm of mass education as preparation of human capital for work. We have reviewed how, at the macro-level, the capitalist world-economy has been structured to distribute global surplus unequally across hierarchical zones, via a global division of labor, global commodity chains, and a process of unequal exchange. Ostensibly independent nation-states, operating within an inter-state system, seek to implement policies within their borders and to influence international and supra-national frameworks and arrangements, so as to maximize their share of global surplus, and in turn their level of economic growth and development within the world-economy, and their capacity to support, maintain and expand this.

This foundational structuring of the capitalist world-economy, we believe, functions to support the concept of education for human capital development across all nation-states, and their multiple political arrangements, as part of their respective projects for national economic development and progress. On this basis, we would argue that there is general support for the policy across social classes, just as we witnessed support historically for such a policy within ostensibly anti-systemic, socialist states. Moreover, as we have also outlined above, the dominance of the geoculture of liberalism, and hierarchical knowledge structures embedded within it, has meant that deviations from this general policy position are constructed as inferior and/or backward-looking cultural positions, and likely to be included in particular causal accounts for nation-states' under-development within the bounds of the world-economy.

How has the structuring of knowledge within the capitalist world-system contributed to this phenomenon? To respond to this question, we need to provide a brief overview of Wallerstein's critique of the separation of knowledge (and in particular the social sciences) across nomothetic and idiographic epistemologies, thus separating the search for truth from the search for beauty, and connect this with his associated conceptualization of timespace.

We have presented the argument about how the geoculture of liberalism entrenched an ideology of linear developmentalism across all parts of the world-economy (Wallerstein: 2005). A belief in development as a possibility for all states, with prosperity for all to be found over the horizon, operated to legitimize political parties, in and out of power, across the system, including what began as anti-systemic socialist parties and movements. Wallerstein's work on the historical structures of knowledge is crucial for understanding how this dominant ideology of liberalism worked through educational structures to also support the inequalities of the system.

The separation of knowledge across the two cultures of nomothetic and idiographic epistemologies rendered scientific knowledge and the pursuit of universal truth as the foundation that would underpin the scientific and technological revolutions that, in turn, once harnessed by rational policy makers, would deliver the development promise. A consequence that continues to be reflected in modern educational institutions, albeit with increasingly porous boundaries and active calls for cross-, inter-, or trans-disciplinary work (Aguirre Rojas:

2000), has been the formalized structure of knowledge into disciplines with particular epistemological understandings, and associated claims to producing generalizable (universal) truths on the one hand, and particular descriptions and insights on the other.

Wallerstein has written extensively about the place of the social sciences within this historical separation of knowledge across the two cultures, beginning with the modern university relegating philosophy and the humanities to idiographic understandings of the good/beautiful, and the hard sciences to the nomothetic uncovering of universal truths. He has written volumes (e.g., Wallerstein: 1996; 2004a) and numerous articles documenting this historical phenomenon—the division of the disciplines within the social sciences across the two cultures—and arguing for both the reunification of nomothetic and idiographic epistemology in favor of a "singular epistemology for all knowledge" (Wallerstein: 2003a, 460), referred to in other work as a "unidisciplinary" (Wallerstein: 2004c, 19) approach to knowledge.

There are multiple dimensions to this work. At the most basic level, the relegation of philosophy and the search for the good/beauty to secondary and inferior status, in favor of the hard sciences, carried with it all of the predictable social, political, and cultural implications of such a change. Having historically been a central focus of formal education, the reduced status changed the very nature and purpose of formal education.

At the broad level, the division of knowledge across nomothetic and idiographic epistemologies directly facilitated the development of dominant Western European Universal knowledge (universalism), under the guise of its scientific and nomothetic status, that provided the historical justification for colonialism and other forms of intervention and domination by core/powerful states. Wallerstein (2006, 27) provided an extended essay on this question, observing that "the interveners, when challenged, always resort to moral justification—natural law and Christianity in the sixteenth century, the civilizing mission in the nineteenth century, and human rights and democracy in the late twentieth century and twenty-first centuries." He added that this occurs "within the framework of accepting the values of the interveners as universal ones. If one observes that these universal values are the social creation of the dominant strata in a particular world-system, however, one opens up the issue more fundamentally."

In opening up the issue more fundamentally, we observe first that the structuring of knowledge in education systems, and its presentation to effectively and efficiently prepare, sort, and allocate human capital, was similarly the creation of the dominant strata of the capitalist world-system. Second, the dominance of scientific knowledge provided the veneer of scientific rationality to the differential allocation of educational credentials, and implicitly endorsed the liberal promise that the correct application of this knowledge could and would lead to national growth and development.

Wallerstein's (1998b) paper on the concept of *timespace* provided a synthesis of some of the other divisions or cleavages of social science knowledge that, along with the epistemological divisions, have facilitated a particular hierarchy and the claims to universal status for particular knowledge, that similarly work to justify intervention and domination, and to maintain policies of mass education for human capital formation. In addition to disciplinary divisions, we see the temporal division of past (history), and present (economics, political science, sociology), and the politically loaded geographical division of the study of the West (economics, political science, history, sociology) and the "Other/non-West" (anthropology, oriental studies), or as expressed elsewhere, the study of "the West and the rest" (Wallerstein: 2003a, 454). A consequence of these divisions was that the dominant knowledge of "eternal timespace," being knowledge involving universal explanations of phenomena with an "assumption of timelessness and spacelessness" (Wallerstein: 1998b, 73), was primarily knowledge of the natural sciences (scientific or European universalism). In this framework, the disciplines of economics, political science, and sociology emulated scientists through the quantifiable study of the immediate present, seeking to similarly produce knowledge as eternal timespace. Thus while nomothetic disciplines tended to use eternal timespace in their analysis, idiographic disciplines tended to use episodic geopolitical timespace, whereby events are tied to the meanings given to them by the immediate, short-term context of time and space.

We can see here how a policy, and an intellectual understanding, of mass education to transfer knowledge and skills to human capital required for national economic activity and development, might become part of eternal timespace, particularly given its roots in economic theorizing about the rates of return on investments in education.

Wallerstein's (1998b) discussion of alternative kinds of timespace, used to approach and make sense of social reality, is linked to the broader argument for the reunification of nomothetic and idiographic epistemology and a unidisciplinary conception of knowledge. The general tendency of social science disciplines to adopt one or the other, he argues, via eternal or episodic geopolitical timespace, "made time and space socially exogenous and, in consequence, in the long run socially unimportant" (79). More sharply, he argued that Time and Space were thus constructed as "formidable realities, colossi to whose implacable constraints we must yield" (79), functioning to present action within the social world to shape and construct social reality as "difficult, if not impossible."

Again, we can see the appeal of a global policy of human capital theory in education, perhaps offering the best opportunity available for human agency to have an impact on implacable space and time via incremental change, while limiting even the intellectual space for alternative educational purposes to be considered.

Wallerstein identified three other kinds of timespace that can facilitate both the bringing together of alternative epistemologies within a unified or unidisciplinary historical social science, and can contribute to understanding and to taking action that can influence future social reality. These were cyclico-ideological timespace, which references long-term cyclical trends to help explain immediate history; structural timespace, which makes long-term explanations by reference to the historical system and its space and time boundaries; and transformational timespace, which, in stark contrast to the concept of eternal timespace, seeks to uncover the exceptional nature of particular events and conditions which contribute substantively to the rupture and transformation of the existing system and its institutions.

The reasoning here is that the alternative kinds of timespace identified necessarily yield alternative interpretations of the phenomenon under investigation, and, as with world-systems analysis itself, argue that some of these provide better understandings of social reality than others. Cyclico-ideological and structural timespace may help to account for the dominance of human capital theory in mass education systems, linked to the cycles and logics of the capitalist world-economy, while transformational timespace offers the possibility for alternative policies to prevail, which may contribute to the wider antisystemic transition. This is the focus of the proceeding chapter.

To conclude here, as briefly noted above (p. 55), it is important to affirm that we believe the general argument for mass education as preparation of skilled and disciplined workers, expected to simultaneously compete in the global economy and deliver national economic development, continues to hold and underpin global policy paradigms, under contemporary conditions (described by many as 'globalization'). We return to this in chapter 4 when discussing key fractures in the dominant ideology of liberalism, but we foreshadow here the argument that in the current context of the capitalist worldeconomy's transition, we continue to see the discourse and associated policies of liberalism put forward by governments/policy makers and (inter)national institutions, and by publics.

Despite the failure of nation-states to deliver on the promises of liberalism, whether under the banner of socialist or capitalist economies and ideologies, the promises and accompanying logics of liberalism continue to be put forward as viable solutions. The promises of mass education to deliver upward social mobility for individuals and for the nation, through the preparation of good and disciplined workers, similarly continues with an apparent high degree of support.

Conclusion

We conclude this chapter by returning to the pivotal point of worldsystems analysis, this being the argument that the capitalist worldeconomy simply has not, and cannot, deliver the development promise to the multiple polities that make up its constituent parts. In the volume *After Liberalism,* Wallerstein (1995a) elaborates the thesis that the collapse of actual existing socialism, of the Soviet Union and Eastern Europe, was a major blow, not to the socialist alternative, but to the world-systems geoculture and its promise of national development for all. Wallerstein (1995a) provocatively concluded that 1989 marked the end of "any serious prospect for the economic transformation of the periphery within the framework of the capitalist world-economy" (121). This view was neatly summarized as follows:

> It is true on the one hand that some so-called national development is always possible, indeed is a recurrent process of the system. But it is equally true that, since the overall maldistribution of reward is a constant, both historically and theoretically, any 'development' in one part of the world-economy is in fact the obverse face of some 'decline' or 'de-development' or 'underdevelopment' somewhere else in the world-economy. (167)

We return to this central premise to emphasise the inherent weakness, in the long term, of the mass education for human capital formation policy. The conditions of the capitalist world-system in crisis and a period of transition, most emphatically manifest in the crisis of global warming, create the conditions for alternative conceptions of development, of schooling, and of education, to be constructed. These conditions highlight the historical disconnect between human capital theories and work in the capitalist world-economy, and like the promise of universal national economic growth and development, the fundamental inability of education to realize this goal. It is to the fuller consideration of alternatives that we now turn.

Chapter 4

Educating Critical Citizens for an Alternative World-System

> *These are our times, and it is the moment when social scientists will demonstrate whether or not they will be capable of constructing a social science that will speak to the worldwide social transformation through which we shall be living.* (Wallerstein: 1999c, 201).
>
> *Critical pedagogy isn't formulaic, it isn't stagnant, and it isn't an is. I believe it is what isn't...*(Steinberg: 2007, x)

Introduction: A New Geocultural Framework?

Referring to the institutionalist branch of global studies, whose educational variant is discussed in preceding chapters, world-systems scholars Boswell and Chase-Dunn (2000, 25) presented the interstate system as promoting and developing over time a world polity, with "shared cultural definitions of what is legitimate among states and other global actors...institutionalizing the parameters of what is a goal worth pursuing." The ensuing world polity is both defined by and defines the operation of the interstate system, and the logics of the world-system that underpin them. Boswell and Chase-Dunn's (2000) interest was in associated strategies for transforming the capitalist world-system by changing the world polity, or in Wallerstein's terms, the geoculture of the world-system.

As we have illustrated, this seemingly straightforward proposal is complicated by the hegemonic nature of the existing geoculture of liberalism or developmentalism. As Wallerstein (1995a, 171–75) argued, within the capitalist world-system nation-states pursued alternatives to the dominant geoculture of liberalism in two main ways. First, they sought alternative paths to the same goal of national development, whether by more or less state planning and involvement in the national economy, through attempted important substitution and/or export-led growth, through structural adjustment packages underwritten by international agencies, or some particular combination. The alternative was about strategy or methods, rather than purpose and goals, and was characteristic even of overtly anti-systemic governments and movements. Second, but less frequently, nation-states sought to elaborate a range of critiques of the geoculture and its transformation in a way that works against the logic of endless capital accumulation, whether by promoting spiritual (traditional or other) over material values, promoting collective over individualist ideals, promoting cultural diversity over the dominance of a limited European universalism, or promoting ecological sustainability over humankind's domination of the natural environment.

In contemporary times, we are witnessing some more developed cases where the elaboration of an alternative geoculture is being explicitly invoked, and pursued, challenging the dominant ideology of liberalism and seeking to construct a viable alternative. These include countries that are part of the move in Latin America over the past 10–15 years to define and implement a twenty-first century socialist alternative to neoliberal capitalism (see for example Burbach et al.: 2013b). This movement includes the construction of international agencies and agreements that directly correspond to and provide alternatives to existing bodies and agencies, promoting and disseminating an alternative cultural framework for international social, political, and economic relations. For example, ALBA (the Bolivarian Alliance of Our Americas) was established in 2004 as a direct counter to the North American-led ALCA (Free Trade Agreement of the Americas); CELAC (Community of Latin American and Caribbean States) was inaugurated in December 2011 to counter the North American-dominated OAS (Organization of American States); the Bank of the South was established in September 2009 as a counter to the World Bank; and UNASUR (the Union of South American Nations) was formalized in 2008 to pursue South American integration. While the anti-systemic nature of this broad movement, and these organizations and their bilateral and multilateral agreements, is necessarily an open and ongoing question, it clearly holds historically significant potential to contribute to a twenty-first century anti-systemic movement in these times of "worldwide social transformation" (Wallerstein: 1999c, 201).

The case of Bolivia is distinctive within this broader movement, in terms of challenging the notion of endless national economic growth, and defining an alternative understanding of "development," driven both in response to the ecological crisis of global warming and by Indigenous values and practices with respect to life and the land (Burbach et al.: 2013a). In other cases, as sympathetic leftist scholars like James Petras (2009; 2010) have observed, the economies of nation-states like Venezuela and Ecuador continue to varying degrees to be driven by resource extraction models to underpin increased levels of consumption, and so to some extent continue to meet the interests of capital and capital accumulation (see also Álvarez: 2010). Moreover, the promises of liberalism, in terms of policy goals of rapid catch-up-style development and growth, with a more equitable distribution of wealth to realize greater material well-being for the previously excluded majority, arguably remains an overarching theme, or at the very least persists in multiple ways, in the policy rhetoric and practice of twenty-first century socialism.

These brief introductory reflections are indicative of the turbulent contexts in which we are living, and from a Wallersteinean perspective, of significant shifts or ruptures in the legitimacy of the dominant geoculture of liberalism and further signs of its decline as significant populations and nation-states actively endorse some sort of anti-systemic alternative. While precisely defining historical turning points is fraught with difficulty, there is much scholarship to support the assertion that these days, years, and decades, are indeed "our times," and that this conscious application of human agency "can in fact determine the shape of the replacement historical system that will come into existence" (Wallerstein: 1998b, 82).

The Critical Pedagogy Heritage

It is not possible to talk of a critical education, whether as critique of existing systems, structures, and practices, or efforts to develop students' capacity for a critical reading of reality, without invoking the long-standing and extensive movement of critical pedagogy. Founded on the work of Paulo Freire, critical pedagogy scholarship has actively been engaged in these dual and tightly connected tasks. Its practitioners consistently and relentlessly analyze existing systems, their curricular and pedagogical practices, to reveal how they "reproduce dominant values that, ultimately, work counter to the very democratic ideals that schools seemingly promote...[and]...prepare young people to live with those contradictions and to accept them and to think they're OK" (Zinn and Macedo: 2012, 121).

Coupled with this critique, critical pedagogy seeks to engage teachers in educational interventions that develop students' critical consciousness, their knowledge and capacities, required to make a critical reading and understanding of society/the world, its injustices and inequalities, in order to act and transform social reality (see for example McLaren and Kincheloe: 2007). Here we can envision a continuum between visions of education that prepare citizens for their functional participation within existing society and its structures, to one focused on preparing citizens to actively transform society.

It is not uncommon to hear Freire's (1970b) critique of the "banking concept of education," which likened the dominant pedagogical practice to banking in the sense of knowledge being deposited by educators into their students as though they were empty vessels, being invoked in contemporary teacher education programs calling on future teachers to adopt a more active view of their students. In a similar way to Vygotsky's work being reduced in initial teacher education to the concept of the zone of proximal development, and in the process stripped of its politics, Freire's work is often reduced to this banking concept of education which, in the spirit of de-politicized student-centered pedagogy, teachers should overcome. Freire's (1970a, 60) foundational critique, however, described how the dominant approach to teaching saw students as

> adaptable, manageable beings... The more completely they accept the passive role imposed on them, the more they tend simply to adapt to the world as it is and to the fragmented view of reality deposited in them.

The result for Freire (1970b) was a acutely politicized pedagogy of oppression, in the sense that the process of education was reduced to the uncritical transfer of knowledge from teacher to student, with no space for students' critical understanding and evaluation of the received knowledge, and hence with no overt space to develop their critical understanding of the world and their place in the world.

The alternative pedagogy advocated by Freire involved authentic dialogue between educator and students, acknowledged and valued students' prior knowledge brought to the classroom, and above all advocated an educative process as one of critical consciousness raising, or *conscientizacion,* in which students' critical understanding of social reality contributed to their capacity to move from this understanding to acting in and on the world in order the bring about transformative social change. Put simply, after discussing the social problem of hunger and the impossibility of charitable initiatives to resolve the problem of hunger, Freire (2007, 7) observed that "we need to approach problems in such a manner as to invite people to understand the relationship between the problem and other factors, like politics and oppression... It is up to us to make history and to be made and remade by it."

These sorts of core concepts of Freire's critique of conventional, oppressive education, and advocacy of liberatory alternatives, have thus been taken up by critical theorists and pedagogues across the world. Given the scope of the critical pedagogy corpus grounded in this work, however, it is difficult, and of course contentious, to simply characterize the entire field. As is evident from these foundations, under the critical pedagogy banner, we find a significant body of scholarship from Marxist perspectives, critically examining the ways in which education systems, their organization, curricula, and pedagogies, function to maintain and legitimize the status quo of capitalist social reality (e.g., Hill: 2006; Allman: 2010).

The critical perspective has similarly encompassed multiple other trajectories and dimensions of this problematic, including critique from feminist, culturally diverse and post-colonial perspectives that highlight particular dimensions or categories of oppression experienced under conventional systems and their dominant pedagogical practices (see for example Darder: 2011).

To return to the heart of the critical pedagogy project, and mindful of Steinberg's (2007) incisive characterization, Giroux (2007, 2) succinctly captures the goal of creating educational spaces in which students learn to "think critically and act with authority as agents" within the classroom, and through this practice develop their skills, knowledge, and capacities to critically examine/question the many "deep seated assumptions and myths that legitimate the most archaic and disempowering social practices that structure every aspect of society." Here Giroux (2007) highlights two key features of critical pedagogy—the capacity for critique and the capacity (and disposition towards) agency and action, or praxis. Critical pedagogical practice then involves teaching students "to believe that democracy is desirable and possible" (Giroux: 2007, 3), and who then are obliged to act, to assert their authority as agents, in the realization of such possibilities. Giroux (2007, 2) also articulates the essence of critical pedagogy's intended outcome—action to transform the world.

> Pedagogy always represents a commitment to the future, and it remains the task of educators to make sure that the future points the way to a more socially just world, a world in which the discourses of critique and possibility in conjunction with the values of reason, freedom, and

equality function to alter, as part of a broader democratic project, the grounds upon which life is lived.

In what follows, we seek to connect Wallerstein's world-systems analysis with the critical pedagogy project. Noting the limited reference to Wallerstein within the critical pedagogy field, we highlight the alignments and potential for what we call a 'critical world-systems education,' building on the critical pedagogy tradition, to contribute further to the task for educating to support more democratic, equal, and just social and political transformations in a world-system in transition.

World-Systems Analysis and Critical Pedagogy

Amidst the diverse trajectories of critical pedagogy theorizing and practice, we have suggested that a major identifiable theme centers on the argument that human agency can be harnessed to struggle for and achieve social transformation and liberation. This is exemplified in the work of Giroux (2007) cited above, whereby individual students are conceived as active critical agents, conscious of their individual and collective power to act on and transform the world. Dominant or hegemonic educational practices are understood in oppressive terms, actively and passively obscuring a critical reading of social reality, while contributing to the maintenance of oppressive and unequal social systems. The critical pedagogy project appears to involve a belief in the potential to transform and overcome such practices through the critically conscious practices of critical educators.

This is not a prescriptive, linear account of inevitable transformation led by enlightened critical agents, however, in the Old Left spirit of an intellectual vanguard, but an aspirational, broader movement that both explores and advances the possibilities for such change through informed critical reflection and action of agents. Critical pedagogy is a movement in the sense that it seeks to constantly challenge established orthodoxies in educational practice, and to expand its reach geographically and across educational sectors, to build a movement of active, critical, authoritative agents enacting social change in and on the world.

At a glance, there are clearly multiple connections between this broad project and Wallerstein's work as presented in this volume. We elaborate some of these below, as groundwork for imagining a critical world-systems education. These connections include an active interest in imagining utopian (or utopistic in Wallerstein's terms) dreams as a necessary part of understanding and acting on reality. As expressed by Freire (2007: 3–4)

> Recently, reactionary forces have obtained success in proclaiming the disappearance of ideologies and the advent of a new history, one devoid of social classes and, therefore, without antagonistic interests or class struggle. At the same time, they maintain that there is no need to keep talking about dreams, utopia, or social justice. However, to me, *it is impossible to live without dreams*. How can we accept these neoliberal discourses that have been preached as if they were real and also keep our dreams alive? One way to accomplish that, I believe, is to awaken the political consciousness of educators.

This sort of invocation resonates with Wallerstein's articulation of the moral task of educators and politically engaged academics to imagine an "alternative, credibly better, and historically possible (but far from certain) future" (Wallerstein: 1998c, 2). Before exploring these alignments in more detail, however, it is striking to first note the limited reference to Wallerstein within the critical pedagogy field. A scan of two recent major collections of exemplary, indeed seminal, critical pedagogy papers (McLaren and Kincheloe: 2007; Darder et al.: 2008) finds not a single reference to Wallerstein's world-systems analysis. The same holds in Allman's (2010, 11) recent volume, although she, too, calls for strategies and alliances "intended to contribute toward the eventual abolition of capitalism and the beginning of a new and better future for humankind."

We could speculate on this limited use of Wallerstein by critical pedagogues, but a thorough account would require a more rigorous investigation of the phenomenon than that provided here. The results may be that it simply doesn't matter. In articulating a proposed reconstruction of the social sciences, Wallerstein (2004a, 181) argued "What I shall do, therefore, is pick a series of cultural prejudices that I think work better than their alternatives and that I hope would serve, in combined form, as the foundation stones of the putatively reconstructed arena I am calling the historical social sciences." Perhaps we are all engaged in some similar process, such that the inclusion of one scholar over another simply reflects these underlying decisions. That is to say, it may simply be a matter of ideological and political preferences. Followers of other major scholars may well ask similar questions of this and other volumes—Why such limited use of David Harvey or Alain Badiou? for example. Perhaps, as we noted in an investigation of the take-up of Wallerstein's work within the field of comparative and international education (Griffiths and Knezevic: 2009), Wallerstein's work is characterized solely as part of the neo-Marxist critique of modernization theory, and so is perceived as a perspective whose time has come and gone in the linear progression of political philosophy. Perhaps accusations of economic determinism leveled at Wallerstein (e.g., Skocpol: 1977) see the work rejected by some critical pedagogues whose emphasis is clearly on human agency and action. There are exceptions, however, such as Cho's (2013) recent volume that we draw on below.

The major point we want to make here is first to acknowledge that the limited connections between these intellectual trajectories is something this work seeks to address. Relatedly, our purpose is to promote the examination and use of Wallerstein's work, to the point that we begin to imagine a Wallersteinean conceptualization of critical world-systems education, based on a belief that his work, and mode of theorizing, has much to offer the field.

To elaborate some of the major alignments then, and building on the shared aspiration to imagine future worlds, the very project of critically examining existing social reality, or 'what is,' as an inherent part of this process, is embedded in Wallerstein's work. We have covered in some detail Wallerstein's conceptualization of world-systems analysis as a knowledge movement or perspective that seeks to unthink established categories of analysis and structures of knowledge, in order to generate a better understanding of social reality. This intellectual project centers on a sustained critique of what is, involving long-term historical analysis to understand the cycles and deeper structures that produced the objects of critique, and a belief that a unidisciplinary approach to knowledge that brings together nomothetic and idiographic epistemology can generate better or more accurate representations of social reality, of truth and beauty. Moreover, it is explicitly based on a particular understanding of capitalism and its development as a world-system, its rise and future demise (Wallerstein: 1974b), advocating the use of cyclico-ideological, structural, and transformational timespace in this analysis (Wallerstein: 1998b).

The world-systems approach, focusing on cyclical trends within longer-term structures of the historical system as an improved way of understanding its trajectory, is subversive of the historical system itself insofar as it raises questions about its assumptions, its structuring of the cultural discourse, and the orthodox, universal, geocultural idea of gradual progress over time.

Wallerstein's focus is on the critical (re)evaluation of existing social reality, its systems, structures, and power relationships that underlie inequalities within and between nation-states, within the historical capitalist world-economy. The broad critical pedagogy project holds similar aspirations. Critical pedagogy is on the one hand focused on the practices of educators within formal education systems, acting within the constraints of those systems and their curricular and organizational frameworks. Much of this research involves case studies of educators making spaces within these contexts to work with their students in ways that develop their critical consciousness and their capacity to become critical agents in the transformation of society (e.g., Duncan-Andrade and Morrell: 2007; Darder et al.: 2008). Other work in the field expands the focus to sites of non-formal and popular education, and the potentials within these contexts to advance critical consciousness raising through critical pedagogical practices by critical education (e.g., Martin: 2005). In this sense, we argue there is close alignment with world-systems analysis, which is concentrated on the content of the critical understanding of social reality that critical educators might engage with in their practice.

The same might be argued for multiple, competing accounts of history and social reality, including post-structuralist positions questioning the capacity of any account to make a claim to truth, or even to claim precedence over other accounts. On this question, we note Wallerstein's (1997a, 1254) unambiguous position that world-systems analysis, as a knowledge movement, seeks to work through the socially constructed nature of knowledge to arrive at better or "more correct" approximations of truth.

> We seek to discover the reality on the basis of which we have constructed reality. And when we find this, we seek to understand how this underlying reality has in turn been socially constructed. In this navigation amidst the mirrors, there are however more correct and less correct scholarly analyses. Those scholarly analyses that are more correct are more socially useful in that they aid the world to construct a substantively more rational reality. Hence the search for truth and the search for goodness are inextricably linked the one to the other. We are all involved, and involved simultaneously, in both.

In another volume, he more forcefully asserts that

> perhaps the problem is the entire thought-system of the capitalist world-economy. The so-called postmodernists have suggested this, to be sure. I am sympathetic to many of their critiques (most of which, however, we have been saying more clearly, and indeed earlier). However, I find them on the whole neither sufficiently 'post'-modern

nor sufficiently reconstructive. They will certainly not do our job for us. (Wallerstein, 1999c: 198)

Without returning to speculation about the limited use of Wallerstein within the broad field of critical pedagogy, we could certainly suggest that some lines of critical pedagogy research adopting a post-structuralist lens would be less than taken by Wallerstein's approach, yet there are key and distinctive elements of his analysis that further support our claim of its alignment with the critical pedagogy project in its broadest sense, and undoubtedly with what Martin (2007) refers to as "revolutionary critical pedagogy."

Wallerstein has developed and maintained a consistent and overt political agenda, in effect built into his world-systems analysis, arguing that capitalism as a world-system will come to an end, and on this basis seeking to identify both the empirical basis for its transition toward an undetermined alternative system, and to take political action to influence this transition. This sort of normative political agenda connects with a critical pedagogy position of identifying, critiquing, and acting to overcome oppressive practices within educational systems and in broader society. Kincheloe (2007, 37), for example, described the sort of identity construction that critical pedagogy sought to advance in terms of producing "conscious individuals who are aware of their self-production and the social conditions under which they live." This sort of call for the formation of particular individuals is made in different ways by Wallerstein, but is a consistent and indeed a central part of his work.

This sort of alignment is evident in Wallerstein's advocacy for politically engaged academics, as outlined in chapter 2. He makes the normative call for academics and educators to engage in, and promote others' engagement in, three distinct areas of activity: the analytical and intellectual task of understanding social reality (as cited above), the moral task of searching for the good and beautiful, of imagining and seeking to articulate how things could and should be, and the political task of taking action to bring together, in practice, the truth with conceptions of the good, and to influence the nature and direction of social transformation (see for example, Wallerstein: 2006, 80). This is a classic call for revolutionary praxis. In this vein, almost two decades ago, Chase-Dunn and Grimes (1995, 414–25) concluded

> This potential for world-systems analysis to enable us to understand social change and act in a collectively rational way to avoid predictable disasters (such as global war and environmental collapse) is the most

alluring aspect encouraging research in the area. Already we know that our current system is wobbling dangerously close to the edge of growth limits. As the best unit of analysis for studying social change on a global level, world-systems theory provides social science with a new purchase that can produce a robust and scientific theory explaining both the past and likely future...But today the study of world-systems promises to wrest our expectations about the future away from theology and into the realm of science. In this respect, sociology may now be able to join with other sciences in demystifying the world.

Given the scope and complexity of the collapse of the capitalist world-system and its transition toward an uncertain alternative, Wallerstein has been typically reluctant to put forward more specific programatic actions beyond the three-pronged characterization of the task before us and the articulation of some broad principles that should guide our action, including: (1) massively expanding "serous intellectual analysis"; (2) replacing the goal of economic growth with the goal of "maximum decommodification"; (3) creating "local and regional self-sufficiencies" to construct an alternative globalization of multiple autonomies and universalisms; (4) abolishing foreign military bases; (5) aggressively pursuing "ending the fundamental social inequalities of gender, race, ethnicity, religion, sexualities—and there are others"; and (6) recognizing that all of these are contingent on our avoidance of irreversible climate change, nuclear war, and massive pandemics (Wallerstein: 2011c). These sorts of general principles, and arguably vague outlines of a normative political project, can be frustrating for those seeking guides to immediate action. In the final words of *After Liberalism*, Wallerstein acknowledged this dilemma.

> You may think that the program I have outlined for judicious social and political action over the next twenty-five to fifty years is far too vague. But it is as concrete as one can be in the midst of a whirlpool. I have said essentially two things about life in a whirlpool. First, know to which shore you want to swim. And second, make sure that your immediate efforts seem to be moving in that direction. If you want greater precision than that, you will not find it, and you will drown while you are looking for it. (Wallerstein: 1995a, 271)

The acknowledgement here, linked to the lack of certainty over the future replacement world-system, allows for human agency in its determination that cannot be predicted in advance. It is, we would argue, entirely consistent for example with Nikolakaki's (2012a, 29) assessment that critical pedagogy in contemporary times must promote the sense of freedom, an inner sense that radicalizes and revolutionizes interpersonal and group relations, an inner revolution, which will express itself outwardly and will transform the existing structures, relations, and modes of communication... This democratic ethos evolves into conscientization, which in turn becomes responsibilization with hope, culminating in solidarity, love, dignity, and mutual support through praxis.

On the need for politically engaged academics/educators in a period of systemic transition, providing and encouraging the serious intellectual analysis of this transition, Wallerstein emphasizes the need to undertake this task in ways that are accessible to the "the vast numbers of working strata" (Wallerstein: 2006, 83), adding that "if the intellectuals do not hold the flag of analysis high, it is not likely that others will" (84). Academics/intellectuals, or we could say critical pedagogues, are thus seen as crucial to the political task ensuring that the transition does not produce "a new hierarchical, inegalitarian world that will claim to be based on universal values, but in which racism and sexism will continue to dominate our practices, quite possibly more viciously than in our existing world-system" (Wallerstein: 2006, 84).

As with the field of critical pedagogy, however, this is explicitly not a call for an intellectual vanguard or elite to assume leadership of the transition and construction of an alternative world-system. This is a crucial point of departure for Wallerstein from the position of orthodox Marxism and its adherence to vanguard parties setting and leading political action. This is evident in Wallerstein's (2003b, 222) critique of the developmentalism of orthodox Marxism, and his characterization of Leninism as a variant of this broader development theory, whose particular account of history was itself a product of the capitalist world-system (Wallerstein: 2003b, 222).

Here we need to remind ourselves of Wallerstein's fundamental critique of orthodox Marxism, or at least of some aspects of orthodox Marxist theorizing, as part of its wider critique of modernization theory. Rather than viewing capitalism as a progressive force, an advance over feudalism, and a sequential stage in the inevitable move toward socialism and communism, Wallerstein (2001a, 167) is unequivocal in his assessment of historical capitalism.

> Capitalism has represented historically moral regression and for the vast majority of the world's population material regression, even while it has ensured for the upper strata of the world (now enlarged from

1 percent to maybe 20 percent of the world's population) a material standard of living and style of life that far surpasses the possibilities of even "oriental potentates" of yore.

Moreover, his critique of ostensibly Marxist and anti-systemic movements' operation within the capitalist world-economy involves, in large part, their two-step operation of achieving state power, or "control of the apparatus of rule of a particular sovereign state" (Wallerstein: 2001b, 179), in order to legislate to transform the world (the nation). The anti-systemic and utopian aspect of Marxism was lost, he argues, in the "Marxism of the parties." It is from this perspective that Wallerstein (1995b, 109) portrayed liberal democratic Wilsonianism and Bolshevik Leninism not as two antagonistic ideologies, but rather as two alternative paths or models for "the political integration of the periphery of the world-system" and for "national development." The experience of historical socialism made it very clear that the sort of utopian dreaming that Freire and Wallerstein propose can "never be brought to fruition by some (a few) on behalf of others (the many). That can only be done by the many on behalf of themselves" (Wallerstein: 2001b, 184).

To conclude then, what we see here is Wallerstein (2001b) advocating educators' direct engagement with students, with social movements, and with political organizations, contributing to the critical consciousness-raising task of identifying and illuminating the historical choices before us, rather than seeking to take power in order to make them. The message is clear that "neither a socially unattached intelligentsia nor a party, any party, can bring about this transformation" on its own (Wallerstein: 2001b, 184). Rather, critical world-systems educators would seek to imagine alternatives, to map out political strategies for change/transformation, based always on the principle that such a transformation requires the active involvement of the majority, that is to say a broad-based, anti-systemic movement.[1]

Accepting the broad analysis of Wallerstein as a framework for understanding the capitalist world-system and its transition into an undetermined alternative system, means accepting the need for a critical pedagogy, a critical education, to extend and expand the potential involvement of populations in these debates and processes. Our elaboration of possible strategies, and a framework for a critical world-systems education in what follows, is premised on this understanding, and on the accompanying belief that underpins the critical pedagogy project—that the central purpose of our education systems ought to contribute to the development of the populations' critical understanding and consciousness of these issues.

Critical World-Systems Education

We would define a critical world-systems education as a program of mass education to deliver mass understanding of the historical development of the capitalist world-system, whose tendencies are approaching or at their absolute limits in ways that underpin its transition, and a willingness to directly participate in the moral and political tasks of this period of transition. Such a program raises these types of educational outcomes as the explicit and primary purpose of our education systems and institutions. It makes no false claims of neutrality, acknowledging the reality that education and its institutions are never neutral. Rather, it defends its purpose in terms of the simultaneous objective and subjective analysis of social reality, past and present, and future possibilities. This is an overt and vital program to put mass education to the service of society, but in a way that appropriates and transforms the conventional, instrumental idea that has characterized education under capitalism and historical socialism in their shared mode of preparing human capital for differential roles and trajectories within the capitalist world-economy. Rather, its primary purpose is to educate populations required to build global anti-systemic movements, to build the "network of universal universalisms" (Wallerstein: 2006, 84) that both constitutes and is shaped by an alternative geoculture.

These ideas are rooted in Wallerstein's argument that the outcome of the transition is uncertain and open to human intervention, and that failure to engage in this work leaves open the way for a replacement world-system that maintains or even intensifies the inequalities and injustices of current arrangements (Wallerstein: 2006). Contemporary ecological crises, including climate change approaching an irreversible tipping point of a two-degree Celsius rise in global temperature that will produce spiraling environmental changes beyond human control (Bellamy Foster: 2013), leave no rational options other than to challenge orthodox capitalist economic paradigms, and apply our available efforts to the construction of viable alternatives.

We acknowledge the ambitious scope of what follows, and of course the almost inevitable critiques of the limited detail, in many contexts the seeming impassable distance between existing politics and institutions and the thrust of what is advocated here, and therefore claims that this is simply unrealistic or naively utopian. On the other hand, we acknowledge contemporary efforts in some countries of Latin America, cited in the introduction to this chapter, which are attempting to define a viable model of twenty-first century socialism for the region and beyond, and to transform education systems to align with these broad social projects (see for example, Griffiths: 2010b; 2013; Muhr: 2010; Muhr and Verger: 2006). The progress of such efforts warrants separate and ongoing study. They are cited here to highlight the contemporary potentials for radical political programs to win popular support and adoption by national and regional governments and organizations.

In what follows, we sketch out such a program under the three areas of systemic organization of mass education, curricular design, and pedagogical practices, to imagine some core principles of a critical world-systems approach. This is followed by discussion of how such a program responds and relates to the dominant ideas of mass education since its inception—human capital formation, social control, and the formation of loyal citizens.

Critical World-Systems Education: Organizational Structure

To suggest that systems of mass education should be universal, free, and secular may seem self-evident. However, despite the history of the expansion of systems of mass schooling, extending to post-school education, as an identifiable global trend (Fiala and Lanford: 1987; Baker et al.: 2005), the achievement of such goals still remains unfulfilled. At the time of writing, the Millennium Development Goals (MDGs) for education—to achieve universal primary (elementary) school education for all, and to achieve gender equity within schooling—remain as aspirational targets for 2015. A current report on the MDGs noted that in 2010, there were 61 million primary school age children, and 71 million youth (between ages 12 and 15) out of school across the world (United Nations: 2012, 16–17). A recent UNESCO (2013, 1) policy paper added that the finance gap (between what has been promised and what is required) to achieve universal primary education has increased since 2010, standing at some $26 billion a year through to 2015.

Alongside the ongoing struggle to achieve mass primary school level education in many parts of the world, the neoliberal offensive of the past three decades has put pressure on the maintenance of systems of free and secular education for all across all areas of the world-economy. This story is well-documented in the existing scholarship that identifies and critiques moves toward 'cost-sharing' in the provision of mass education, privatization of education, inadequate and declining finances and resources for officially universal and free systems, and a broader tendency to wind back this initiative as part of the broader neoliberal program of winding back multiple aspects of the welfare state across the globe (for a nice summary see Klees: 2008a; 2008b). These tendencies are seen across some of the wealthiest nation-states of the world-economy, as national governments struggle to reconcile the basic tensions associated with demands to reduce taxation and maintain or improve levels of public services, including education.

These processes highlight the strength of the neoliberal agenda and its logics, and their capacity to enter national policymaking and implementation globally. Notably, they bring into stark contrast such moves away from universal, free, and secular education, with the experience of nation-states located outside of the core of the world-economy that were able to achieve universal, comprehensive, school education for all under a variant of socialist ideology (see Griffiths and Millei: 2013c). One of the most emblematic remains the experience of Cuba, which has maintained its universal system, from childcare through to undergraduate university education, and catering for adult education, in the decades since the collapse of the Soviet Union (Griffiths: 2009a).

We are not putting forward the Cuban educational system as one to be emulated globally, and we acknowledge critiques of even sympathetic observers about the limited autonomy for educators and boundaries on free political expression (Carnoy et al.: 2007). However, there are principles underpinning educational provision in cases like this that are worth identifying, defending, and extending, including the massification of all levels of education via free, public systems, the extension of this to adult and lifelong education, and some commitment to developing students' sense of vocation rather than provision of an educational credential for personal economic return. Perhaps above all else, the experience of a relatively poor country like Cuba demonstrates the potential for nation-states to deliver and maintain such goals with the commensurate political will.

When we imagine a critical world-systems education, we are talking about an approach to the provision of education at all levels/sectors. Hence we imagine universal, free, quality, secular educational programs from childhood through to post-school/tertiary levels, however they are named. All we are really doing here is taking seriously the liberal discourse of the United Nations (1948) Universal Declaration of Human Rights that posits education as a basic human right, both as a social good in and of itself, and as a necessary condition for individuals' achievement of other human rights. Pushing back against tendencies to commodify education, this stance endorses a liberal conception of education for self-fulfillment, to identify and realize one's interests and capacities as far as possible, alongside developing one's awareness of how these relate to and may complement and be conditioned by one's contribution to society at its multiple levels of scale. It is one that provides opportunities for all to pursue so-called 'further study' throughout their lifetime, in response to changing interests and vocations, in accordance with the underlying liberal conception of maximum human fulfillment and contribution to the social good. This conceptualization acknowledges the ever-present tensions between multiple demands on publicly financed services, but rejects the logic of individuals paying for education based on the personal remuneration benefits received in the workforce. Moreover, it observes that these tensions exist within choices made by governments everywhere on public spending priorities, and that some reprioritization makes this sort of goal affordable.

The principle here then gives precedence to the social good that higher levels of education of populations brings. It also asserts that a critical world-systems education stands to contribute to a transformation of society whereby income inequalities within and between occupational groups, and within and between nations, will be reduced, such that the social benefits are distributed in a more egalitarian fashion.

Under this sort of approach, the basis for entry and participation in systems of childcare and schooling would be simply one of residency. Again, in accordance with human rights conceptions of education, entry to such systems would thus be the exercising of this basic human right. Boundaries would need to be set to ensure that other barriers to residents' exercise of this right do not make it unviable in practice. Here we are referring to particular arrangements with respect to, for example, physical distance from educational centers/institutions and associated travel impediments, particularly for populations in regular geographical movement within and between nations. The basic principle, in line with policy rhetoric and aspirations globally, is universal access to and participation in, in practice, quality childcare and schooling.

At the post-school level, this principle could be extended, as again occurs in many parts of the world where university education, for example, remains free. In terms of systems' organization to determine access, we would draw inspiration from the approach that countries like Venezuela have adopted as part of its Bolivarian Revolution, whereby entry requirements to new universities are minimally set at successful completion of secondary schooling, effectively facilitating a mass expansion of university education. The guiding principle here is succinctly expressed by the founding director of the Bolivarian University of Venezuela, Maria Egilda Castellano (2004, 53), who observed, "We believe that everyone is capable of learning, that everyone has talent, abilities, and skills, and that the thing that needs to be done is provide the conditions in which these can be developed."

In short, the emphasis is placed not on restrictive selection systems and criteria to limit the number of students according to predetermined quotas, but on providing the scaffolding, support, and resources required for all who have achieved the base entry requirement to pursue further study according to their interest and sense of vocation. These same principles could be applied to what is currently organized as alternative, technical, or vocational post-school education. Moreover, this relatively open system of entry into post-school education could and should be cumulative, supporting adults' lifelong education and opportunities to further their level of skills and education, and potentially retrain for new occupations throughout their working life.

As we have suggested, these broad principles to facilitate universal education at all levels, from childcare to post-schooling, do not in and of themselves constitute a critical, transformative, world-systems education. Rather, they can be read as a further extension of the liberal promise, pushing for the universalization of these liberal principles as a part of the process and struggle to influence the world-system's transition. Readers will no doubt identify tendencies in this broad direction across the globe, frequently in policy aspirations/rhetoric and to significantly varying degrees in practice. Ideas of more education for more people are hardly controversial in the twenty-first century, while the mechanisms to achieve this and the underlying purposes continue to be contested. Pushing for this sort of extreme liberalism, or revolutionary reform (Griffiths: 2013; Rodríguez-Garavito et al.: 2008), in the context of neoliberal logics pushing toward commodification and privatization of education, is we argue a push to establish the pre-conditions for a critical world-systems education.

Another key question with respect to the organization of education is about universal access to what types, systems, or forms of education. We have relied to date on existing terminology of pre-schooling childcare, primary (elementary) schooling, secondary schooling, and post-school university or technical/vocational education. In practice, writers like Tomasevski (2003) have highlighted that even under the banner of Education for All (EFA) and the efforts to achieve the MDG of universal primary schooling, there is significant variation in what passes for primary education, for example, across different countries. This variation includes the nature and quality of the education, however measured (e.g. physical infrastructure, teacher-student ratios, teacher qualifications, class sizes, learning resources), but also the number of years of schooling deemed to constitute primary schooling. Despite these variations, there is a strong global tendency to equate education with formal schooling, and to seek to institutionalize a model of national schooling involving approximately six years of primary/elementary schooling, three years of junior or basic secondary, and then three years of upper or senior secondary schooling (a 6+3+3 model). Different countries will have varying arrangements at the pre- and post-school levels, and of course in the precise duration of these different sectors of mass schooling, but the broad tendency remains, as does the organization of students within such systems into age-based and subject-based classes.

A critical world-systems education would question separation of knowledge into separate discipline-based subjects (see below), but in the spirit of un-thinking, the social sciences would be similarly open to alternatives to the logic of age-based classes, and indeed the administrative concept of organizing education into prescribed years of primary and secondary schooling. The ways in which the formal organization and operation of schooling has disciplinary effects on students are also well-documented (see for example, Symes and Preston: 1997). Our primary concern here, however, is with the central purpose of mass education as we have articulated, such that the re-purposing of mass education should be the starting point for any organizational change, including the administrative organization of educational systems/sub-systems and distributions of students within these. Our intent here is not to map out a prescriptive alternative, but rather to highlight that a critical world-systems approach would insist that we begin from this position and resist establishing systemic structures that are driven by practical and administrative rather than by critical educational concerns.

Critical World-Systems Education: A Unidisciplinary Curriculum

The historical development of knowledge structures, and their relationship to the capitalist world-system in which they have emerged, lies at the heart of Wallerstein's scholarship and characterization of it as a knowledge movement (Wallerstein: 2004b) and a protest against established divisions and categories of knowledge (Wallerstein: 1999d). As we elaborated in chapter 3, he argues that that a critical understanding of social reality and its transition requires a unidisciplinary conception of knowledge that reunites nomothetic and idiographic epistemology, such that the claimed search for scientific truth is not and cannot be separated from the concurrent moral search for the good or beautiful. Wallerstein (1997a, 1250) cites the examples of cultural studies in the humanities and complexity studies in the sciences to assert that "knowledge is in fact a singular enterprise, and there are no fundamental contradictions between how we may pursue it in the natural and in the human world, for they are both integral parts of a singular universe."

Connections between knowledge, whether conceived of as a cross or interdisciplinary approach, are widely accepted and frequently operationalized in some form in educational systems and their teachers' pedagogical and curricular practices. This is the case in systems of primary/elementary schooling in which classes have a single teacher, and learning tasks are often organized as thematic ideas or projects rather than subject discipline-specific activities.[2] Similar project-based approaches are found in secondary school systems as explicit attempts to draw together knowledge from across school curricula and apply it to immediate and relevant problems in an integrated fashion. Beane (1995, 616) articulated this approach by arguing that "the sources of curriculum ought to be problems, issues, and concerns posed by life itself." He went on to assert that an integrated curriculum

> is rooted in a view of learning as the continuous integration of new knowledge and experience so as to deepen and broaden our understanding of ourselves and our world. It concerns the active construction of meanings rather than the passive assimilation of others' meanings.

The potential connection here with a critical Freirean approach is evident in the shift of focus of curriculum content selection away from that which is deemed necessary for transmission to students, and toward that which is generated and accessed locally by students to apply to their engagement with relevant problems and issues, and to their construction of particular understandings and responses. The starting point becomes the locally relevant and tangible social problem, rather than the subject discipline, with an explicit concern for student engagement with curricula in ways that enhance their understandings of themselves in the world. In the spirit of Postman and Weingartner's (1969, 183) classic text, teachers might begin by asking themselves, "What am I going to have my students do today? What's it good for? How do I know?"

A critical world-systems education would build on such an approach, here again radically extending and appropriating this quite mainstream policy agenda of linking knowledge together for students in ways that connect to their knowledge and experiences outside of the school. It would conceptualize curriculum as knowledge to be engaged with and by students, in order to develop deep understandings of the world and students' place in the world, including the localized, contemporary social, political, and economic challenges that students confront, as a basis for exploring ways to respond to and act on these issues in order to transform the world and one's place in the world.

In addition, a critical world-systems education would incorporate Wallerstein's core principles of engaged academic work into curricular design, and so view knowledge in terms of the key tasks of developing an intellectual understanding of social reality in all of its complexity, the moral task of thinking and engaging in the work of imagining and articulating alternatives that improve equality, peace with justice, and democratic participation in governance, and the political task of acting and intervening in the world to achieve such goals.

Tomasevski's (2003, 192) comprehensive review of global education noted that "What children are taught can amount to indoctrination, advocacy of racism or sexism, war propaganda, or stultifying regurgitation of useless bits of information," and added that "Human rights education ought to be located at the top of the educational ladder." We cite this as another example to illustrate the potential to build on these existing discourses and policies, toward a critical world-systems education centered on the analysis of social life and its potential to maximize human rights in terms of maximizing social justice, social equality, and democratic participation.

With respect to the question of what/whose knowledge to include, a critical world-systems approach would advance several key responses. First, it engages explicitly with the constant historical tension between what is deemed as universal and particular knowledge, with particular reference to the cultural and political debates that are associated with such differential status. For example, Wallerstein (1990, 47) details how groups' assertion of their particular cultural status has frequently operated to support social and economic inequalities based on/directly correlated with this status, by socializing members into "cultural expressions which distinguish them from the dominated groups, and thus into some at least of the values attributed to them by the racist and sexist theories."

By highlighting the complex or intricate ways in which debates about recognizing cultural difference/diversity play out within institutions, within the structures of the unequal capitalist world-system, we need to assess our curricular practices to recognize and respond to such outcomes. This task might also build on well-worn educational debates about the recognition of social and cultural diversity, its representation in curricular systems, and the implications for equitable participation and achievement in formal education for all social groups. A further radical push will be required, however, through a unidisciplinary approach to curriculum knowledge that is harnessed to alternative curricular questions (see below).

We have foregrounded the critique of European dominance or hegemony with respect to knowledge and epistemology, and the ways in which this dominant status has been used to justify intervention, oppression, and domination under banners of enlightened development, progress and modernization (Wallerstein: 2006). Similarly, we have reviewed the call for a new epistemology that overcomes the divide of nomothetic and idiographic ways of knowing (Wallerstein: 1997b), linked to a unidisciplinary conceptualization of knowledge. It is precisely this unified approach that has the capacity to make a decisive break with prevailing systems and their negative effects on identified equity or disadvantaged groups. A unidisciplinary approach aligns with historical and radical calls for a democratic and integrated curriculum that sets, through an inclusive process, the common curriculum content: that is to say, the curriculum content that is considered to be of such importance that all members of society ought to access and engage with the knowledge.

A critical world-systems approach has set the key normative principles for this process, but by definition the approach also insists that we resist the creation and imposition of new sets of supposedly fixed universal knowledge. Instead, we must engage with the more chaotic processes of simultaneously particularizing universal claims and universalizing particular claims (Griffiths and Knezevic: 2009; Wallerstein: 2006, 49), without end, to arrive at new, tentative iterations of a "multiplicity of universalisms that would resemble a network of universal universalisms," which are always provisional and immediately subject to critique.

So, a unidisciplinary curriculum for a critical world-systems education would build on these premises, overtly reintegrating the search for the (scientific) truth with the search for the good, and for beauty, about which Wallerstein (1999d, 191) observes

> The good is the same as the true in the long run, for the true is the choice of the optimally rational, substantively rational, alternatives that present themselves to us. The idea that there are two cultures, a fortiori that these two cultures are in contradiction to each other, is a gigantic mystification. The tripartite division of organized knowledge is an obstacle to our fuller understanding of the world. The task before us it to reconstruct our institutions in such a way that we maximize our chances of furthering collective knowledge.

The goal of reintegrating nomothetic and idiographic epistemologies is dependent on the reconfiguration of curricular disciplinary boundaries of knowledge. This task is a part of the rejection of the dominance of nomothetic epistemology linked to scientific universalism, as well as the accompanying imperative to incorporate and value particularist knowledge, experiences, and perspectives in ways that consciously avoid the (re)construction of hierarchical knowledge to the benefit of the dominant social groups in society.

To operationalize such a conception of unidisciplinary knowledge, and based on it a seemingly indeterminate conception of curricula within a critical world-systems education, we argue for the need to revisit progressive and radical traditions that have sought to organize school curricula and activity around a series of key questions and associated learning tasks. These, too, by definition, would be open to ongoing critique and debate, this indeed being a systematic part of the learning processes facilitating democratic participation by communities and populations in the articulation of guiding questions that all members of society need to engage with.

This may be seen as a contemporary variant of the working class conception of identifying *really useful knowledge* for effective and consequential participation in contemporary, post-(historical) socialist, neoliberal capitalist crises and contexts. At the same time, a critical world-systems perspective has an overt normative agenda as we have emphasized throughout, and sees this position both as defensible and capable of winning mass public support. Hence, we offer a conceptualization of such questions as follows, as examples of the types of organizational questions that could guide such an approach.

1. How can I understand the world in which we live, how we live in this world, and my particular place in this world (in my home

or family, my local neighborhood, town, state, country, region, etc.)?
2. How has the world (at these multiple levels) created and tried to solve major problems confronting the world (environmental crises, poverty and inequality, war and the displacement of people, living together with diversity)?
3. How have positive changes been achieved, how can we know, and what can we learn from these histories?
4. How can we imagine, describe, and plan, alternative communities, ways of being, and understandings of good and beauty in and for the world, at multiple levels of scale (local community, state, nation, region, world), that are more democratic, more equal, more peaceful, more just, and more sustainable in the full sense of the word (environmentally, socially, economically, politically, culturally)?
5. How can we know what we can change in the world, to change the world and our ways of being in the world, and what can we do to enact such changes?
6. What actions can we take to influence the nature and content of an alternative world, and ways of being in the world, that is needed to overcome the major problems confronting our current world?

These questions consciously reflect Wallerstein's characterization of the primary tasks that confront us in this period of systemic transition. We need to argue that our systems of mass education must be directed to the urgent questions and dilemmas that confront the world. It may sound, and will certainly be characterized by some, as melodramatic, but the very future of our continued existence on the planet depends on our collective responses to such questions, and of course on our collective awareness of consciousness of our capacity to understand, act on and transform the world.

As Freire (2012, 45) observed,

> It is certain that men and women can change the world for the better, can make it less unjust, but they can do so only from the starting point of the concrete reality they 'come upon' in their generation. They cannot do it on the basis of reveries, false dreams, or pure illusion. What is not possible, however, is to even think about transforming the world without a dream, without utopia, or without a vision...World transformation requires dreaming, but the indispensable authenticity of that dream depends on the faithfulness of those who dream to their historic and material circumstances and to the levels of technological scientific development of their context.

Wallerstein's perspective, like Freire's (2012, 46), steadfastly refuses to "renounce our ability to think, to conjecture, to compare, to choose, to decide, to envision, to dream." Wallerstein, however, also refuses to remain in the realms of utopian dreams, in favor of a sober and rational approach to exploring alternative, credible, and realistic or viable utopistic alternatives to actual social reality (Wallerstein: 1998b). Guiding curriculum questions generated from this grounding have the capacity to connect with the diverse cultural, historical, and political contexts of the world, and so to directly engage themselves in the global/local, universal/particular dialectics, in ways that can generate new, provisional, universal ways of understanding and being in the world.

Critical World-Systems Education: Pedagogical Praxis

Advancing critical world-systems education, inspired by Freire, by the depth of revolutionary critical pedagogy, and by Wallerstein's world-systems analysis, involves an overtly politicized pedagogical practice, or praxis, given the overriding normative commitments to influencing the transition of the contemporary capitalist world-economy toward a more equal, democratic, just, and peaceful alternative. This is a call for systems of mass education and the praxis of their educators to be politicized in a way that will undoubtedly be critiqued and rejected. Such critiques will almost inevitably claim that we are advocating a proposed program of mass indoctrination that is reminiscent of the failed and discredited approaches of historical socialism. Arguments that education should be value-free, or neutral, or at least balanced to present both/all sides of debates, would be sure to follow. We are not so naïve as to suggest such a program would easily win popular support, nor that existing education systems, institutions, and governments would readily accept such a program and write it into policy. We would again note, however, that some contemporary systems, countries, and regions are explicitly seeking to do so. What we are seeking to do then is to put forward more radical alternatives and models that appropriate and move beyond existing policy frameworks.

A radically reformed conception of curriculum as unidisciplinary, and organized around democratically debated and shaped guiding questions, sets the grounds for a critical world-systems practice that is consistent with the political, moral, and epistemological assumptions of a world-systems approach. As we have elaborated in this chapter, the pedagogical approach here has many parallels with that advanced under the banner of critical pedagogy, amounting to "more than just a theory. It is a way to be in this world" (Nikolakaki: 2012b, xi). The pedagogical approach is not about the transmission of a new, politically radical set of content, but about actively and consciously contesting the prevailing and dominant narratives that are a part of mass schooling, whether it be representations and understandings of the past, present and future, the identification of issues and problems, or the terms of the associated debates.

Freire (2012) was careful to note both the realist nature of a process of long-term struggle to move toward such utopian dreams, and in these processes the potential for counter-dreams to prevail. On this question, Wallerstein's work is even more conscious of the potential for utopias "to rebound. For utopias are breeders of illusions and therefore, inevitably, of disillusions. And utopias can be used, have been used, as justifications for terrible wrongs" (Wallerstein: 1998c, 1).

More importantly, Wallerstein (2010, 141) has consistently and forcefully argued that the nature of the current struggle in which we are all engaged is chaotic, and its outcome inherently uncertain, with some forces intent on instituting a program to "change everything so that nothing changes," putting forward for example a "green universe, a multicultural utopia, meritocratic opportunities for all—while preserving a polarized and unequal system." Whether conceiving of this in binary terms as the battle between the spirit of Davos (home of the World Economic Forum) and Porto Alegre (founding site of the World Social Forum) (Wallerstein: 2010; 2011c), or in more explicitly nuanced terms, a critical world-systems education would by necessity invoke a pedagogical praxis that brings such debates to the forefront of educational activity, guided by the principle that we educate to develop and facilitate our individual and collective capacities to think outside of the restrictive parameters established by dominant historical systems, and coupled with this thinking to take action in order to transform these realities.

Pedagogy then should always be about informed praxis, in the sense that it explicitly involves students in a critical understanding of both what is, and consideration of what could and ought to be, developed through concrete projects and tasks in which they act on specific phenomena that consciously break boundaries between school knowledge/schooling and that beyond the school. It ought to be an active process, whereby students exercise real decision- making power and control over the content of their learning and the associated activities, and where and how they apply their learning to concrete social problems and issues, in their local communities and beyond, in ways that keep these real-life applications of learning at the forefront. These sorts of principles are commonly found within contemporary education systems as generic pedagogical or learning frameworks that advocate models of authentic pedagogy/instruction/assessment practice (Newmann et al.: 1995; Hayes et al.: 2006; Gore et al.: 2004). In this respect, we see real opportunities in contemporary times to expand and push for a radical pedagogical practice within established global policy initiatives and discourses that emphasize making learning relevant to students and their experience of the world, and preparing students for their active participation in the world.

Critical World-Systems Education and Human Capital Formation

Critical world-systems education is firmly based on a critique of human capital logic that reduced education to the formation of specialized and disciplined labor. In addition to the critique from more humanitarian grounds and a fuller conceptualization of the human experience beyond being located in production processes, Wallerstein's critique is a rejection of the global division of labor and differential distribution of global surplus value that is inherent to the capitalist world-economy. This is a relentless task of unthinking established divisions of knowledge, which have been a feature of specialized learning for occupational categories, in favor of unidisciplinary approach that expands common learning experiences for all students. This approach invokes a broader vision of education and its purposes beyond the narrow bounds of preparing human capital for participation in the capitalist world-economy, whether in peripheral, semi-peripheral, or core economic activities, or in ostensibly socialist or capitalist national polities.

Once again we see broad support for a more expansive conceptualization of education that includes the more generic social good that education can provide, and which includes some sense of preparing students for participation in social, political, and economic life beyond the school, and for their participation in generating solutions to social problems that they will experience.

However, we acknowledge the power of human capital logic globally, and its resilience in the face of long-standing critique from educators, policy makers and practitioners over decades. Contemporary contexts of an array of economic crises across the world, accompanied by social and political turmoil, as part of the broader processes of neoliberal capitalist globalization, have arguably reinforced and further intensified competition between nation-states seeking to maintain and/or improve their relative share of global surplus required to maintain and/or expand levels of remuneration and material consumption locally.

There is an obvious irony here in the sense that the very system of a hierarchical and differential distribution of surplus across the world-economy both structurally requires the sorts of inequalities that help to reinforce attempts within national polities to improve their relative share through a logic of education supporting national economic growth and development. Moreover, as Wallerstein highlights, both ongoing cyclical crises of the capitalist world-economy, and those associated with longer term trends or tendencies, operate to weaken the legitimacy of national governments and the nation-state, and their perceived capacity to deliver on promises of increased well-being for all through national development projects. As alluded to elsewhere (Griffiths and Millei: 2013a; 2013b), a consequence is a resurgence of human capital theory logic and policy rhetoric around educational reforms to deliver national economic growth within the volatile global economy, in contexts of extreme and seemingly permanent economic crisis that is beyond the control of national governments and their state institutions.

The resultant tensions and contradictions can be seen across the globe. In countries primarily located within the core of the world-economy's division of labor, like Australia, for example, we see ongoing and heightened policy rhetoric about the importance of education to deliver ongoing economic growth, coupled with cuts to public funding for education as participation in the global-economy impacts on government revenues. In semi-peripheral or peripheral contexts, we find similar policy rhetoric about the importance of education to the nation and its performance, but this is seen alongside new levels of protest, questioning the capacity of either the State, or of education, to deliver either individual and national prosperity as parallel austerity measures are imposed in response to the global financial crisis.

Critical world-systems education would make explicit the critique of human capital theory in education, and overtly seek instead to prepare students for their full participation in social life within and beyond formal education. Clearly this involves developing knowledge and skills that will facilitate effective participation in the world of work, in particular occupations, in future studies, etc. The intent is not be to ignore these realities, nor the pressures that are likely to continue from populations for an education that enhances their employment opportunities and possibilities. It would unambiguously, however, ask very different questions about work, and work with students to enhance their understanding of work in society, and their capacity to reconstruct the nature of work in an alternative world-system that aligns with broader goals of human liberation.

Critical World-Systems Education and Citizenry

The idea of mass education to assist in the creation and formation of particular types of citizens has been a part of the educational enterprise since its beginnings. Under the modern nation-state, the gradual expansion of systems of mass schooling across countries, politics, and cultures, has in part been justified in the name of creating citizens of the modern nation-state (see for example, Ramirez: 2006). In addition to creating good workers, the intent is also to create citizens who share some sense of loyalty or affiliation to the nation-state of which they are members. Here we see the intended function of mass schooling to contribute to social order and stability by instilling in students these beliefs or dispositions, and so a sense of belonging to the imagined community of the nation.

Recent scholarship in the comparative education field has explored the growing trend in national education policy to instill a sense of global citizenship in students (e.g., Niens and Reilly: 2012; Moon and Koo: 2011). The debate here is about the nature and extent to which systems of education can develop some sort of cosmopolitan identity or supranational identification in students that transcends national loyalties and boundaries.

A world-systems perspective adopts a political, realist, conflict approach to the question of citizenship and its functions within the capitalist world-system. While equilibrium or consensus perspectives see processes of the linear expansion of citizenship, and corresponding expansion of citizenship rights across the world, we concur with Ramirez's (2006, 439) acknowledgement that

> a historically grounded comparative education needs to recognize both contestation and the reality of elite segmentation in many countries (Rubinson: 1986). The contestation took place not only between elites and masses but also among the elites and masses themselves. The crucial battles were over the question of who was to be included as a citizen. In educational terms, the corollary question was who was to be schooled.

For Wallerstein, this contestation has developed over centuries, and has centered on the capacity (and inevitable reality) of legal concepts like citizenship to include and exclude, and with each expansion of inclusion to make the exclusion of others more acute.

> What was new in the nineteenth century was the rhetorical legitimacy of equality and the concept of citizenship as the basis of collective governance. This led as we have seen to the theorizing of the binary distinctions, the attempt to freeze them logically, to make de facto transiting across the boundaries not merely against the rules of society but against the rules of science. What was new as well was the social movements created by all those excluded by these binary reifications in order to secure their liberation, or at least a partial liberation, from the legal constraints. Each success of a particular group seemed to make easier by example and more difficult in practice the attempts of the next claimants of liberation. Citizenship always excluded as much as it included. (Wallerstein: 2002a, 673–74)

The broader context from a world-systems perspective is the continual process of state institutions, their legal frameworks and institutional practices, operating to publicly proclaim equality and inclusion on the one hand, while having to resolve this public position with the realities of persistent and systemic inequalities and differential opportunities. Like the democratic pressure of meritocracy against the realities of non-meritocratic outcomes, the tension here arguably sees faith in the promised democratic process of inclusion decline. The push for equality and inclusion, in this case for universal suffrage and full citizenship rights, has and continues to be a political conflict in these broad terms.

Contemporary expressions include acute struggles to create new classifications for those seeking asylum in the core-states, other than full citizenship, in efforts to contain and actively discourage the movement of some people from one nation to another. Thus, in addition to xenophobic reactions to immigrant populations, we see phenomena from governments like systems of mandatory detention, 'Temporary Protection Visas' being granted even to those found to be genuine refugees in need of asylum, rather than full and ongoing residence and/or national citizenship, with a view to returning refugees to their country of origin when conditions there are deemed to be safe.

In this sort of world-systemic climate, a critical world-systems education invokes the critique of the concept of formal, national citizenship, in the sense that it has functioned in the capitalist world-system to both reinforce and legitimize inequalities within and between states. Within the intellectual agenda of constructing alternative and provisional universalisms, a critical world-systems education would engage with these critiques, and consider the tensions between the tendency for greater equality through formal citizenship within nation-states, and the systemic requirement of the capitalist world-economy to establish hierarchical categories of peoples (within and between states) to justify inherent social inequalities of its operation. It would of course critique the appropriation of internationalist or global citizenship rhetoric by policy makers that is reduced to preparing a select and mobile workforce to compete globally as part of a strategy of improving national competitiveness in the world-economy. Moreover, it would make explicit the contradictions between calls for a sense of global citizenship, or supranational citizenship, and the realities of more restricted possibilities of movement for the majority across national borders.

Introducing a special issue on the political economy of global citizenship, Andreotti (2011: 310) referred to "possibilities of global solidarities beyond class-divided internationalisms." In the same special issue, Camicia and Franklin (2011, 321) concluded that "students are being prepared to participate as global citizens, but the meaning of this citizenship is complicated by a tension and blending between neoliberal and critical democratic discourses." At one level we see the tension as simply between the discourses of global citizenship and material realities of legal citizenship impacting on actual rights and physical movement within and between nationally bounded territories. This leads into the sorts of critical discussion of what is invoked and meant in the discourses of global citizenship education. A full range of alternatives may be explored: a push for radically open borders and some form of legal membership of the global community with corresponding rights, a liberal push for a cosmopolitan or global outlook from national citizens, an instrumental push for participation in the global economy (for some national citizens of some states). We could of course cite many other variations. It is the formation of citizens ready to advance these sorts of debates and alternative understandings that a critical world-systems education would aspire.

Conclusion

The central point that we have been making here, and throughout this chapter, is that a critical world-systems education, and so educators inspired by this broad position, must always engage in the rigorous and unidisciplinary historical analysis of what is, consideration of what could and should be, and take action to direct our efforts in this broad direction. It advocates rational and modernist principles of greater equality, democracy, and justice in our collective construction of alternatives, with the caveat repeatedly stated here that as a universal project in this sense, it is also by definition open to and inviting of critique, and of course is overtly conscious of its own biases and uncertainties.

We are taking a position of provisional certainty. We are opposing as unviable and politically destructive an alternative of absolute relativism, but taking a heavily qualified and critical approach to the search for a "more correct" and "more socially useful" analysis and framework from which to build a "substantively more rational reality" (Wallerstein: 1997a, 1254). Here it is worth quoting Wallerstein (2004c, 21) at length.

> Of course, world-systems analysis is a grand narrative. World-systems analysts argue that all forms of knowledge activity necessarily involve grand narratives, but that some grand narratives reflect reality more closely than others. In their insistence on total history and unidisciplinarity, world-systems analysts refuse to substitute a so-called cultural base for an economic base. Rather, as we have said, they seek to abolish the lines between economic, political, and sociocultural modes of analysis. Above all, world-systems analysts do not wish to throw the baby out with the bath. To be against scientism is not to be against science. To be against the concept of timeless structures does not mean that (time-bound) structures do not exist. To feel that the current organization of the disciplines is an obstacle to overcome does not mean there does not exist collectively arrived-at knowledge (however provisional or heuristic). To be against particularism disguised as universalism does not mean that all views are equally valid and that the search for a pluralistic universalism is futile.

Chapter 5

Mass Labor: Reviving the Concept of Community and Collectivity

In many ways, Mészáros has sought to maintain a 'traditional' view of collective action in that people with a specific class interest still have the capacity to act in their own interests for the good of the collective. This view of collective action is grounded in the philosophical anthropology of early Marx. Mészáros discusses human communities and human collectivities as having a 'natural propensity' for collective activity as well as having a universally understood desire to develop trade. Mészáros' analysis is one in which the philosophical grounding can be found in Marx's early work, and is combined with a Gramscian view of hegemony as well as Polanyi's idea of the destruction of the commons in England.

Bringing back the idea of collective action that is positive collective action and that can further develop, we examine how this might be a productive way forward by looking at non-performance model schools, and those sorts of school systems that rely on a collective concept. Mészáros' work has a number of interesting convergences and divergences with the work of Wallerstein and we argue here that Mészáros' background is fundamental to understanding how and why he arrives at his critique of modernity, and in what ways he intends to have his analysis employed in order to effect a realized global transformation.

Before visiting the concept of mass labor, we need to develop Mészáros' view of the concepts of unity and universality. A major problem with philosophical analysis, according to Mészáros (2010a, 205), is the inescapable individuality that pervades all of the thinking around human action in the modern period as defined by the inception of the industrial revolution. A historically situated view of this problem demonstrates that dualism remains as a core construct; unit and universality is assumed and postulated, but never established, according to Mészáros. In this case, we see the necessity to establish a philosophical anthropology of what constitutes human nature. Before doing so, the specific version of critical Marxism, and the ways in which Mészáros uses early Marxist thought to develop his critique of modernity, is discussed below.

Mészáros is very much like his counterparts in the 'Budapest School' and has remained in this strand of Marxism throughout his work. The Budapest School was a group of Marxist-humanist philosophers who were working with Georg Lukács in the 1950s in Budapest, Hungary. They developed their ideas via a convergence of both 'critical Marxism' as well as a particular strand of cultural/humanist Marxism that we analyze in chapter 6.

Critical Marxism

Mészáros' version of critical Marxism developed during the same time period as the Western versions of critical theory in the late 1960s and early 1970s. Even though he left Hungary in the 1956 Revolution, the approach to Marxism remained in line with the early work of the Budapest School. Along with the Frankfurt School and the Budapest School, Habermas and Heller, and German and Hungarian versions of sociology, there emerged new forms of social criticism that diverged on many fundamental issues. A main reason for this divergence was their respective interpretations of Continental philosophy and Marxism, as well as their different historical experiences that set the stage for the theoretical problems and solutions that developed distinct perspectives. For example, the negative dialectics of Adorno (1973) were in opposition to any form of a positive reconstructive aspect of Marxism and the possibilities of modernity. Habermas developed his theory of communicative action and ideal speech situation. German sociologists, such as Schutz (1972), shifted their focus toward the development of systems theory in contrast to their Hungarian counterparts who analyzed the needs structure and value systems of society in order to 'humanize' the social sciences. Thus, the Budapest School developed a form of humanist Marxism that was different in character from their counterparts, who were engaged in similar emancipatory social criticism.

Mészáros' early work was a particular form of critical Marxism that, in part, embodied an attempt to reconstruct the East European leftist tradition of social criticism. The development of the Praxis Marxists in Yugoslavia (Markovic and Petrovic: 1979), the radical democrats in Czechoslovakia, and the union movements in Poland and East Germany were similar attempts at creating participatory democratic structures within existing socialism. In some cases, this quest for democracy in East-Central Europe caused the political situation to move toward outright revolt against the existing orthodox Marxist governments in the post-World War II era. The October Revolution in Budapest in 1956, the Prague Spring in Czechoslovakia in 1968, and a series of uprisings in East Germany and Poland from 1954 to the Polish Solidarity movement in 1980 were examples of attempts at creating social democracies in the region. These political events and organizations were part of a reaction to the orthodox Marxism existing in East-Central Europe and the search for a Marxism which was not based on the scientific empirical reductionism of the contemporary Marxists (Markovic and Petrovic: 1979, vi).

The early critical Marxism of Mészáros is similar to his counterparts in the Budapest School, especially the early work of Agnes Heller, in the interpretation of East-Central European political philosophy. We argue that this original problem context was the Marxist orthodoxy in Hungary during the 1950s and 1960s. This was coupled with the problem of German Idealism in that the political structures for emancipation were always 'ideal' in a Kantian sense and never 'real' in a revolutionary Marxist sense as we explain in this chapter. This meant that the fundamental assumption was that philosophy must attempt to make the world a home for humanity by examining the relationship between human beings and their world. In attempting to understand how to go about making the world a home for humanity, Mészáros continued to base his work on an analysis of the relationship between human beings and the way in which they perceived their respective worlds. The three main themes in this development were contingency, dialectics, and the Marxian idea of praxis, each of which are dealt with in this chapter. Thus Marxism, as a philosophy, had a specific relationship with society as a whole understood via a particular understanding of theory and practice.

Contingency, Dialectics, Praxis

Mészáros argued that German Idealism played a major role in the development of philosophy in East-Central Europe and that this presented a problem for Marxism. For Mészáros and the Budapest School, this tradition of philosophy maintained that the central problem was humanity's relationship to the world (Kolakowski: 1978a,

1–70, 173–74). Mészáros' interpretation of both Kant and Hegel stated that it was necessary to examine the relationship between human beings and their understanding of their existence (Mészáros: 1970; Mészáros: 1986; Mészáros: 1995), similar to Agnes Heller's early work (Heller: 1978a; Heller:1979a; Heller: 1981). For both thinkers, Marx had a similar focus in the attempt to analyze social conditions in order to reveal the truth of their possibilities for human emancipation. The view of the Budapest School was that in East-Central Europe, Marx appropriated the entire tradition of philosophy in order to transform this central problem into a concern with practical issues that had immediate social consequences.

The appropriation of philosophy through Marxism as such developed three categories relevant to the understanding of possibilities of human emancipation through which to view these immediate social problems. These three categories were contingency, dialectics, and praxis. They formed the basis from which both Mészáros and the Budapest School began examinations of the problem of humanity's relationship to the world.

Contingency

In discussing the problem of contingency, the original starting point is Aristotle (Kolakowski: 1978a, 1). The Aristotelian argument was that human beings were created entities that began and ended at finite points in time (Barrett: 1962; Aristotle: 1941 [Mkeon trans]). This was deduced from the fact that at some point in time human beings did not exist. The human individual was thus a finite being who did not necessarily have to exist (Aristotle: 1941, 231). This meant that the relationship to the world was bound by history and made human beings, by their mere existence, immediately problematic in that there was an element of human existence that could not be known.

This is in contrast to the Aristotelian interpretation of contingency with the Platonic notion of humanity's relationship to the world in history through temporality. For Mészáros, Heller, and the Budapest School, the difference of interpretation was Plato's conception of the atemporal ideal form (Plato: 1945 [Cornford trans], 117). This ideal form was considered by Plato to be an external and unrealizable concept toward which humanity was destined to move in a quest for perfectibility. As a result, human beings were always conscious of their waning physical nature in comparison to the immutable ideal (Plato: 1945). Other thinkers such as Kierkegaard suggested that the existence of a similar ideal form could be reached through a leap of faith into the religious sphere (Kierkegaard: 1973 [Bretall trans], 119). In his recent work on Sartre, Mészáros (2012) argues something similar in the modern individual's capabilities to choose from among a variety of possibilities that would eventually aid in the creation of a new self. For Kierkegaard, this embodied a leap of faith toward the possibility of change, or in Heller's words, the acceptance of human contingency as a part of modern reality. This existential theme was taken up later by Sartre (1956) and Camus (1956) in their emphasis on self-creation through accepting the responsibility of one's own contingent nature. Individuals were thought to have reached a stage in modernity in which they had realized they were alone in the universe and were forced to deal with the possibilities that they lived. The Kierkegaardian leap of faith was a leap of faith in and for themselves as individuals, and Mészáros suggests that this theme is taken further in Sartre's position on modern human beings.

For Mészáros, existential philosophy continued the examination of contingency. Heidegger took an ontological approach in dealing with the facticity of the Dasein (Heidegger: 1962), Camus called for human beings to take on the task of Sisyphus (Camus: 1955), and Sartre created the categories of en-soi and pour-soi to illustrate the relationship between humanity and the world (Sartre: 1956). For the Budapest School, there was a direct link between existential philosophy and those postmodern writers who attempted to show contemporary human reality through the fragmentation of the grand narratives of modernity (Best and Kellner: 1991; Heller: 1977; 1980a; 1988). In particular, Richard Rorty (1989) illustrated the dissolution of the human being as a subject, Foucault's (1980) work on power and knowledge illustrated among other things the positive potential of power, Derrida's (1978) writing dealt with privileged discourses in western metaphysics, and Lyotard's (1984) defense and promotion of heterogeneity of discourses were all different forms of the many approaches to the problem of the contingent nature of human beings.

These approaches to contingency were more than important guiding themes in European philosophy through to contemporary debates about postmodern discourses, since they framed the real conditions for possible human freedom. For Agnes Heller, contingency meant that human beings were born within a particular point in history (Heller: 1980b; 1987). This was the condition of historicity, which meant asking questions about "the way in which we are in fact historical beings" (Bellhierz: 1994, 127). People were born into a concrete society with concrete genetic characteristics and were left with the responsibility of their own potential for self-education. This notion remained at the core of Mészáros' understanding of the universal condition of each individual person. For Heller, this concept of contingency became fully developed in modernity, and some philosophers had claimed to be able to solve the problem of human contingency by solving the problem of the concept of history (Heller: 1980a; 1987), a notion that Mészáros grapples with throughout his work. It was by coming to understand the laws of history that human contingency could be made certain. This meant that once these fundamental human characteristics were understood, individuals could then solve their own particular context by overcoming their own particular contingent natures and realizing their full potential as human beings. This solution came about as a result of a process known as dialectics.

Dialectics

The beginnings of the dialectical approach to philosophical problems were grounded in the concept of contingency. The Marxism of Lukács had continued to use dialectics as a part of historicity that was in turn a part of history (Heller: 1980a). As students of Lukács, both Mészáros' and Heller's logic was that since all individuals found themselves in history in that events and circumstances changed over time, then the discovery of the laws of the process of history could lead to overcoming the problem of human contingency. This meant that the individual, as a finite unit in history, could actualize their potential through both predetermined genetic characteristics and a predetermined set of cultural norms by understanding the way in which human beings developed through history. The key to this was the existential philosophers' focus on the finite nature of human beings, or the knowledge that we are all moving to our final solitary experience of death. Human beings could overcome the uncertainty of their lives by understanding the dialectical process of change and thus understanding their own situations. This was very much the same as Barrett's (1962) position on existentialism: "if human finitude is not understood, neither is the nature of humanity" (14), and what Mészáros would later claim in his work on Sartre.

The problem of contingency as a historical embodiment of change remains as one of the recurring philosophical themes for Mészáros. This meant that historical change occurred without any form of logic or determinism guiding this change. Kolakowski's three-volume work on the history of Marxism was an analysis of Marxism from an East-

Central European perspective and illustrates the divergence between Eastern Marxism and its Western counterpart (Kolakowski: 1978a; 1978b; 1978c). According to Kolakowski, in East-Central European Marxist philosophy, the focus became one of the appropriate method by which to come to know, and be involved in, the constantly changing human circumstance. This involvement in the contingency of the human condition came to be dealt with through the philosophical category of dialectics.

Dialectics was a point of contention between Hegel and Marx in their respective approaches to the role history played in the changes that humanity experienced over time. In the understanding of Hegelian philosophy in East-Central Europe, the examination of contingency was formulated in the question "How can the human mind be at home in the world?" (Kolakowski: 1978a, 135) and the answer was in the development of history in which the human spirit progressed toward freedom. This freedom was part of the Spirit, and the Hegelian dialectic is not a method that can be separated from the subject matter to which it is applied and transferred to any other sphere. It is an account of the historical process whereby consciousness overcomes its own contingency and finitude by constant self-differentiation (Kolakowski: 1978a, 70).

The problem of human contingency had to be solved, and in Hegel's philosophical system, the solution was in sublating the contingent nature of human beings. "This overcoming of contingency is the same as freedom of the spirit," and Hegel's philosophy of history is an account of the search of the spirit for freedom through a variety of past events (Kolakowski: 1978a, 71). According to Hegel, the meaning of past events can be discovered, but it is a meaning not indicated by history. Freedom is a property of the Mind, but the Mind must elevate itself to freedom for itself. Thus, the self-knowing freedom can move toward a true emancipation and an overcoming of the problem of contingency. For the followers of Lukács, contingency was equated with human possibility, and since this contingency was part of history, history could not be left with the task of maintaining that possibility by necessity. This meant that there were no guarantees of historical development toward a particular goal. Dialectics did not guarantee development toward human freedom. It ensured that there was historical change, or change in history, but that was all.

There were some important distinctions, however, that some followers of Lukács and the Budapest School argued could help in realizing emancipatory goals in philosophy by interpreting the development of philosophy in Eastern and Western Europe. Agnes Heller articulated her position on the interpretation of the dialectical method in an article entitled On *The New Adventures of the Dialectic* (Heller: 1977). Heller's article was based on her examination of Sartre's *Critique of Dialectical Reason*, Lukacs' *Ontology*, Adorno's *Negative Dialectics*, and Karel Kosik's *Dialectics of the Concrete*. Heller differentiated between the East European and the West European understanding of the philosophical category of dialectics. In a comparison between Adorno and Sartre on the one hand, and Lukacs and Kosik on the other, Heller demonstrated the significance of different approaches to dialectics (Heller: 1977). Heller stated that Sartre's *Critique of Dialectical Reason* and Adorno's *Negative Dialectics* displayed the West European penchant for self-reflection as a central function of philosophy (Heller: 1977).

For Heller, this led to the fragmentation of the main grounding of their position on dialectics, the "thing-in-itself" (Heller: 1977). Heller's evaluation of the similarity between Adorno and Sartre was an important point. For Heller, Adorno's dialectical position led to the postmodern interpretation of the fragmentation of the subject and a rejection of the modern constitution of the individual. Furthermore, Sartre's conclusions in his work led to the concept of the central epistemological position of the idea of the self was a nullity; that as human beings we all die alone since we are all limited by our historical contingency; and that this nullity and freedom-unto-death leave human beings with nothing except for their choices precipitated by their individual will.

By contrast, Lukács' "ontology" and Kosik's "dialectics of the concrete" "rely on their perception of the 'thing itself' and allow their ideas to float in a clear and unrestrained manner, thus leaving their methods unthematised" (Heller: 1977, 134).This meant that for Lukács and Kosik, philosophy was a kind of historiography that allowed for an amalgamation of approaches to a particular problem. Since the umbrella under which all of these concepts fell was Marxist dialectics and Marxist historical materialism, the question of methodology was not necessary to ask. The implication was that the subject to be examined would be able to possess possibilities beyond just the process of change. Philosophical self-reflection would not lead to the reduction of the importance of philosophy itself in Lukács' and Kosik's respective philosophical systems. Even though dialectics was problematic, this did not mean that the despair of the death of philosophy was to be adopted. Freedom-unto-death was not the Eastern conclusion.

The significance of this was that Heller has viewed the Western tradition of Marxism and philosophy as divorced from their practical implications. This is a problem that Mészáros grapples with throughout his work. Since the concern in the West had been with the use of logic and method to refute possible arguments against a particular philosophical position, this application of philosophy in the West was in danger of becoming merely an exercise of competing logic games divorced from any practical consequences.

By contrast, Eastern European philosophy confronted an extremely simplified thought, a litany of dogmatized tenets. Questioning these tenets was thus the prerequisite for emancipating thought. The turn toward a philosophy of essence implied probing the limits of one's own independent thinking (Heller: 1977, 134). This 'philosophy of essence' was a way to critique the idealist concept of the relationship between humanity and the world, and this ought to be the focus of philosophy. It was the philosopher's attempt at independent thinking, independent analysis, and the limits of these analyses, oriented toward humanity's relationship to its world that can be seen as a practically oriented philosophy. For Eastern Europe, this meant that thinking about the world embedded philosophical discourse in everyday life rather than abstracted from their immediate political consequences. The obvious conclusion of this approach to philosophy was human emancipation, and Mészáros arrives at the same conclusion.

Similarly, for Heller the conflicting attitudes of Adorno and Kosik portrayed very different conclusions—conclusions for which Heller clearly indicated her prejudices.

> This is partly revealed through "existential metamorphosis," that is, a change in one's relation to the world, but it is accomplished primarily through revolutionary praxis. For Kosik, the meaning of history consists in the constitution of man and humanity. The task of philosophy is to grasp the totality of human reality and to reveal the truth of that reality. This is why philosophy is so indispensable. (Heller: 1977, 136)

The despair of Adorno reduced philosophy to a position without immediate consequences and thus a partial involvement in the daily activity of change. It was this daily activity of change that was so important for Mészáros. Western existentialism and some proponents of the Frankfurt School had reached philosophical 'cul-de-sacs' or 'dead-ends' as a result of their abstractions from everyday life, their assumptions of despair as a driving force of human beings, and their inability to remain connected to their practical universe. This was in contrast to those theorists who had maintained the opposite prejudice of the stagnation of the Eastern Left and the vibrancy of the West. The manner in which it was possible to remain centered on certain problems at hand emerged through this philosophical category of praxis.

Praxis

Fundamental to Mészáros' thinking on the role of dialectics and eventually the praxis of Marxism, is the development of the relationship between theory and practice. This relationship was best described as an attitude towards a praxis that was always social in form and content and had to do with the changing social conditions of human beings. Mészáros' reading of the tradition is one emphasizing a kind of positive potential to clarify contemporary problems. Marx's eleventh thesis on Feuerbach which stated that the philosophers, "have only interpreted the world in various ways; the point is to change it" (Marx: 1845), illustrated the attitude toward philosophy which had the potential for emancipation.

For Marx, the eleventh thesis on Feuerbach illustrated a position toward philosophy and philosophical discourse that involved bringing the socialized human being to the fore of discussion. Marx's criticisms of Feuerbach and Hegel in the 1844 manuscripts revolved around the lack of reference to human activity based on human sensuality or those of practical activity. For Marx, sensuality was meant to oppose abstraction. This meant that any analysis of society had to begin with human experience and not philosophical or scientific theories. This has operated as a guiding principle for changing social conditions toward the 'good': an involvement in an examination of the social conditions by living and participating in those social conditions, must be attempted. This interpretation of the role of Marxism means that history must be made subordinate to everyday life. In this system, the individual and everyday life became the necessary focus in any understanding of human activity. The logic of individuals and the various collectivities could not be understood unless the daily practices were at the fore of discussion. One needed to move beneath theory and description to the fundamental political activities involved in this everyday life. Mészáros' understanding becomes very Aristotelian in this sense since this was the world of the general human condition that had the possibility of orientation toward the 'good.' Revolutionary praxis thus becomes a politics of everyday life.

These three modes of analysis—contingency, dialectics, and praxis—were the main categories that comprised the tradition of Marxist social science in Hungary. Mészáros remains concerned with praxis as an accepted form of both social criticism and social change.

Orthodoxy

The East-Central European intellectual heritage focused on Marx and the various interpretations of Marx's work. The development of philosophy in the region had a number of influences including Kant, Hegel, and the work of Lukács. It was assumed that Marxist social theory was the culmination of a development of philosophy that was to transform social relations and provide an organization that would allow individuals to fulfill their potential as human beings. Marxist philosophy had appropriated all other forms of inquiry and social science disciplines to the point at which the debates were centered on 'socialist realism.' This meant that philosophical questions and answers had to be posed and solved through a Marxist discourse. This was the prevailing theoretical orthodoxy in Hungary in the 1950s and formed part of the original problem context of critical Marxism for Mészáros.

This orthodoxy in social and political theory in Hungary began just prior to World War II. While Marxist theory played an important role in East-Central Europe since his works first began appearing in the region, it was in the period immediately after World War II that Marx began to be considered as the theorist with the most highly developed ideas regarding humanity. For the Hungarian Communists, supported by the Soviet Union, Marxism became the dominant ideology.

The conditions for such political orthodoxy occurred when Admiral Horthy had established himself as leader of the nation with the expulsion of Béla Kun and the Hungarian Communists in 1919. The authoritarian Horthy regime became increasingly pro-fascist in character and eventually allied with Nazi Germany in order to regain Hungarian territory lost at the end of World War I. Hungarian Jews faced the same systematic extermination as was the case in the rest of East-Central Europe during World War II.

At the end of World War II, Hungary fell on the Soviet side of the division of Europe between Stalin and Churchill. Agnes Heller has described this as an "immoral bargain" (Heller and Feher: 1990) that subjected East European countries to further fascism and totalitarianism. The limited attempts at democratic reforms in the region were immediately quashed by the Stalinist Soviet Union and the political system in Hungary became a "dictatorship over needs" (Heller et al.: 1983). The Hungarian Communist Party was one of a number of political forces in Hungary and between the years 1945 and 1948 became increasingly Stalinist in character. Under the leadership of Mátyás Rákosi, the Stalinist faction, supported by the Soviet Union, consolidated its domination of Hungarian politics and remained in control until 1953.

The period from 1953 to 1955 was a time of reformist politics in Hungary. Rákosi lost a leadership challenge by Imre Nagy who had taken the reins of the Communist Party after a similar political shift in the Soviet Union had occurred under Khrushchev's reforms. The Soviets had moved away from Stalinism and began to liberalize and acknowledge that political expression could involve some criticisms of the government as well as the necessity of economic reform to maintain certain levels production. Nagy met the approval of his Russian counterparts, and he began reforms that extended into social, cultural, and economic life and began to exert some national autonomy for Hungary.

Politics in the Soviet Union became totalitarian once again as Khrushchev and his allies began to lose their hold on the Soviet Union government. Nagy was forced into exile in 1955, and Rakosi came back to lead the Communist Party in Hungary once again. For many Hungarians, the new crackdowns were intolerable. The chance for greater levels of self-determination was lost, as they had been at the end of 1945, and protest escalated. In the fall of 1956, a crisis point was reached, and student and worker protests culminated in a full-scale revolt that forced Rákosi to flee the country. In October of 1956, Nagy was reinstated as leader.

Many Hungarian intellectuals such as George Markus and Ferenc Feher had argued that the successes of reformist politics outweighed those of major social upheavals. For these people, revolution unleashed uncontrollable social forces that, in many cases, would lead to situations worse than previously experienced. In terms of Agnes Heller's moral philosophy, this meant that if a revolution would posit a value system that placed the sacrifice of a generation above the satisfaction of the needs of the people within that society, then the revolution should not occur. On the other hand, if a revolution could bring about the construction of a new society that immediately met the needs of the people who participated in such a drastic change, then it was the correct moral and political decision.

Immediately after Rákosi was forced out of power, workers councils were set up and genuine moves toward social democracy had begun. Nagy declared Hungary a neutral country and announced the intention to withdraw from the Warsaw Pact. On November 4, 1956 Soviet tanks occupied Hungary, and Nagy was executed. János Kádár was made leader of the Hungarian Communist Party and remained as premier until 1988.

Lukács was usually out of favor with the Hungarian authorities for advocating political criticism of the regime. In the aftermath of 1956, while Lukács was interned in Romania for complicity in the Revolution, Mészáros left Hungary permanently. The immediate philosophical consequence for the Hungarian intellectual Left was an examination of the development of modern moral philosophy, questioning the prevailing orthodoxy that argued for Marxism as the main determinant of morality.

In 1958, all of Lukacs' associates who did not denounce his political position of being critical of the government were threatened with termination of employment. This was the initial problem situation in which Mészáros found himself in as a Marxist critic of Marxist regimes. For Mészáros, this concern with humanity's relationship to the world was central to German Idealism, and as a result of this intellectual heritage, the development of social theory through the analytical categories of contingency, dialectics, and praxis had profound effect on the analytical stance he took.

The idea of contingency was a problem that dealt with the finite nature of human beings and their limited capabilities as individuals in history. The main method through which to approach humanity's contingent existence and provide guidance to humanity's relationship to the world was through dialectics. This process of dialectics provided an understanding of historical change that helped the individual deal with their contingent nature. The role of the social theorist was defined by the Marxist category of praxis, thus demanding an immediate form of involvement in society. It was thus that Mészáros' work turned toward moral Marxism and the examination of the development of ethical categories as the way to emancipation.

Moral Marxism

The central problem of the early intellectual work of Mészáros was the lack of freedom in orthodox Marxist philosophy that led to the lack of freedom in existing Marxist societies such as Hungary. Mészáros and his contemporaries argued that this was caused by the inability of Marxism to provide guiding moral norms for contemporary society. Mészáros believed that there was an intellectual space for an argument capable of illustrating the necessity of maintaining the values of life and freedom within Marxist philosophy. This eventually led to the Budapest School program of the renaissance of Marxism. Before discussing the Budapest School in more detail in the next chapter, there are two further categories of philosophy that Mészáros uses as a foundational approach to his work.

First, the development of a moral philosophy remaining within the Marxist paradigm was a key component of the work of a number of social theorists, and this was certainly an initial problematic for Mészáros. This was similar in character to the earlier attempts by the Austro-Marxists and the Kantian Marxists to deal with what was considered to be a lacuna in Marxist philosophy in its inability to deal with ethical questions (Kolakowski: 1978a). Second, it was an elaboration on the development of a sociological position which was an attempt to provide an analytical framework capable of including this moral Marxist position as well as empirical Marxist methodology of examining specific social conditions. The tradition of sociography in Hungary was quite different than that of the empirical social sciences emerging from the Anglo-American circles (Haraszti: 1977) and Mészáros sought to ensure that an ethical construct was part of these emerging trends. Third, the Budapest School agenda that contained elements of both of these positions as well as the larger project of arguing for a radical democratic alternative to socialist societies is discussed in the following chapter. These three philosophical positions were united by the attempted renaissance of Marxism through a return to what Mészáros, Heller, and many of their contemporaries believed to be the original insight of Marx's work: that history was about human suffering and philosophy ought to be about human emancipation.

The original problem situation for Mészáros revolved around the reform Marxism of the political regime of Imre Nagy from 1953 until the revolution in 1956 in which he sought to restructure social relations around democratic participation while maintaining aspects of socialist organization. Part of this was the problem of the concept of revolution, and this remained a central problem for Mészáros throughout his work. Revolution was a central tenet in the East-Central European Marxist philosophical system, and the reality of the failed revolution of 1956 made this central tenet questionable as to its legitimacy as a focal point for emancipatory philosophy.

The development of moral philosophy as a critique of Marxism had its origins in the Austro-Marxists and the Kantian philosophies of the turn of the century (Kolakowski: 1978a). Kolakowski's work analyzed the development of Marxism in the region and illustrated the connection between moral philosophies that sought to reconcile a specific value system with the Marxist view of social change. This meant that Kolakowski was able to show that the possibility of merging Marxism with ethical questions had existed for some time on the continent, and Mészáros was able to continue these examinations and remain within a Marxist paradigm. For Mészáros, using the philosophical precursors of Marx such as Kant and Hegel, as well as other Marxist philosophers such as Lukács, who had pointed out the need for examinations of moral philosophy, was fundamental to an analysis of contemporary social and political conditions in the modern world.

For Mészáros, the importance of an epistemological position dealing with the problem of freedom was evident in his early work on alienation as well as his work on Lukacs' views of the dialectic. In both Marx's *Theory of Alienation* (1970) and Lukacs' *Concept of Dialectic* (1972), Mészáros sets up a critique of the epistemology of Marxism, and in many ways it is a direct response to the 'established socialist' states in East-Central Europe. This disagreement with the epistemological position of the Hungarian Marxists in the 1950s was not part of an anti-Marxist agenda since Mészáros (1978) sought to reform the philosophical disposition toward a 'truer' version of Marxian social theory that would ensure a transformed set of social relations and ensure liberation for all people: a theme he takes up in *Neo-colonial Identity and Counter-Consciousness: Essays in Cultural Decolonisation*. This was part of the fundamental value of humanism, of which the first immediate consequence was human emancipation, and was assumed to come directly from Marx. The development of the theme of Marx's 'original' idea of human emancipation meant that early Marx was the starting point for an emancipatory philosophy.

The Hungarian Communist Party maintained throughout the 1950s that in order to be able to achieve a certain level of industrialization, there needed to be a series of 'sacrifices' by individual people for the greater good. This greater good was the collective transformation of social relations. Agnes Heller and the Budapest School also critiqued this call for a sacrifice by a whole generation of people and had always sought to repudiate this truth-claim via Marxist social theory (Heller: 1966), rather than make a counterpoint via liberal social thought built around the individual. Heller's argument was that once an individual acceded the power of decision-making to an organization, it became a form of totalitarianism.

> One generation should not exist for the sacrifice of another: this would be fundamentally anti-humanist. The revolutionary generation seeks to better the situation of the coming generation, thus their situation is more difficult. But in this difficulty lies the claim—and rightly so—that their lives are always enriched and made more beautiful. (Heller: 1966, 205)

The difficulty with the concept of revolution was in the legitimation of a social process of radical transformation. Heller maintained that if we adopted a moral position in which every individual had a right to their own freedom and a control over their own lives, then this could ensure that any social process would not sacrifice any one person for any reason. If a 'revolutionary generation' sought to transform their social conditions, Heller maintained that they must do so only if their own material conditions were made better or more beautiful. Mészáros has claimed similar things in his work on Sartre, from the original article in *Telos* in 1975, which became 1979's *The Work of Sartre: Search for Freedom* to the reworked version of the book, *The Work of Sartre: Search for Freedom and the Challenge of History* published in 2012. Mészáros (2012, 240–41) has consistently maintained that this human creative force, revolutionary action, must be about individuals and not some form of totalizing historical force. Further, the normative position is that people should not engage in revolution if they could not see immediate practical change for themselves, otherwise they were dangerously close to giving away their freedom. This is also similar to the Arendtian position in revolution, and indeed Arendt drew a number of conclusions regarding this philosophical position from the Hungarian revolution in *The Origins of Totalitarianism* (1951), much as Mészáros and the Budapest School did.

Marxists like Mészáros maintained that Marxian organizing categories were correct in their insight, but the application of categories such as class and superstructure should not be employed to argue for the moral position of revolution as it went against the fundamental principle of emancipation in Marx's work (Mészáros: 2012; Heller: 1966, 7–8, 162–64, 247). Revolution, like generational sacrifice, was an anti-humanist ideal, as individuals were asked give up their freedom or their lives in order to further enhance a higher good. Heller argued that since there were no higher ethical goods than life and freedom, any philosophy that claimed to be subordinating it for a higher ethical good could not be historically correct. Thus Mészáros can maintain his support for the 'existential-Marxist Sartre' rather than the 'Marxist-Sartre.'

For Heller, this humanism was part of the historical progress of ethical development. At this stage of her work, Heller claimed that morality had evolved toward two specific contemporary conditions. The first was the universalization of ethical norms. This meant that normative aspects of human moral life, what ought to done, had undergone, and were still experiencing, a growing universal or global character in modern history. The second was the humanization of those categories considered to be human. This meant that those categories that were assumed to constitute the essential characteristics of human beings, for example emotions, were involved in a simultaneous process of 'humanization' or regulation for the purpose of the positive development of the human species. Socialist morality, as a result, had to be reconciled with these social facts. Heller argued that Marx realized these developments and the science of Marxism was the inheritor of this tradition of thinking about human beings (Heller: 1978a; Heller: 1979a). Heller concluded that it was indeed possible to maintain a Marxist critique of morality and ethical categories.

For Heller, the idea that a generation should not be sacrificed for the betterment of the coming generations was grounded in the idea of the unquestionable autonomy of the individual. Heller believed that this was a Kantian position that assumed that all individuals had the capacity for rational choice through reasoned reflection (Heller: 1980c; 1985b, 117). Furthermore, ethics was an autonomous sphere and experienced a development apart from historical phenomena. Since the individual was an autonomous unit in history, and the ethical sphere was in the process of a separate development, there was an interaction between these two as historical processes. Also, since human beings all had the potential for rational reflection, there existed an ability to live as an 'active-reflexive' person with regard to moral decisions. This freedom of the individual was the starting point from which praxis was to occur and thus lead to the fundamental value of humanism. This was how human emancipation became the guiding principle since it was part of a logical historical development consistent with Marxism.

From these assumptions about the abovementioned historical processes, Heller argued for the Marxian idea of the free development of the individual. History was not the main focus of investigation at this point, as Heller sought to analyze what she considered to be developments preceding historical processes. For Heller, there needed to be a social structure in place that would aid in such development and guarantee free association for individuals to proceed along the path to a self-chosen development. Heller chose the ideal polis, from Aristotle, and stated that public life must be open and democratic to ensure that the individual could participate in his or her own freely chosen development (Heller: 1966; 1985a). The polis as a whole would naturally move toward happiness since Heller assumed that happiness was the highest form of both ethical and non-ethical good. Even though modernity was involved in a process of a dissolution of norms and a dissolution of the hierarchies of norms associated with them, happiness was the goal of this development as a universal norm (1988). Furthermore, since the ethical sphere was an autonomous one, there was a question of where to place them in relation to other human endeavors.

This is precisely the argument put forward by Mészáros a couple of decades later. And it is interesting that Mészáros sees a need to continue to return to Sartre, as a core existentialist position, to effectively rescue Marxism from the dichotomy of structural Marxism and the political economy alternative that Sartre's philosophical descendants see as such an important element of contemporary Marxist practice. For example, Mészáros' work is at odds with Badiou's interpretations of socialism and the world-view that espouses a different form of collectivity engaging in the kind of unity demanded by Badiou's philosophy (There is not space here to treat this issue in full, see Imre: 2010 for a brief discussion of a piece of Badiou's work).

Heller's solution to the normative problem was to demand that morality not be used for political ends, in that the Hungarian Communist Party should not be able to claim to have made correct political decisions based on their moral authority. For Heller, this meant that politics had to be guided by a set of norms, and since the free individual was to be involved in a free association, public life could not demand that individuals be involved in those systems not of their choosing. For Heller, there could be no coercion in the political arena as political decisions had to be subject to openly discussed and freely chosen moral imperatives. It was this phase of Heller's work that led to her original problems with the authorities in Hungary in the late 1950s. Heller's demand that moral questions be discussed openly in public meant that each individual had the capacity to think about the decisions that the Communist Party had made. Practical decisions about distribution of resources to meet the needs of people were to be questioned and evaluated based on what Heller considered to be fundamental human values above political or pragmatic decisions. As a result she, and some of her contemporaries, were asked to stop teaching.

Sociology: Humanizing Empiricism

Heller returned to a teaching post in 1963 at the Institute for Sociology in Budapest where she began her work on the problem of the relationship between value systems and the social sciences. For Heller, social science inquiry was always value-laden, and questions involving human beings were always subject to particular forms of prejudices, depending on the social contexts from which they originated. However, Heller was not a proponent of cultural relativism. For Heller (1964), all cultures had a value system of one form or another, and the examination of these value systems became the focus of analysis.

The question was not Weber's dilemma of the fact-value dichotomy, since for Heller all facts had the fundamental guiding position of a value system that underlies the choice of the actual fact. Reality was always guided by a structure of norms and values that prejudiced the kind of questions people would ask as well as the kinds of answers people would accept (Heller: 1975). Since there was a plurality of values and a development of the primacy of the individual in modernity, there had to be questions of how to go about conducting social inquiry that was compatible with these developments.

One aspect of these contemporary theoretical developments was the growth of American sociology (Heller: 1975; Heller: 1964). For Heller, American empirical sociological inquiry as well as the individual psychological perspectives were important additions to critical theory. However, these forms of sociology were inadequate in providing the cultural guidance and the moral norms necessary for emancipation and had not solved the problem that Heller believed was inherent in modern social theory. This problem was the lack of discussion about value systems. Thus, the realization of the potential of the human species needed greater elaboration than relying on the 'assured' methods of empirical analysis.

For Heller, the problem with Marxist analysis and existing socialism in East-Central Europe was a lack of adjustment to contemporary circumstances. This meant that examinations of economic data that were used to guide social planning in East-Central Europe were not taking into account contemporary value systems. Since moral questions guide individual decisions, and freedom was part of the development of value systems in modernity, the adjustment to contemporary circumstances had to incorporate these changes. At this stage, Heller continued to emphasize life and freedom as central values that would lead to happiness. This underlying value system was, for Heller, the starting point in constructing the social situations that had the possibility of creating the conditions for human emancipation.

The question remained as to how to conduct sociological inquiry. If the individual was the main unit category in history, and the reasoning capacity of that individual allowed for choices to be made toward the development of human freedom, then what should the social theorist focus on if not the actions of that individual? What was the alternative to empirical sociology? For Heller, there needed to be a method by which one could come to understand the developments of the choices that people made that would reconcile their actions with historical development. For Heller and her contemporaries, this became a complex series of philosophical problems that were embodied by the renaissance of Marxism that brought together Heller's positions on moral Marxism and the social sciences.

Conclusion

For Mészáros, this set of problems represents an issue with community and collectivity. Mészáros is still working to revive and strengthen this concept of human collective action and is doing so via Marxian categories. The next chapter discusses in more detail how Mészáros has worked to achieve this, and how everyday life in the modern world can be made to be part of a non-alienated future. An important aspect of the development of this kind of Marxist thought is a continuation of the work of the Budapest School. This aspect of Marxist thought is treated in some detail in the next chapter.

Chapter 6

Work in the Post-Industrial World

Mészáros' analysis of the contemporary capitalist system is one in which he emphasizes how the utility-maximizing thesis has worked to destroy the marketplace. Rather than create efficiency, or the "best price/best value" for produced goods, having convinced individuals to act in their own narrow interests in order to maximize this personal utility has created a set of difficulties in the post-industrial world. These difficulties have exacerbated the traditional Marxist view of human alienation and taken them to a much higher level. Mészáros claims that work in the contemporary world needs to be thought through in a different way, and that mass education and mass society can provide avenues for that "working through."

We challenge the idea that schooling and work are linked. This challenge is brought about a number of ways, including normative questions about what we ought to deliver in schools, practical ways in which we examine what has worked in schools in terms of teaching content, and in ideological ways in terms of what sorts of theoretical groundings make sense for students in terms of facing this human alienation.

The Budapest School

Moral Marxism and the critique of the development of social science were symptomatic of a larger movement in Hungary and East-Central Europe that adopted a critical Marxist position (Gehlen, Schutz, Habermas, the Frankfurt School, the Praxis Marxists in Yugoslavia). During the late 1950s through the middle 1970s, a group of social theorists in Hungary engaged in a project of examining the philosophical problem of human emancipation that encompassed Mészáros attempts to address the same problem. Mészáros' role in this movement led to an elaboration of a position on a series of problems dealing with alternatives for Marxism in Hungarian society and the rest of East-Central Europe, and eventually a global position on how to create change.

Marxian historical determinism presented a problem for philosophers looking to employ a Marxist analysis using categories described by Marx, while simultaneously escaping from historical determinism. Mészáros work on this problem runs through all of his writing, and in order to arrive at a practical position in which Mészáros is ultimately discussing the problem of work in late modernity, he felt he needed to develop a particular reinterpretation of Marxian history. This is grounded in the interpretations of Lukács in Mészáros' work, *Lukacs' Concept of Dialectic* (1972). Straight from the Budapest School interpretation of Lukács, Mészáros analyzes history from a point of view that emphasizes the contingency introduced in our previous chapter. This is based on similar work done by others in the Budapest School, and is very similar to Agnes Heller's early work on the topic.

In *Renaissance Man*, Heller (1978a), began to articulate a form of accidentality of history consistent with pre-Hegelian and pre-Kantian notions of history that focused on particular narratives that did not fit together as a unified process. Mészáros had similar arguments contained in his work on Sartre as well as the second volume of *Social Structure and Forms of Consciousness* (2010). The value systems articulated by the people during the European Renaissance, whom Heller referred to as European humanists, did not fit the pattern of class antagonisms or the articulation of economic interests which drove change on the European continent. For Heller, this meant that the renaissance ideals represented a series of responses by various social strata to various social conditions given a number of historical precedents that did not necessarily correspond to the progressive development of a unified value-system. The claim here is that the irreducible plurality of values provided the room for individual decisions that were loosely surrounded by a system of socially constructed rules and regulations and not determined in a fixed and unchangeable pattern. This led Heller to conclude that the historical evolution was a process that involved the growth of the autonomy of various cultural spheres that Heller sought to bring together under the single categorical imperative of human emancipation. This is a very similar approach found throughout *Social Structure and Forms of Consciousness* as Mészáros' (2010, 159) analyzes work toward building a dialectic that privileges diversity rather than a predetermined pattern of history.

These concerns summarized the position of the Budapest School as these thinkers expressed "a common concern not only for the application of Marxian social theory to contemporary issues but also for the elimination of alienation" (Brown: 1988, 15) and they attempted to make the "distance between the potentialities of the human species and its individual richness the smallest" (Lukacs: 1971, 664). Apart from Mészáros these people included Heller, Ferenc Feher, Mihaly Vajda, and Georg and Maria Markus.

Ivan Szelenyi was also considered to be a contributor, but he had repeatedly gone against some of the moral positions discussed above. His concern for pragmatic economic policies over the moral Marxism of the other members was considered to be a difficulty by the Budapest School and illustrated a divergence of opinions about the role of democracy in East-Central European society. According to Szelenyi, "the correct question is not whether East European societies are becoming capitalist, but rather what kind of capitalism is likely to emerge" (Szelenyi: 1991, 167), and he had repeatedly argued for the need for private property in a mixed economy. The acceptance of the inevitability of capitalism was a tenuous connection with the rest of the School, but the necessity of private property was a definite break from the position of the Budapest School.

Szelenyi had also repeatedly disagreed with the radicalizing of democracy in the region in that he believed that the complete democratization of the workplace in an industrial society would lead to higher wage demands, decreased productivity, and inflation, as has been the case for several of the former communist states in East-Central Europe. The pragmatic implications outweighed the value choice for Szelenyi as he remained an economist before any other consideration. For Heller in particular, this was a philosophical position that ought not be adopted, and for Mészáros, the ultimate human freedom was not to be found in the economic sphere.

The Budapest School analyzed the development of capitalism as it was embodied in political and economic relations in free market economies in Western nations. The Budapest School analysis of capitalism concluded that Western societies were not products of class struggle but rather societies "characterized by a stratified distribution of power over social decision-making mechanisms" (Brown: 1988, 68; Heller, et. al.: 1983). The discussion of existing socialism also rejected the orthodox Marxian notion of the class struggle as the single explanation for activity. The Budapest School theorists believed that Soviet societies were inexplicable by Marx's basic class-based categories and that the East-Central European region must be seen as "new social formations requiring a fresh approach" (Brown: 1988, 97; Heller, et. al.: 1983; Heller and Feher: 1986). Consequently, the Budapest school suggested the radical democracy alternative based on a mixed economy. Feher and Heller repeatedly argued that the revolution in Hungary in 1956 was one example of the possibility of a spontaneous radical democracy that could emerge in Eastern Europe (Heller et al.: 1983).

The Budapest School rejected the Marxian conception of capitalism in that the dialectic of wage-labor and capital was not sufficient in explaining the history of capitalism. For these theorists, the economistic logic of Marx was a valuable organizing tool, but it remained insufficient in explaining the results of various capitalist systems. Mészáros has often pointed out that alienation is the result of surplus labor being exploited and not a condition of surplus value being created (Mészáros: 2001, 87–89). Coupled with this, the Budapest School refused "to view the activities of the capitalist state as an epiphenomenon of the class-constituted property relations in Marx's base-superstructure dichotomy" (Brown: 1988, 94). Simply put, this meant that the Budapest School did not accept the idea that activity of and by the capitalist state was a result of the clash of class divisions between a lower working class and an upper elite. For the Budapest School, there was a tendency and an organizing process of capitalism that indicated such characteristics. The Budapest School did not believe that it was the single tendency, it was not the lone organizing process, nor was it a single explanation of capitalism. The process of capitalism was a stratified process.

The Budapest School's neo-Marxism was based on Karl Polanyi's revision of Marxist economics. Polanyi supported the idea that Marx's economism analyzes one tendency within a total process of "disembedding the economy from society" (Brown: 1988, 94; Polanyi: 1957). For the Budapest School, "the historical process through which formal democracy evolved, that is, the protective response, indicates serious problems in Marx's economistic method" (Brown: 1988, 53; Polanyi: 1957). Formal democracy, the structure of Western political democracy, came to be as a result of this counter-movement in the form of the protective response that sought to check the development of capitalist relations. "Capitalism became an economic society through a process that was largely political—the disembedding of the economy simultaneous with the protective response" (Brown: 1988, 45; Polanyi: 1957). Thus the protective response was a spontaneous attempt by society to re-embed the economy through a repolitisization of the economic sphere.

Polanyi stated that "the dynamics of modern society was governed by a double movement: the market expanded continuously but this movement was met by a counter-movement checking the expansion in definite directions" (Polanyi: 1957, 132). The history of capitalism, according to the Budapest School, was one in which "power over social decision-making mechanisms was neither democratized nor dichotomized by the double-movement of the nineteenth century" (Brown: 1988, 65). It (power over decision-making) was not allowed equal access to all individuals, nor was it split into the base-superstructure, capitalist-proletariat dichotomies. Instead, the power was stratified, and thus decision-making processes were unevenly distributed. In his work *The State and Socialism*, Mihaly Vajda writes,

> Without a counter-trend, that is, without a trend toward repoliticization of the relations within civil society, the society would not be viable. Nevertheless, as long as these counter-trends, merely limit (without becoming subject to) the basic trends of capitalism, in order to maintain in existence the relations of private ownership, capitalism remains capitalism. (Vajda: 1981, 143–44)

This meant that the system of power distribution, which was based on the profit motive, remained unequal, even though the state acted in such a manner as to redistribute power in ways other than a capitalist economic system dictated. This did not indicate that there existed a state of completely free competition in the economic sphere, but instead it meant that "the fundamentally private nature of ownership" continued to dominate (Vajda: 1981, 144).

The Budapest School claimed that the economic sphere had not been democratized, but rather created a stratified power structure. The role of the state in capitalist society "has not been to undermine or directly subvert conditions of private capital accumulation or the existence of dominant business interests and social groups," but rather, the position of the state "has been to respond to those less powerful social groups threatened by the market" in a reactive rather than a proactive fashion (Brown: 1988, 67). Thus the democratic state in western societies acted to alleviate market problems without violating business interests through the protective response, and in this system of stratification, the power remained with those who dictate the greatest amount of resources. Simply put, those with the proportionately largest access to capital commanded the most political influence in terms of decision-making in civil society. Thus capitalism, for the Budapest School, was still fundamentally undemocratic, and as Vajda tautologically puts it, "capitalism remains capitalism" (Vajda: 1981, 143).

Continuing to draw on Polanyi's dialectic, however, the Budapest School argued that this clash between the market forces and the countermovement of the protective response did have potential in that it was not static.

> Formal democracy is still in the making and can be the basis for a transformation in its content, a transformation toward a radical democracy in which the right of equal participation in social decision-making is paramount. (Brown: 1988, 53)

As Heller wrote in *Past, Present and Future of Democracy*, "formal democracy is precisely the great invention ensuring continuously the democratic character of a state" (Heller: 1978b, 869).

The break with Marx went further as the Budapest School stated that transcending capitalism did not mean transcending bourgeois society. Again, this is similar to the problem articulated by Mészáros' (2012, 178) work on Sartre, most especially in Sartre's critique of Heidegger. The Budapest School argued that bourgeois society had kept alive the idea of the free individual with the potential for complete development as Mészáros points out in the recent version of *The Work of Sartre*. This was the crucial difference because it implied that Marx was not 'the greatest philosopher of the Enlightenment' but rather a part of Enlightenment philosophy. Further, Marx was an incomplete thinker who had approached some problems with great clarity while missing the point on others. As a result, these thinkers believed that the social inequalities of capitalism could be changed without sacrificing individual freedom, but this would require a major revision of Marxist social theory. This revision began in the renaissance of Marxism that placed the concept of Marx's species- essential individual at the center of its critique. As these thinkers viewed Marx, individuals and their respective freedoms realized their full potential in a condition of absolute abundance of resources. Since this condition of absolute abundance was not possible, there was a necessity to place constraints on the individual through state authority. Thus, for the Budapest School, a revision of Marx was necessary in that the individual freedoms of capitalism could be maintained through limits imposed by the state. Furthermore, bourgeois society could not be transcended but, like the capitalist economic system, could be democratized.

In her article *The Dissatisfied Society*, Heller (1983) discussed these ideas of individual freedom and analyzed the basis for this democratization. Heller stated that, "we cannot conceive of the continuously expanding individual need structure and the simultaneous satisfaction of all human needs in the same breath, for several reasons." The natural resources of the planet were not unlimited, and even in the "case of a continuously expanding demand for material goods a state of complete abundance" could not exist (Heller: 1983, 369). Furthermore, Heller stated that "even the satisfaction of the so-called spiritual needs presupposes a certain amount of material investment," given that material goods such as books and pianos had to be constructed out of these raw materials (Heller: 1983, 369). But some external body had to intervene to guarantee equal self-determination for all individuals. Mészáros (1995) makes similar claims throughout *Beyond Capital*, and had maintained that the hegemonic interpretation of the historical development of capital on a global scale provides little in the way of de-alienation and individual freedom. Invoking Lukács, Mészáros (1995) states,

> This is how Lukács...ended up proclaiming with undialectical one-sidedness the earlier quoted proposition according to which ideological crisis of the proletariat must be solved before a proactical solution to the world's economic crisis can be found. (321)

And Heller (1979a) concurs:

> Later rationalizations of capital's social metabolic order—especially in the twentieth century—lost even the relative justification of the Kantian illusions which could be maintained in the eighteenth century. The beautiful and plastic idea according to which all we need is for man (sic) to develop his essential forces, and all he needs for this purpose is to bring about a human society which will make this possible for everyone is something I myself accept, with one qualification: that "all he needs" is indeed everything." (3–4)

Heller's "beautiful and plastic idea" was the notion of equal self-determination, which was, she admitted, her version of a modern construction of the rational utopia. In capitalism, however, the stratified social decision-making process limited the expression of this equality. This limiting occurred "by allowing the formally free individual with potentially unlimited needs to emerge out of society and simultaneously by allowing the emergence of a self-regulating market economy based upon consumer demand" (Brown: 1988, 89). It was by this process that a capitalist society was organized around need fulfilment based on commodities rather than some "higher" form of social interaction.

The Budapest School argued for a democratization of the relations of production, or as Polanyi might put it, to 're-embed' the economic sphere in society. The productive capacity of a capitalist structure was to be maintained but radically democratized. The Budapest School suggested the liberalization of access to capitalist relations of production, rejection of the commodity-based production cycle, and the promotion of human freedoms through the democratization of production. This was to occur in East-Central European societies as well since all of these thinkers maintained that a new form of analysis of the region was necessary. The Budapest School critique of existing socialist states attempted to establish a link between the economistic approach of Marxist analysis and the characteristic of domination in these societies. The Budapest School believed that the Western Left had avoided the possibility that there might be a definite connection between Marxist social science and the obvious denial of human freedoms in these countries (Heller and Feher: 1977). Furthermore, they (Western leftist analysts and thinkers) have avoided serious study of Eastern Europe, resulting in explanations of Eastern European societies "that have not fully explained the repression and social domination in these self-reproducing systems of unfree paternalism" (Heller and Feher: 1977, 42). These two factors—the inherent repressive character of the economistic approach and Western ambivalence and misunderstanding—necessitated both a revision of Marxism as well as a change in the approach to analyzing East-Central European societies.

The Budapest School maintained that the economism of Marxian analysis was still a valuable organizing tool in terms of a paradigmatic approach to the analysis of Soviet societies. They employed a critical theory paradigm, similar to the Frankfurt School, since "the task of the critical theory of these societies is to discover the specific rationality of the system and thereby the tendencies, strains, and contradictions of its development" (Markus: 1982, 308). For Markus, the "Marxist tradition in its historical totality does retain its critical potential with reference to the societies of Eastern Europe" (Markus: 1982, 295). The main reason for this was that the Budapest School argued that liberal social theory and the analysis of authoritarian political systems offered little in the way of explaining the complexities of the regional problems experienced by these societies. This theory of authoritarianism simply stated that Soviet societies were the result of two factors contributing to their authoritarianism. The first was a 'natural' predilection for an authoritarian system, and the second was the strong military presence of the Soviet Union in the region.

Clearly, this was an insufficient explanation, however, as the complexity of the political structures of the region maintain a huge variety of characteristics which are the result of many different political, economic, and social forces. The Western analyses that employed such a theory fell well short of the mark in the eyes of the Budapest School, regarding a process of explanation of activity in these societies. It was here that the Budapest School begins to branch out and create its own analytic school. They sought to go beyond the totality of Marx's economism while rejecting the Western approach of the liberal theory of authoritarian political systems. The emphasis was on the value of economism as an organizing rather than a totalizing mode of analysis, and if the reductionism of the economistic approach is given up, then "the class division of society ceases to be the only important and decisive factor in the constitution of social groups" (Vajda: 1981, 6). Furthermore, Vajda (1981) stated that even though these class divisions have been officially eliminated in these Soviet societies, they still "may have a definitely hierarchical structure." In terms of an organizing process, the "new inequality comes to permeate all of social life: i.e., that between those who distribute and those who are distributed" (Heller and Feher: 1977, 12).

For the Budapest School, the Euro-communist or Western Marxist approach was indicative of a general ambivalent characteristic of most Western analytic approaches to Soviet societies. "Soviet society represents the historical embodiment of...the Babeuf option" which means "the eliminat(ion of) the inequality of capitalism by sacrificing individual freedom" (Brown: 1988, 86). The Budapest School constructed the argument as such: the separation of the economic sphere from capitalist society greatly increased the degrees of freedom over previous societies. This resulted in the creation of a civil society that advanced the freedom of the individual. In Soviet society, however, there was an attempt to eliminate inequalities generated by capitalism through sacrificing the individual freedom generated by capitalism. This type of anti-capitalist structuring of society operates on the assumption that capitalism and bourgeois society were inseparable. Therefore, directly as a result of Marx's economistic method, the elimination of capitalism meant the elimination of civil society.

Western Euro-communists according to the Budapest School did not take this development in East-Central Europe seriously enough.

There was an attempt by the Euro-communist social theorists to salvage socialist thinking, as the inability of Western Communist critiques to fully explain Eastern European societies had left the socialist movement with a vast analytic deficiency. The Budapest School operated on the premise that there was nothing socialist about these soviet societies in the region, and Euro-communists who had attempted explanations based on the premise that some aspect of socialism remained in existing soviet societies were responsible for advancing theories which had "largely transformed and degenerated" (Heller: 1984b, 235–36). These Western analysts had failed to realize that the movements in Eastern Europe "produced regimes which are in fact anti-capitalist but which are not socialist" (Heller: 1984b, 235). Instead these regimes were "an abominable caricature of everything socialists have lived and fought for" (Heller: 1984b, 236). This emotional response from the Budapest School meant that soviet societies in East-Central Europe were anti-capitalist in that they maintained the primacy of historical materialism and a collectivization of resources in order to achieve human emancipation by sacrificing the human beings presently living in these societies.

Socialism was in a state of analytic delegitimation for the Budapest School. The Euro-communists had failed to explain Eastern Europe as a unique historical phenomenon and had, instead, attempted an explanation in terms of authoritarianism or a simple acceptance that the class struggle was incomplete. The idea that Hungary, for example, was a communist state in the midst of a process of completion was a common argument among Marxists. Since socialism, by definition, was a historically more advanced phase than capitalism, there could be no question that the Soviet system had to be maintained. Following this argument, the transition to socialism was still continuing, and the dialectic of historical materialism was proceeding toward the completion of a socialist phase of development. Markus wrote that it was this type of analysis that was indicative of the mistaken totalization of the Marxian dialectic if "socialism, as a whole...is to ever transcend its miserable state (it) needs radical self-criticism of what has happened in the last sixty years" (Heller: 1984b, 222).

> Thus every militant with a will to genuine socialism is confronted with a situation which is far more complex than the first day of World War I, when socialists whose moral integrity was still intact felt that the idea and the movement had already become hopelessly compromised. (Heller: 1984b, 235–36)

There remained hope for the Budapest School in the burgeoning leftist opposition in East-Central Europe during the 1980s. There was a political development of a "better consciousness of what socialism may be, must be" since "the emergence of a leftist opposition in Eastern Europe by its very existence...has compelled some segments of the Western left to face the reality of what socialism is not" (Heller et al.: 1983, 293).

In seeking a form of change toward a real socialism, the Budapest School emphasised the idea that there was no historical precedent for the political and economic phenomenon of East-Central European societies. The formerly Soviet societies must be treated as unique in the historical unfolding of the region. These critiques of capitalism and existing socialism led the Budapest School to prescribe their version of a radical democracy alternative that included advocating a type of social democratic mixed economy. This form of mixed economy promoted by the Budapest School meant that while capitalism needed to be democratized, this did not mean that bourgeois society ought to be transcended. The importance of the idea of the free individual had to be preserved in the manifestation of bourgeois society and the productive capacity maintained, but the stratified political relations inherent in a capitalist structure must be left behind. It was here that the Budapest School made the break from free market advocates such as Szelenyi in that the mixed economy of a radical democracy ensured the existence of a "non-capitalist civil society divorced from the state...(with) the features of the capitalist system...no longer the primary resource allocating principles" (Brown: 1988, 161). This meant that private property had to be abolished in what the Budapest School referred to as a 'positive' abolition. This was the greatest split from Western mixed economies, recommendations by liberal theorists such as Szelenyi and Kornai, and free market reform advocates, all of whom viewed the relations of private property as indicative of dynamic production. The radical democracy alternative of the Budapest School necessitated its own version of a mixed economy that attempted to transcend capitalism and the relations endemic to such a system through a democratization of the relations of production. This was to occur through the separation of state and civil society and the use of markets for the recognition of all the needs of individuals living in that society. Since the limited resources of society required a certain degree of state intervention, this intervention was to be used to distribute these limited resources based on the idea that there must be an equal recognition of the needs of all people. This was the moral imperative that guided the interventionist position of the state.

The Budapest School's version of radical democracy maintained that humanity ought to be liberated from certain authoritarian impositions and guided by other external constraints in order to ensure the fulfilment of equal self-determination. There was a necessary liberation required to achieve the objectives of freedom and need fulfilment in this kind of a society.

> The 'liberation of humankind' cannot possibly mean liberation from all kinds of constraints...it cannot mean liberation from all kinds of authorities, norms, and duties, only from specific kinds of external authorities, norms, and duties. (Heller: 1982b, 369)

The unequal distribution of goods and opportunities within a stratified society could be changed through the creation of rules and norms—a society in which "everyone could equally participate in the process of conflict-solving" (Heller: 1983b, 368). In order to do so, there needed to be a commonly recognized set of ethics. These ethics or "'moral maxims' provide...(the) foundation for political practice in a radical democracy" (Heller: 1983b, 368).

The three moral maxims adhered to in the Budapest School's radical democracy model were freedom, justice, and an end to suffering. They believed that these values had historically evolved throughout humanity's development and were repressed through the inequalities generated by capitalist and soviet societies. Any such expression of these values presupposed the participation of "good citizens" (Heller: 1983b). For Heller, this Aristotelian notion of "good citizens" cooperating to maintain the proper functioning of a participatory democracy necessitated the acceptance of equal self-determination. For the Budapest School, if freedom and justice could be provided, then the potential for equal self-determination could exist in society. Furthermore, if these concepts could be posited as norms experienced in everyday life in the society in question, then a true socialism could be achieved. Following this acceptance, there could be a society that guaranteed the expression of equal self-determination. For the Budapest School, this moral philosophical analysis could provide the social stability necessary for the achievement of a radical democratic alternative to both socialism and capitalism.

The Budapest School sought to maintain a civil society in their radical democracy model that was separated from the economic sphere. In this version of the mixed economy, the capitalist economic sphere was maintained for its value as a productive mechanism but would not be the main allocating system in the mixed economy. The existence of a non-capitalist civil society provided the possibility of preserving individual freedom and maintaining bourgeois society as the Budapest School had previously suggested, thus eliminating the inherent inequalities produced by capitalism. Rather than attempting to eliminate the capitalist system by taking away individual freedoms, as had been previously tried in East-Central Europe, the capitalist economic system was to be subject to the social goals of equal distribution.

The change in the role of wage labor in such a system through self-managed enterprises illustrated the possibility of accomplishing the goals of the radical democracy alternative. "Wage-labor and capitalist become 'roles' played by the same individual" (Vajda: 1981, 90) thereby eliminating the opposing roles among individuals. This is a form of self-management in which workers participate in greater degrees of decision-making in the operation of the productive unit in which they work. The freedom of the individual was maintained along with the "dynamism of production" (Vajda: 1981, 34). The direct democratization of the economic and productive spheres characterized this form of a mixed economy in which ownership was changed in two ways. The first was the "rational administration of property as the source of the rational satisfaction of needs" and the second was "the direct relation of decision-making to ownership" (Heller and Feher: 1977, 17). Thus wage-labor would become a self-imposed and self-regulating system of production ensuring democratization in the economic sector.

This was a fundamental point for Mészáros' thesis in *Beyond Capital* and his analysis of the attempt to "overcome the power of capital." For Mészáros (1995, 980) this meant that "the object, the target, of socialist transformation" is precisely this "overcoming of the power of capital" and without this approach, it was not possible to effect real social transformation. Further, Mészáros (1995, 489) states, "undoubtedly, Marx's advocacy of attacking the *causes* of social evils, instead of fighting necessarily lost battles against the mere *effects* of capital's ongoing self-expansion, is the only correct strategy to adopt". As such, Mészáros' work on the problem of capital was different than a dismantling of 'capitalism' in that he has consistently demanded that the examination of the growth of capital as a hegemonic world-view be challenged, rather than create a critique that sought to mitigate problems with capitalism. This was in many ways similar to the interpretation of the Budapest School when dealing with the development of socialism, or 'realized socialism,' in East-Central Europe.

The Budapest School had the main objective of providing a new perspective for analysis of East-Central European societies. They began with the premise that neither Western liberal nor Eurocommunist analyses had produced sufficient insight on the region to be able to prescribe and recommend a course of action for political, economic, and social policies. The three specific areas of contention for these thinkers were the critiques of capitalism and socialism, and the resulting prescription for the mixed economy of the radical democracy. They drew on highly specific political histories of Soviet societies and Western capitalist formal democracies, respectively, leading to a discussion of a mixed economy. They rejected the totalizing of economism, in much the same way as Mészáros, as they maintained that capitalism was a stratified society with a hierarchy of power and could not be explained solely through a class struggle dialectic. They sought to analyze existing soviet societies apart from a totalitarian critique, and to , these societies as a derivation of what they believed was an incorrect application of Marxian ideas. The complexity of the Eastern European region necessitated a discussion based on the acceptance of the idea that the problems experienced in these nations were unique.

The radical democracy alternative of the Budapest School stated that the relations of production needed to be democratized. Mészáros continued to seek similar alternatives throughout his work, and in particular the economic critiques found in *Beyond Capital* develop this position. The prescription was premised on the idea that each individual had the right to participate in the decision-making processes of their respective lives. This could not occur in existing capitalist or soviet societies, and there had to be a central authority that guaranteed the right to participate in all sectors of society. This was based on the moral philosophy employed by the Budapest School in which they believed that life and freedom were the categorical imperatives for thinking about their world.

The analysis of capitalist political and economic relations concluded with the need to preserve the productive capacity in order to fulfil the needs of all individuals equally. These needs were to be guaranteed by a governing body that promoted the values of freedom, justice and equal self-determination. Heller concluded that the next direction for her work was to continue to elaborate upon the problem of the human individual. While the Budapest School claimed they were not 'third way' theorists seeking a combination of socialist government and capitalist economics, their program of radical democracy was quite similar in its insistence on subordinating the economic sphere to the political sphere which was in turn to be subordinate to the moral sphere. This was in line with Mészáros' view of 'existential-Marxism' and the basis for his analysis of Sartre's work. For Heller, a system of immanent critique that employed Marxism to analyze societies was becoming increasingly problematic. Heller's philosophical system eventually developed in a direction away from the renaissance of Marxism, and quite unlike Mészáros, Heller moved away from these forms of Marxism to turn toward another version of philosophical inquiry altogether. Mészáros continued his Marxist-Marxian line of questioning and developed his work on *The Structural Crisis of Capital* in 2009 and his two-volume work on *Social Structure and Forms of Consciousness* in 2010 and 2011.

Conclusion

The renaissance of Marxism was a movement throughout the Left in both Western and Eastern Europe, when that false divide reigned supreme in the Cold War. It provided internal dissidents such as Agnes Heller with a philosophical position that could remain committed to Marxism and also provide external dissidents such as Mészáros a way to question the capacities of Marxist theory to account for the great changes occurring on the European continent and the world over. Moral philosophy, sociology, and the Budapest School's larger project of reviving a critical and emancipatory Marxist philosophy in Hungary made it possible to analyze social conditions in the region within a slightly altered Marxist paradigm. However, all of these philosophies challenged Marxist epistemology by finding it insufficient for contemporary social criticism for Heller and Budapest School, and Mészáros saw Marxism as continuing to be rich with possibilities of analysis. For Mészáros, the structural development of global capital was the main problem to confront, and capital, not capitalism, was to be resisted as the contemporary form of domination. In moral philosophy, Heller found that Marx's lack of an elaboration of the development of an ethical position left a lacuna in the tradition of East-Central European thought. Furthermore, the development of sociology pointed to the fact that there was a belief in an increasing amount of knowledge about human beings. The program of the Budapest School encompassed these two objectives and also dealt with a kind of political economy which demanded a radical democracy—the kind of participation that Stalinist regimes could not tolerate. The outright acceptance of a positive value of capitalism was problematic for the Budapest School as it became increasingly difficult to remain within a Marxist social criticism. On the other hand, Mészáros remained a structural Marxist, determined to find human emancipation precisely in that form of resistance that the Budapest School eventually found futile.

In Heller's philosophical system, human emancipation needed a greater elaboration upon the active subject. Moral philosophy was taken for granted, as if there were significant components of society that would, out of their own volition, attempt to live a moral existence. The science of sociology became a way of tracking what had happened at a superficial level by producing statistical data about the behavior of individuals. Without attaching meaning to these social changes, it became difficult to understand what was happening in human development.

Philosophical Anthropology

Conceptions of human nature are central to all political philosophies. Most moral, social, and political philosophies have a set of assumptions about the constitution of human characteristics that act as the basis for their theories. Similarly for Mészáros, Heller, and the Budapest School, the composition of individual human beings became the focus of their epistemological position. Mészáros continued to examine a series of ethical, political, and social problems, eventually turning to a detailed examination of the problem of the individual human being. Mészáros sought to show that the possibility for social change rested in Marx's concept of the species-essence of human beings. The project of human emancipation thus became grounded in the interaction of the individual with their 'life-world' and the possibility of achieving abundant individual human capacities.

In this chapter, we argue that Heller developed three main categories in addressing the problem of the human individual. These categories were everyday life, neo-Marxist philosophical anthropology, and social anthropology. In each particular stage of development, Heller sought to reorient questions of the constitution of human beings around the epistemological imperative of emancipation. The first stage involved the argument for the possibility for change in the everyday life of the individual. The second involved a neo-Marxist philosophical anthropology in which Marx's concepts of need and value, both of which were produced in everyday life, were reworked around Heller's epistemological position of human emancipation. The third phase, social anthropology, illustrated the beginnings of Heller's move away from Marx and the eventual dissolution of Marxism as the fundamental ordering paradigm. The development of these three characteristics lead Heller to abandon a 'system-immanent' critique and embark on a new philosophical focus which would remain true to her original position of human emancipation.

The Science of the Human Condition

During this Italian Renaissance, Florentine culture began to concern itself with the development of the possibilities of the human individual, or what Marx was to later term the 'species-essence.' For humanist-Marxism, this period of human history was the birthplace of modern conceptions of human beings. For Heller, science, philosophy, art, and knowledge were removed from the sphere of everyday life in antiquity, and their movement into this sphere was a result of the process of the humanization of everyday life. Heller's description of the development of the sphere of everyday life began with her analysis of feudal society in which, according to her, science and philosophy were separated from everyday life (1978: 148–69).

In antiquity, the stratification of the sciences ensured that ideas remained in the realm of the privileged. Heller argued that in the Renaissance this changed, as ideas were no longer for privileged people. The Platonic Academy in Florence was open to those who had the desire to study and not just to those who had the birthright to be educated. Science and magic became differentiated in that the control over the elements of nature had to be demonstrable and reproducible, thereby accessible and visible to all people. Art was no longer done for the glory of God, but for the sake of the production of beautiful objects. This production was open to public criticism and a hierarchy of artists developed which, according to Heller, indicated an interest in the multiple capacities of human beings. For Heller, this indicated a move toward the realization of individual capacities within the sphere of everyday life and the beginnings of the Marxist project to engage in the same realization.

This "genealogy of cultural modernity" (Markus: 1988, 12) Heller produced in Renaissance Man illustrated the evolution of particular concepts regarding the human individual in the Italian Renaissance. According to Heller, two interrelated themes needed elaboration in order to clarify the development of the theoretical disciplines that had human beings as their focus. The first theme was everyday life, and the second was philosophical anthropology. Heller argued that in modernity, everyday life became the fundamental social category from which all other social categories derived. The study of the everyday life of human beings led to the examination of the categories of experience within this sphere. The elaboration of these categories became the concept of philosophical anthropology. "The Renaissance created philosophical anthropology, the science whose subject is man as a species being" (Heller: 1978, 373), and this science became the focus of Heller's work. Thus, for Heller, everyday life became the unit category for historical change.

Everyday Life

In her work on everyday life, Heller developed the main categories through which an understanding of individual and collective action was possible. Her approach was one that showed how individuals were involved in a dynamic process of self-realization that was mitigated by norms and values. Within this sphere of everyday life, the individual person was involved in appropriating norms as norms which were taken for granted as well as those norms which were self-created or appropriated out of volition. It was this self-reproduction that had the capacity to change the everyday life of the individual and thereby change social conditions. At its most fundamental level, this represented the possibility for change toward the good. For Heller, her attempt to argue for this change was part of the process of change itself. Since the attitudes for such change existed, it was possible. Since it was possible, it ought to be generalized in other individuals. This meant that the generalization ought to be non-coercive and rational, thus producing the impetus for social change.

Heller stated that in "modern times norms and rules are not taken for granted and traditional values are dismantled thus the 'phenomena' themselves must be constructed" (Heller: 1984a, 3). For Heller, the individual in everyday life had needs and the elaboration of the needs of the individual indicated that people, as individuals, were not reducible to a series of fixed rules about social interaction. Finite individuals were certainly socially conditioned, but this did not mean that at a general level there should be coercion that pushed individuals to conform to a single externally determined pattern.

For Heller, the implications of this approach did not allow for an anti-historical or anti-rational philosophical stance. The emphasis on human emotive characteristics was not the same as some of the postmodernist emphases on these kinds of human qualities. Heller's position was decidedly against nihilism, negative dialectics, and the politics of despair. Heller recognized the historically contingent value systems of human beings, but the question remained as to how the species-essential individual was to affect emancipation against instrumental reason.

In *Everyday Life* (Heller: 1984a), it was this humanization that Heller argued for in that she saw the possibility of changing social life by changing everyday life. She stated that the attitude for such change existed and only needed to be generalized in individuals. Furthermore,

> if individuals are to reproduce society, they must reproduce themselves as individuals. We may define everyday life as the aggregate of those individual reproduction factors that, pari passu, make social reproduction possible. No society can exist without individual reproduction and no individual can exist without self-reproduction. (Heller: 1984a: 3)

Everyday life existed in all societies and every human being had their own everyday life. Reproduction of the person was of the concrete person, and the concrete person occupied a given place in a given society. Reproduction of a society did not follow automatically from the self-reproduction of persons. People could reproduce themselves only by fulfilling their social functions, and self-reproduction became the impetus for social reproduction. Thus, at the level of the category of the person, this everyday life depicted the reproduction of a current society in general as it depicted the socialization of nature and the degree and manner of its humanization.

This was Heller's articulation of a philosophical category that Heidegger had referred to as "thrownness" in his work, *Being and Time*. Heller stated that concrete social conditions, concrete sets of postulates and demands, concrete things, and concrete institutions existed prior to each individual's birth. A person had to learn to use these things by acquiring customs and meeting societal demands. Thus the reproduction of the person was always of the historical person existing in a concrete world. This characterization was problematic in Heller's philosophical system as it still did not solve the problem of human emancipation. Heidegger's category of thrownness led him to conclude that individuals living an authentic existence would eventually reach their full human potential by overcoming their environment. Since such an environment also consisted of social conditions, and social conditions consisted of other human beings, most likely inauthentic human beings, this opened the door for an 'overcoming' of other people. This conclusion was a philosophical position with which Heller disagreed, since placing human beings and their needs at the fore of a discussion about human beings was the first step in changing everyday life. As a result, Heller began an examination of the relationship between individuals and their world to reorient everyday life around emancipation.

In analyzing the sphere of everyday life, Heller produced a set of categories that emphasised the primacy of the individual. Heller (1984a, ix) wrote that "I...(have) established the very framework of my philosophy which I have never changed since, short of elaboration or occasional modification". The method of *Everyday Life* was a phenomenological approach and an Aristotelian analytical procedure. This meant that Heller used the ordering categories of Aristotle, such as conceptions of goodness, truth, and beauty, that were to be realized in an ideal polis composed of good citizens in a civil society. Furthermore, Heller stated that in modernity, norms and rules were not taken for granted, and traditional values were dismantled which meant that, for Heller, the 'phenomena' themselves had to be constructed before implementing an Aristotelian analytical method. For Heller, this was a phenomenological approach that relied heavily on both Husserl and what Heller referred to as a "critically modified" Heidegger (Heller: 1984a, ix).

This 'continental categorical system' included the Hegelian in-itself, for-itself, in and for itself, and for us (we-consciousness) that were the categories applied to the three spheres of objectivation and respectively to their appropriation. Species-essence or species-essentiality was taken from Marx's *Paris Manuscripts*, and Heller stated that all spheres of objectivation were termed 'species-essential.' This meant that all of these categories were dynamic human categories common to all individuals. Heller termed these spheres of objectivation as species essential in-itself, species essential for-itself, and species essential in- and for-itself. The species essential in-itself was the empirical human universal that was appropriated as taken for granted by individuals in their life-worlds. The species essential for-itself was a sphere of objectivation that was appropriated out of free volition and reflection by individuals. This occurred because the for-itself involved a crystalization of previously willed and reflected acts.

Objectivation provided the means of appropriating phenomena through the sphere of objectivation "in itself." "Since this sphere of objectivation is an empirical universe, all social categories can be understood by having recourse to this objectivation and this procedure of transcendental reduction could be avoided" (Heller: 1984a, ix). This sphere, in the main, regulated everyday life. It was an anti-historicist position but not an anti-historical one since, for Heller, there remained a historical variability of social structures and simultaneously the historical variability of the content of the norms and rules presented by the sphere of objectivation in itself. This obvious tension ensured that Heller had great problems in working out a philosophy of history that could remain consistent with her philosophical anthropology. Furthermore, Heller's view of history at this stage of her work meant that there was a great tension between her attempt to maintain a categorical imperative of human emancipation and her analysis of everyday life.

For Heller, it became clear that a philosophy of history in which humanity continues to evolve and progress toward higher states of being over time would not be able to remain consistent with her analyses. As Heller (1984a, ix) stated, "I then shared the evolutionism of Marxism in full and subscribed to a philosophy of history, characteristics which I have since abandoned".

The sphere of objectivation in-itself and thus the patterns of everyday life included historical constants, and these historical constants had to be reflected upon in conjunction with the historical variables. In spite of the constancy of some patterns of everyday life, it had the possibility to be changed, humanized and democratized (1984a, x). This was intended as a challenge to the Heideggerian position of providing the possibility of overcoming other aspects of social conditions through a process of dialectics. Heller sought a form of historical change in everyday life in which the appropriation and continuation of patterns of behavior could never involve the negation of the needs of other human beings. Since she argued that Heidegger provided such a philosophical opening in rationalizing overcoming specific aspects of human social life, her work was definitely anti-Heideggerian. The practical issue that *Everyday Life* addressed was how everyday life could be changed in a humanistic, democratic, and socialist direction. For Heller, social change could not be implemented on the universal scale alone, and the change in human attitudes was part of all forms of social change and had to begin in everyday life with individual attitudes rather than imparted from above or externally.

Heller (1984a, x) argued for "the possibility of a change in attitudes on the grounds that the attitude essential for the change for the better does exist, and that it only needs to be generalized". Heller used the term "individual personality" in contrast to "particularist person" when referring to this attitude and argued that the point of using such categories was not to illustrate individual perfectibility. Heller's "individual personality" had the potential for goodness and was thus capable of experiencing a humane everyday life that was, by definition, a non-alienated experience. It was in this way that Heller's particular version of phenomenology was able to maintain a philosophical position in which it was not possible to ask whether or not an individual was living an authentic or inauthentic existence. This meant that individual suffering could not be made valid in Heller's philosophical system.

However, Heller began to encounter difficulties with many of the categories of analysis that were used in her philosophical system. Due to Heller's categorical imperative of human emancipation, individual suffering could not be validated in her philosophical system. Heller argued that Lukacs' theory of everyday life was fundamental to understanding the development of the concept of human freedom. Lukacs was concerned with everyday life as a social category that provided the possibility of liberation through art. Aesthetics had the possibility of providing a forum for self-realization and eventually liberation in the everyday appropriation of, and subsequent production of, art. However, since the continental subject-object dichotomy was a strong element of Lukacs' philosophy, this remained as a problem for libratory philosophy. If the world was to be appropriated by the individual in his or her particular everyday life, then this necessarily objectified the outside world and by implication other people. Constructing art did not guarantee that people could avoid objectification, nor did it guarantee, as the Zhdanov doctrine of the 1950s illustrated, that art itself could not be used for anti-emancipatory purposes. Since liberation through art was not a guarantee of human freedom, Heller sought to redefine Lukacs' concept of everyday life and argued that individuals were both born into a specific culture as well as taught themselves new and different aspects of their world through experience. As a result, individuals were involved in their particular worlds through life experience rather than in a subject-object relationship.

Furthermore, Heller stated that she used a "critically modified" Heidegger, and in appropriating some of these ideas encountered problems in avoiding the negative characteristics attached to them. For example, Lukacs had great difficulty avoiding Stalinist orthodoxy in his Marxism and in seeking to use the categories of *History and Class Consciousness* (1971), as did Adorno, these categories needed to be changed to the extent that they become free of the philosophical system that produced them (Heller: 1966; 1977).

This was the difficulty with Heller's use of Heidegger. Heller's categories of objectivations suffered problems similar to Sartre's

(1956) *Being and Nothingness* and Heidegger's (1962) *Being and Time* in their use of the same categorical systems of the individual objectivations. The authentic life, according to Heidegger, was one in which the individual involved in their particular being in the world (Dasein) was to fulfil their potential. The use of this kind of existentialism abdicated responsibility beyond individual will. The freely taken choice became the primary motive force as well as the main category for action. This was certainly something that Heller sought to avoid as the human condition experienced in everyday life was a social experience.

Heller's version of everyday life was an attempt to clarify the "inner" symbolic system of this everyday life (Heller: 1984a, 24). Once again, this was the opposite of the project of Adorno's negative dialectics and also very different from Habermas' focus on the "symbolic" forms without clarification of where these human characteristics came from. Heller dealt with the concrete life-world and not from a form of state of nature or some kind of first principles. Heller's "image of a person does not derive from a side glance at God" (Heller: 1984a, 17), and thus her philosophical anthropology was both anti-metaphysical and anti-theological. Her work was an examination of the dynamic process of being, which was interested in showing human tendencies and possibilities as they are real (Heller: 1984a, 3).

Heller argued that her conception of everyday life was in fact quite different from the concept of the "life-world" that became one of the basic categories for continental European social theory (Heller: 1984a, 5; Schutz: 1972). Heller claimed that the life-world was the natural attitude of individuals in their action and thinking that was to be contrasted with institutionalized or rationalized action and scientific thinking. By contrast, everyday life in Heller's philosophical system was not a singular attitude, as it had the possibility of encompassing different attitudes including reflective theoretical ones. This category of social analysis was the "objective fundament of every social action, institution, of human social life in general" (Heller: 1984a, 33).

For Heller, the sphere of objectivation in-itself, as the backbone of everyday life, was to be contrasted with all objectivations for-itself. This meant not only science but also art, religion, abstract moral norms, and ideas, as everyday life itself was not necessarily conducted under the guidance of the sphere of objectivation in-itself alone. In everyday life, the possibility existed for a recourse to higher objectivations as well as the possibility to test and query norms and rules that were taken for granted.

The practical intent of Heller's elaboration of everyday life was at odds with those theories that employed similar concepts (such as Schutz: 1972). Heller's work was a specific type of critical theory that had as its main goal human emancipation. This was in contrast to those theories that sought a better system within which the human individual could realize their capacities (Schutz, Luckmann, Habermas to some extent). For Heller (1984a), "everyday life always takes place in and relates to the immediate environment of a person" (6). This meant that the sphere of everyday life provided the "testing ground" in which human beings could come to realize their full capabilities (7). This meant that every individual had the capacity to realize any particular aspect of the species rather than achieve a kind of ideal character of generalized humanity. The plurality of potentials illustrated in everyday life, that is the numerous possibilities of realization of human capabilities, were limited by the assumption that there existed a kind of natural and universal set of laws of need and value.

The next stage in the development of Heller's work became associated with the analysis of the problem of how to make these laws subject to human beings in order to allow a fulfilment of their potentials. It was here that Heller turned to the examination of Marx's concepts of need and value and eventually the generalized personality structures of individuals who became engaged in such value-decisions. This is where we take up the next chapter.

Chapter 7

Global Capital: From the Polanyi Thesis to World-Systems and beyond Capital

Karl Polanyi's work, *The Great Transformation*, analyzed the way in which the inception of the Industrial Revolution changed social life in Great Britain. Polanyi demonstrated how 'the economy' was an aspect of social and productive life that was embedded in societies around the world. His claim was that this was a universal truth, and while this may well be contested, the idea that a process of disembedding this economic sphere from human activity had great traction in the post-World War II global economic reconstruction. Polanyi's approach was based on the 'enclosure' phenomenon, or what later became known as the 'tragedy of the commons' in which modern productive life could no longer maintain the idea that resources could be used 'in common' without ownership attached to it. This major innovation in thinking about the political and social place of economic activity needs highlighting here and will show how both Mészáros and Wallerstein develop their critiques in a similar fashion.

Neo-Marxist Philosophical Anthropology: Needs and Values

There is no philosophical or economic work of importance by Marx in which he does not repeatedly try, often in several different passages, to classify types of need. (Heller: 1976, 27)

For Mészáros, everyday life was the fundamental category of analysis for social conditions in the modern world. Everyday life was the single organizing category that could provide an interpretation of events that remained closest to Marxist philosophical anthropology. Mészáros' elaboration of the different aspects of everyday life remained part of the project of the renaissance of Marxism with the emphasis on the early writings of Marx. Everyday life also dealt with the value systems and needs structures of individuals. The purpose of Mészáros' work on needs was to radicalize the potential for social praxis.

The discussion of everyday life left Mészáros with a problem regarding Marxist philosophy. Heller claimed that since her interpretation of praxis involved a radicalization of everyday life, there needed to be a reworking of the Marxist interpretations of the concepts of value and need in order to arrive at a different interpretation of the relationship between theory and practice. The argument for this relationship was intended to show how the concepts of value and need could be oriented around the categorical imperative of emancipation and remaining within the Marxist paradigm while simultaneously radicalizing social theory. Furthermore, since needs emanated from everyday life and values were historically and socially conditioned, Marxist philosophy needed to be reconciled with these social facts. Mészáros argued for the reorientation of the universal (Marxist) laws of value and need toward the fulfilment of human capacities.

Needs

> It now seems unavoidable to subject the concept of "social need" to a brief analysis especially since "need" is an indeterminate, vague, and merely empirical concept, though one of the most frequently used. (Heller: 1974, 365)

A fundamental idea of Mészáros' analysis of needs was that social groups could only have interests and not needs. As a result, values and needs as Heller defined them could not be compatible with orthodox Marxism. It was in the analysis of the concept of need in Marx's writing that Heller solidified her move beyond Marxism and all forms of system immanent critique. This meant that through her analysis of the Marxist concept of need, Heller was able to illustrate how the categories of the science of the relations of capital that grew out of Marxism worked against the original intention of Marx's philosophy. This produced a twofold consequence within Heller's philosophical system. First, this analysis of the concept of human need meant that philosophical anthropology ought to be about the furthering of human emancipation. Second, philosophical anthropology ought to enable humanity as a whole to further enhance the abundance of the species-essence: that is, the possibilities inherent in humanity as a whole. Although the neo-Marxism of this aspect of Heller's work was obvious, these interrelated consequences would change the direction of Heller's philosophy away from Marxism permanently.

For Heller, the concept of need was an elaboration of the human condition in which Heller sought to analyze those conceptions of needs which were beyond concepts of natural needs and the most basic conditions of existence. "Any clarificatory analysis of needs presupposes a philosophically elaborated value-concept of need which alone can provide the basis for an evaluation of needs" (Cohen: 1986, 171; Heller: 1976, 38). Furthermore, Heller argued that there was a direct relationship between the theory of need "to the normatively based philosophy of history as the unifying thread of Marx's project" (Cohen: 1986, 171). For Heller (1976, 130) this was the fertile utopia in Marx's writing that provided the possibility of individual self-realization. As a result, Heller's work continued to have problems with the theory of history and historical change, since the suggestion that there could be a concept of historical change which was both normative and evolutionary as well as remaining consistent with historically situated value choices was in danger of becoming a 'chicken and egg' argument which Heller sought to avoid. That is to say that, if human history could change and should change toward a particular goal, then the articulation of a need was both the normative foundation for change as well as the goal of such change. The question of the possibility of a human history that was capable of reconciling all the diverse needs of individuals in a complete theory remained. Mészáros' work on the theory of needs in Marx is similar. Mészáros' work on the theory of value and the modern construct of surplus value of labor and capital is discussed in detail in *Capital* and remains a pivotal point of his work (Mészáros: 1995, 739–44).

In Cohen's analysis of Heller's concept of need in Marx, it was pointed out that it was the idea of praxis that Heller sought to redefine as she attempted to make the radical social praxis of Marx the locus of change rather than creating a theory of capitalism that was abstracted from Marx (Cohen: 1986). Heller was not reproducing Marx's mode of theorizing and then looking for a new revolutionary subject with new radical needs. Instead, the purpose of her work on the theory of need was to "retain the concept of radical need while avoiding any ad hoc categorisation from the arbitrary standpoint of their satisfiability within capitalism" (Cohen: 1986, 171). The implications of Cohen's analysis pointed to the problems with theories of class and class interests which had to be re-examined since the concept of need was examined as both an independent and more fundamental idea in

Marx's work (Heller: 1976, 27). Furthermore, since Heller claimed that the theory of need was the focal point for the development of the concept of human essence in Marx, the argument became primarily philosophical. This meant that philosophy, and not history, was the driving force of change. Once again it was the act of thinking about the world which was real praxis, and history was the result of what individuals, actualizing their potential to meet their radical needs, thought the world ought to be (Heller: 1976, 46–48). For Heller, history was subject to human agency.

Cohen argued that the genesis of need was always a historically and culturally mediated act (Cohen: 1986, 172). Heller maintained that the analysis of need must encompass more than the most basic of human needs that an individual needed to survive. For Heller, all natural physiological needs were defined as those beyond which no life could be sustained and all other needs were culturally produced and limited (Heller: 1976, 32, 51, 28). Furthermore, the possibility existed for these culturally produced and limited needs to be necessary for the survival of human culture and necessary for creating the possibility of human freedom. As a result, Heller was able to argue that alienated need could in fact be found in the very interest structure of class. This was a radical step for Marxist theory for two reasons. First, Heller was able to argue that the concept of radical need was actually beyond the (class) interest structure in civil society. Second, in Heller's philosophical system, arguing for social change by placing class interests as the main goal, objective, or reason for such change was actually a process of alienating individuals rather than freeing individuals. These class interests could not be brought about by coercion nor by education and did not exist as unconscious forces within individuals. For Heller, the individual either possessed and knew consciously their needs or did not. These needs did not necessarily have to correspond to a kind of class interest and forcing needs to do so, making class interest the main object of social change, contributed to alienation.

> For there are no needs that are not conscious needs. Either one had and is conscious of radical needs, and is willing to struggle with others for their realization, or one does not. No one, neither a party nor a theorist can claim to have better knowledge of the needs of an individual than the individual himself. By demonstrating that Marx considered solely needs and theory that relates to needs, to be radical, Heller has grasped what remains valid in Marx's critical orientation and what must inform any non-authoritarian theory and praxis today. (Cohen: 1986, 178)

Thus Heller's conclusion that class interests militated against individual freedom directly stemmed from the analysis of need.

In *The Theory of Need in Marx*, Heller argued for "a reading which posits at its centre the concept of finite individuals always socially conditioned but never reducible to some combination of general social determinants" (Markus: 1978, 17). If emancipation were to be effected, it would have to be reconciled with the infinite capacities of individuals. Heller's argument was that within Marx's species-essence there was to be found the plurality of needs. This was a radical interpretation in that it allowed diverse social groups to be able to make an argument for different needs from within a Marxist system. This was intended to lead toward the emancipation of social groups and individuals who were held prisoner by universal laws, such as the concepts of class, interest, and class interest, which did not apply to their particular circumstances. For Heller, it was clear that being part of a specific social category did not guarantee that a particular individual would be the same as all of those individuals within the same category. One could be part of a 'class,' using the term as a social organizing category, and not have the same needs as others of the same class. Furthermore, Heller claimed, one may or may not have the same interests as others in the same class.

Since emancipation was to come from social transition, the question for Heller was the form that this social transition was to take. The Marxist answer was in the collectivization of resources. The development of the human species was for Heller the direct method of social transition but "is this concept synonymous with the centralisation of the means of production and the socialization of labor. . ? The answer is without a doubt, no" (Heller: 1976, 84). For Heller (1976, 84) "the development of the human species" she argued for in everyday life was not a "mere consequence" of this form of collectivization in Soviet-style societies. It was instead fundamental to the composition of human beings and their activity. This argument was, of course, quite dangerous in concluding that the best way to progress socially was not in the form of Marxism experienced in East-Central Europe.

Furthermore, this argument called into question the idea of universality of need. Heller stated that beyond the basic needs of food and water all other needs were socially conditioned. The basic needs for sustenance were considered to be those conditional needs that limited the actual existence of individuals and thereby had little to do with social transformation toward the development of human capacities. Simply put, if one did not eat and drink, then one died, and there was no longer an argument for human capacities. All needs were subject to the everyday experience of individuals. In fact, Heller argues that even the basic needs for sustenance were socially conditioned since there were a great variety of kinds and amounts of food and drink that human beings consumed. The conclusion was that "there is no question... of any 'natural law' that leads society into the future. The necessity of this transition is not in fact guaranteed by any natural law but by the radical needs" (Heller: 1976, 84). Since even the most basic of human needs were changed through human interaction in everyday life, all human characteristics were subject to some form of socialization.

Heller's work on the theory of need argued that a fundamental Marxist category needed reworking in order to remain consistent with her project of a radicalization of everyday life. Heller began to argue for a philosophical position that was different from both Eastern and Western European interpretations of Marxism. In Eastern European Marxism, orthodoxy was the prevailing ideology. This meant that the universal laws of historical materialism were the driving force behind social theory. The fulfilment of the needs of social groups was to come from the state, and these needs were all of the same character. In Heller's interpretation, Western Marxism had inherited the problem of negativity from the Frankfurt School through Adorno's version of hegemonic capitalism and had attempted to compensate by moving toward systems theory to provide a better superstructure to meet the needs of social groups. Neither of these options suited Heller's version of human emancipation in which the needs of individuals must emanate from everyday life and were always legitimate, not to be subordinated to the interests of a class. Heller's analysis of a Marxist theory of value was the next topic of her philosophical anthropology.

Values

Heller's position on Marxist conceptions of value was similar to her work on needs. In *Towards a Marxist Theory of Value* (1973), Heller argued that since the concept of value was a socially conditioned concept, there needed to be a closer examination of those values that were assumed to be universal in character and thereby applicable in every circumstance. Heller's problematization of the concept of value in Marx was a contributing factor, along with the analysis of needs, in unravelling the primacy of orthodox Marxism. The problem began with the question, "How can historically conditioned values be universally valid?" (Heller: 1973, 7).

Once again, Heller returned to the process of philosophical questioning as both the vehicle of, and method by which to test, social change. "Philosophy always operates with categories of value which it does not only spontaneously 'use' as in everyday life, but it consciously questions their function, origin, interrelations, foundation, etc." (Heller: 1973, 7). Heller sought to argue for the necessity of this kind of questioning within everyday life. The radicalization of everyday life and the expression of radical needs and thus the transition to a socialist society could not take place without this aspect of discourse imbued in everyday life. For Heller, the universal human condition was not the particular value itself; it was the act of questioning and discussion that surrounded these particular values that existed as a universal law of value.

The primary assumption for Heller regarding the relationship between the work of Marx and the universal law of value revolved around the idea "that Marx's theory about the constituents of the essence of the species itself is based on a choice of values" (Heller: 1979a, 18 [n22]). Once again this caused a number of problems for Marxism as a social theory since the fundamental building block for human emancipation was called into question in that Marx's understanding of the constitution of human beings was a historically and socially conditioned understanding. Heller remained faithful to her attempt to reorient her epistemology around human emancipation, and since she had made earlier attempts to rework the concept of the species-essence, the possibility for such Marxist social transition remained. However, if these values were socially conditioned, and thereby Marx's values were socially conditioned, the question for Heller (1973, 7) became "can we speak of the development of values from the viewpoint of a theory based on a communist society, i.e., from the Marxist viewpoint?"

Heller (1973) attempted to remain within the Marxist paradigm and claimed that her study on Marx's ideas of value elaborated only one possible Marxist theory of value that corresponded to Marx's original intentions. Furthermore, the choice of the kind of social inquiry the theorist could undertake remained an important consideration for Heller since it had to correspond to the fundamental value premise of human emancipation. She acknowledged this by stating that "there is no value free social science, and our theory is based on value preferences, (thus) it is all the more important to openly and unambiguously establish our Marxian value premises and axioms" (Heller: 1973, 14).

For Heller, the idea of abundance in Marx became a turning point. Abundance was considered to be a concept that referred to the infinite capacities of individuals to express themselves. Lukacs looked to express this abundance in everyday life through the aesthetic life, or the life dedicated to the creation of beauty (Heller: 1966; 1976; 1984a). It was in this way that the plurality of potential in human beings could be encouraged and eventually achieved in everyday existence. The commodifying and reification processes of capitalism had to be changed to a socialist society in order to achieve such a goal for Lukacs, as it was not the external abundance that late capitalism could provide that would give human beings the capacity to fulfil their potential. Heller's interpretation of Marx was similar in that she emphasized the need to change social relations in order to realize this inner abundance of the species-essential person in everyday life.

Heller also claimed, however, that values could not be derived from needs. For Heller, this internal abundance meant that values had to be derived from the human condition to meet human needs. These human needs were diverse in character and added to their radical nature. "Need is a category of the individual; it is an internal necessity: a desire for something. This 'something,' i.e., the object of need, is always heterogeneous" (Heller: 1973, 17–18). For Heller's form of Marxist social theory, the decision became one of choosing to take on the Marxian project of liberating human beings through meeting radical needs emanating from social conditions because it was a value choice. One of the problems associated with this idea was that her position regarding the socially conditioned nature of human activity left out of the discussion some of the modern conceptions of human beings which were considered to be innate propensities. For example, Heller and her contemporaries were not yet exposed to American versions of political philosophy in which values could indeed be derived from needs. Heller would later find herself at odds with Nozick and Rawls, for example, precisely for this reason.

Heller stated that Marx's decision to argue for conditions that would create the possibility for realizing human freedom was a value choice. This value choice was historically conditioned, but arguing for meeting the needs of human beings was the fundamental form of social praxis for Heller. Since all needs were legitimate by definition, and the needs of individuals superseded the perceived interests of classes of people, this begged the question of the place of other innate human propensities. The social praxis advocated by Heller did not address the issue of those characteristics with which human beings were born. What, then, was a critical Marxist such as Heller to do with human instincts and human feelings?

Social Anthropology

The next phase of Heller's philosophical anthropology involved the elaboration of problems within a discipline Heller classified as social anthropology. Heller claimed that this classification was a misnomer since, as we have examined previously, anthropology was the 'science of human beings,' and since all human interactions were fundamentally social in character, there could be no other kind of anthropology other than 'social' anthropology.

The problem with social anthropology, for Heller, was directly connected to her previous work on the Marxist concepts of need and value. The character of the concepts of value and need were shown to consist of socially conditioned propensities and appropriated by individuals in everyday life in order to attempt to realize their human capacities. Since there was no natural law of value and need, Heller addressed the question of whether or not there were natural laws pertaining to the innate propensities of human beings. Heller's examination of social anthropology addressed the problem of human nature with the presupposition that innate characteristics of human beings had the possibility of being molded. This meant that choosing to argue for a particular aspect of these innate characteristics was a value choice in itself.

Heller organized the examination of social anthropology around the concepts of human instincts and human feelings. Similar to her work on the concepts of need and value, Heller assumed that both instincts and feelings were fundamentally social in character. As Heller argued in her work on everyday life, individuals appropriated their personalities from their environment, and all of the available options were socially constructed by previous generations. In this form of social anthropology, Heller showed how empirical sciences, such as the biological sciences, reaffirmed the Marxian concept of species-essence since human beings were involved in a constant process of change (Heller: 1979a, 18; Benhabib:1980, 211). Heller argued that a science that was a catalog of what was in the world ought to be rejected, as it was inadequate in providing insight into the human condition (Heller: 1979a, 18; Benhabib: 1980, 212). Heller sought to understand humanity's place in the world as a citizen of the world, which meant that the social anthropology of Heller became the pragmatic anthropological position of a science of humanity that examined "what human beings are, what they ought to be and what their possibilities are" (Benhabib: 1980, 212). The value choice of this examination was human emancipation.

Instincts

For Heller, the label for 'social anthropology' was a tautology. Heller (1979a, 1) claimed that since human individuals were social beings, and the science of anthropology was an examination of human interactions, there could be no other anthropology but a social anthropology. Heller (1979a) argued that everything specifically human in the biological makeup of the person had evolved socially and was socially determined since through "millions of years of auto-domestication" (ix) human beings changed to become what they are today. According to Heller, there was a 'first nature,' consisting of the genetic-biological makeup of human beings, and she sought to transform the 'second nature' that was the psychological-social composition of the individual human being.

The social anthropological project began as a reworking of the categories that were supposed to be fundamental to human experience. For Heller, these categories included instincts, feelings, needs, morality, personality, and history (1979a: 1). Her assumption was that all of these fundamental categories developed through the process of socialization. Heller sought to move beyond what she saw to be the 'chicken and egg' arguments offered by anthropologists and social theorists who have debated the primacy of either nature or nurture in the actions of human beings. Heller (1979a, 95) sought a third alternative which she argued ought to begin with the practical reality of modern processes of mechanization of labor which did not provide self-actualization but pushed people to use others as means. The 'building-in' of the 'species-essence' into 'second nature' was thus both possible and desirable. Since Heller believed it was possible to argue for this kind of emancipatory social theory, she attempted to do so through an examination of the changing nature of the concept of human instincts.

Heller claimed that the formation of the idea of 'man' was the history of the demolition of instinct guidance (Benhabib: 1980, 213). For Heller, individual humans were distinguished from animals in that human beings were teleological beings and not simply responding to inner and outer stimuli. Human beings had the possibility, the "plasticity" (Heller: 1979a, 17), for an infinite number of changes and developments. Heller's system of species objectivations in itself and for itself meant that for her, "those self-conscious works of art, law, morality, and religion in which, presumably, the human species makes itself into its own object of reflection and expression" (Benhabib: 1980, 214) proved that virtually all characteristics could be socially appropriated. Human freedom, as the central goal of Heller's philosophical system, could not be argued against by a claim to possess an instinct that superseded this categorical imperative.

This was consistent with her general position on philosophical anthropology. In Heller's philosophical system, human beings had no characteristics that did not work toward the possibility of the 'good' of human freedom. For Heller, it was not possible to make the claim that human beings possessed an innate set of characteristics that militated against the possibility of reorienting them around a human activity that worked toward emancipation. Concepts such as 'the species-essence,' or 'human beings,' or 'the individual,' were all classifications that Heller claimed were defined by their possibility. These social beings were molded and changed by the influences of their environment. The social limitations and guidance imposed on all people and through all cultures ensured that all human beings engaged in an everyday life in which the process of appropriating characteristics superseded any basic instinct.

Heller claimed that it was a social fact that individual experience, which was a combination of self-chosen and externally imposed values, would shape human beings in ways that were not simply predictable immutable instincts. There was a non-changing character of human instincts indicated by their very presence. The social fact remained that aspects of the character of human instincts changed over time, thus allowing for yet another aspect of human nature to be made part of the universal value of freedom. This was Heller's (1979a, 17) concept of human instinct that allowed for the "infinite potential of human nature".

Feelings

In her analysis of the concept of human feelings, Heller sought to continue her arguments for a human nature that was flexible as a result of the socialization process in the everyday lives of human beings. In Heller's philosophical anthropology, the theory of feelings was analyzed in such a manner as to argue for the possibility of enriching the lives of human beings. As in her analysis of the concept of instincts, Heller argued against the conception that feelings were innate, unchanging, and common to all human beings. Heller argued that while some of these characteristics were part of the process of human feeling, this was far too simplistic an examination of the idea of feelings since it explained little about the possibilities that human beings encountered.

Heller once again maintained that this human characteristic, like all other human characteristics, was primarily social. This meant that through the combination of innate propensities and socially determined actions, different forms of emotions emerged in the human condition over time. Once again it was experience that was the driving force in changing human beings, and as a result freedom and emancipation could be made part of the social anthropological project. For Heller, this meant that human beings were greater than the sum total of a series of reactions to external stimuli, and thus the possibility of human emancipation as the main human virtue remained.

Heller's work on the idea of human feelings was based on the premise that the act of feeling meant being involved in something (Heller: 1979b; 1979c, 1). Heller claimed that in antiquity, feeling was principally an ethical issue stemming from virtue. Plato illustrated, according to Heller, that there were different virtues for different strata of society; therefore, different feelings were developed. Aristotle illustrated, according to Heller, that the most virtuous man was the good citizen, and feelings were measured by the standard of this good citizen. In modernity, it was the actual process of being involved in something that defined a particular feeling. This process was part of the sphere of everyday life, and the involvement provided the possibility of guiding individuals to their self-chosen enlightenments.

Since these instincts and feelings were socially constructed in Heller's philosophical system, the modern condition was one in which the individual as a whole could also be constructed. Heller argued for a particular aspect of human nature in which the human ego was thought to work for a homeostasis. This homeostasis was the preservation and extension of the ego system that ensured the continuity of the ego: "The Ego selects that which insures its preservation (as a social organism) and extension. These factors are not only selected; they are selected in a manner appropriate to the task. The Ego which is incapable of performing this selection would be incapable of life" (Heller: 1979b, 11).

But Heller (1979b) also claimed that the "Ego's relation to the world is intentional: the Ego not only selects but actively creates its own world." (11). This meant that consciousness was always general social consciousness since there were no private concepts, private language, nor private relationships since all human endeavours involved some form of social interaction. It was in this social interaction, even though each individual worked toward a kind of homeostatic position, that Heller sought emancipatory possibilities through universalizing human identity.

In Heller's philosophical system, the elaboration of the characteristics of generalized human beings concluded with her discussion of the relationship between individuals and their experience of pain and suffering. For Heller, the difference between pain and suffering signified the realization of the universal ego-identity. Heller claimed that once human beings had the capacity to identify with the pain of others through the realization that the other was suffering, this would indicate that freedom had become the main virtue for human beings. For Heller, a form of mental pain characterized human relationships in all their manifestations since it signified something was not in order about the relationship (Heller: 1979b, 244). This meant that the painful experience signified the possibility of generalizing the human condition through another moral imperative: "Help yourself—help others" (Heller: 1979b, 244). This aspect of Heller's philosophical anthropology began to change her focus once again as Heller's conclusions began to sound like a justification for a particular form of social theory rather than the constitution of human nature. Benhabib referred to this shift in focus as a "return to social theory" (Benhabib: 1980, 212).

Heller's return to social theory in the latter stages of her philosophical anthropology was part of the attempt to construct a general social theory that was based on human emancipation. Heller (1979a) wrote that the possibility

> of appropriation of the species-essence by every individual—something which remains yet to be proved—is according to Marx and in my own opinion "real history," and thus becomes absolutely necessary for the further development and building-in of the capacities of the species, in a process that is intended by, and conscious to, everyone. (18)

This generalized social theory that was intended to be accessible to all humanity was based on Heller's assumption that it was the flexible possibility of the species-essential human being that could lead to its own emancipation. This process of appropriation did not mean that every individual could realize all of the potentials of the species. It meant instead that individuals had the possibility to "realize any of these potentials...and to develop a conscious relationship to...(their) species character" (Heller: 1979a: 18[n22]). And through this, freedom could be realized.

Heller's philosophical anthropology went through three phases. The first phase showed how everyday life was the locus of activity in history. For Heller, all forms of social change, as well as individual self-chosen change, occur within the sphere of everyday life. The sphere of everyday life, however, had the potential to produce social characteristics that were beyond Marxism. The second phase of Heller's philosophical anthropology elaborated upon this problem by showing that the theories of need and value in Marx were products of historical conditioning themselves. Furthermore, the concept of value could not be derived from human needs, and there were plural versions of both ideas emanating from everyday life. The third phase illustrated the way in which Heller's work sought to transform conceptions of human nature toward a practical alternative away from the argument for the primacy of either innate or socially acquired characteristics.

The form of argument Heller used in her philosophical anthropology was intended to provide an active theory of social praxis. Developing the conception of what constituted the basic presuppositions of human activity and human nature implied a different form of relationship between theory and practice. This form of social praxis was intended to orient all types of philosophical inquiry around human emancipation. In Heller's philosophical system, changing and organizing such action, however, must always begin with the self-chosen individual. There could be no change that was coerced, as all individuals must participate in this kind of activity. Heller's work was also intended to argue against an epistemological position that accepted instrumental reason and historicism. Her philosophical anthropology was part of a search for a level of analysis that began with the individual but did not lock the individual into preconceived categories that inhibited positive change. This phenomenological approach argued for the possibility of involving human beings in social praxis without coercion, without imputing needs and values from outside, and by arguing for the advancement of human capabilities.

Benhabib (1980, 213) has suggested that there is an implicit view of history and historical change (Heller refers to it as 'historicity') which needs to be elaborated in order to illustrate how the 'species essential' individual is to achieve emancipation. Indeed this is a portion of what needs to be elaborated upon, but a reworking of the fundamental categories of what makes us human beings, how we experience and appropriate things in our everyday existence, implies a rethinking of a number of things as well as history.

Heller focused her attention on philosophy as 'queen of the sciences,' which would examine the universal categories of knowledge and employ them for the good. This was the next phase in her work. If one were to address the question of 'how' the Hellerian individual was to affect emancipation, the immediate answer would not be historical; it would be through reason. The categories of reason and rationality were the fundamental tools, the basic starting points, which could be used in a practically active fashion to move toward emancipation within everyday life. The basic category for human action was the Hellerian species essence. This individual within these categories had the potential for self-development. But individual and collective action, as Heller defined them in her philosophical system, ought be mitigated by reason, and this reason would guide people through history. Philosophy, as human science, was to examine the given possibilities and suggest the course of action based on the categorical imperative of human emancipation.

Heller's version of critical Marxism developed through three phases. The first phase involved an examination of the intellectual tradition of East-Central Europe and the role of Marxism within that tradition. Heller and her contemporaries had concluded that basic socialist principles of the free development of the individual were valid and could be used as a philosophy furthering human emancipation. For Hungarian social theorists, 'correct' meant that within the historical boundaries of modern human development, fully realized socialism was the best possible avenue for the full realization of individual human capacities. In the second stage of critical Marxism, Heller worked to clarify those points of Marxist philosophy that needed elaboration or expansion into contemporary issues. By reorienting Marxism to the concerns of the early humanist Marx rather than the later scientism of Marx, Heller sought to recapture the focus on individual human experience embodied in the earlier philosophy of Marx. Radical democracy was to come about by meeting the needs of individual human beings before assessing the interests of a class. The final phase of Heller's critical Marxism dealt with philosophical anthropology. It was in the elaboration of the universal characteristics of human beings that Heller attempted to argue for a particular interpretation of Marx. The conclusion of philosophical anthropology was that individual human beings were malleable enough in their social conditions that virtually all characteristics had the possibility to be changed. It was through this theoretical opening that Heller sought to argue for an orientation of all philosophy around the categorical imperative of human freedom.

The primary implication of the combination of conclusions within Heller's critical Marxist philosophy was that a system immanent critique was no longer possible. Heller's reworking of concepts that Marx did not deal with, or dealt with in a peripheral manner, did not explicitly preclude the possibility of Marxist social theory. But the conclusions from the arguments about philosophical anthropology ensured that there could not be a renaissance of Marxism. Heller's conclusion that the individual was the main focus of analysis, that this individual appropriated his or her characteristics through social interaction, and that all needs were legitimate and not to be subordinated to class interests, proved impossible to sustain in an orthodox Marxist setting.

This resulted in the expansion of Heller's critical theory to include universal concepts outside of Marxism. This occurred due to Heller's argument for philosophy as the most important method of thinking about the world. Since human thought ought to be about more than merely cataloging what was in the world, Heller argued that the discipline of philosophy was the method by which human beings could transcend material conditions and live the possibility of their emancipation. It was here that Heller expanded her critical theory into radical universalism.

Chapter 8

Conclusion

World-systems analysis is a perspective in creation. It is a holistic, unidisciplinary view of social reality. Its future development and its future intellectual utility will be a function of how plausible its empirical conclusions prove to be and how useful its analytic insights will be to those engaged in the real struggle over the transition to a new world order (Wallerstein: 2004b, 23).

In this book, we have set out some of the major contributions of two contemporary and historical scholars, Immanuel Wallerstein and István Mészáros, to the analysis of contemporary capitalism and its trajectories. A primary purpose of this work has been to highlight and extend attention to their work and its value for research and analysis across the social sciences. We have done this in light of long traditions of comparative and critical educational research that has dealt with issues such as the rise of mass education globally and its primary functions under conditions of capitalism, and particularly in recent decades under conditions of neoliberal globalization. This literature is extensive and important, but our intent in this volume has not been to provide another analysis of the impact of neoliberal thinking and policy paradigms on systems of schooling/education. Rather, we have sought to provoke those engaged in that work, and others, to (re)consider the value of the global analyses Wallerstein and Mészáros bring to understanding mass education.

This type of project, like any research project, produces its own tensions. Perhaps the most striking of these for the authors has been the tension between the normative call to consider, to pay due attention to, and to apply these scholars' work in our research endeavors, alongside the reality of there being a wide range of alternative and often directly competing ways to approach the study of social reality, including perspectives rejecting, or at least problematizing, our capacity to ever know social reality. On what basis do we call for attention to these scholars over others?

The substance of their scholarship adds to the complexity here. Wallerstein overtly defends the need for meta-narratives, and spends considerable attention elaborating both a critique of dominant, Eurocentric, scientific universalism and the need to construct new, alternative, conditional universal perspectives and narratives that resemble some sort of network of (often competing) perspectives. Similarly, for Mészáros, a grand narrative holds in the face of post-modern challenges to our understanding of how to achieve a liberatory analysis of social situations. For Mészáros, the organizing principles of Marx, the hegemony of capital, and the development of alienation via capital(ism) in the modern world, are all part of the 'real' social conditions of the everyday world inhabited by people in all kinds and types of societies. Moreover, in both cases, the normative position of these scholars is grounded in a belief or faith in Western rationality, and the possibility of creating a rational, viable world order that is more equal, just, democratic, and peaceful than that which is possible under capitalism.

In this project, we are also forced to confront the nature and content of these scholars' work, which provides particular analyses of capitalism, its crises, and its contradictions. These include the argument that we have reached some point of no return for capitalism as we have known it, which makes the establishment of an alternative system, however uncertain, almost inevitable. What we are highlighting here is that the meta-narrative of capitalism in crisis and transition advanced by these scholars is one that effectively demands that all who engage with this meta-narrative adopt a position in relation to the analysis of what exists currently, and in relation to potential futures. In raising this, we are not attempting to deny the inherently political nature of all knowledge, nor the problematic nature of research in the broad social sciences that claims not to advance some sort of normative position, whether under the banner of neutrality or the negation of the viability of such positions. In keeping with their Marxist heritage, Wallerstein and Mészáros make explicit their call for a non-capitalist and less unequal, unjust, and exploitative future, phrased at times as a socialist alternative that breaks both from capitalism and historical (real, existing) socialism. In contemporary conditions, the ongoing pursuit of such alternatives holds substantial appeal.

Consistent with the work itself, we find compelling the identified dilemmas confronting the capitalist world-system, whose resolution required some sort of fundamental, systemic change, and hence the need to return to questions about how systems of mass education might be re-purposed and reconstructed so as to prepare populations globally to attend to these historic phenomena. Advocating such a position could be seen as going directly against dominant trends toward ever greater levels of disciplinary divisions and specializations, and of course against critiques of, and the explicit push against, the whole project of generating meta-narratives for reading and acting in society.

Making claims about the importance of the work of Wallerstein and Mészáros risks becoming a circular argument, invoking their articulation of current crises and the absolute limits of capitalism's secular trends to justify using and applying their analysis of these phenomenon in order to create alternatives. These scholars are hardly alone, however, in documenting cyclical and qualitatively new crises across the globe, whether focused on global warming and the associated environmental challenges confronting humanity, or the full ramifications of the ongoing global financial crisis and current rounds of austerity programs for nation-states that lie beyond heightened levels of protest and instability.

To conclude, therefore, we first want to re-affirm the broad argument elaborated through the text in the terms of Wallerstein and Mészáros: that global capital, or the capitalist world-system, is facing structural crises that are leading toward its collapse or transition toward an undefined, alternative system, and that using education systems to engage larger numbers of people in the analysis of these problems, and in the consideration and construction of replacement system(s) with logics that are alternative to those of endless capital accumulation and growth, are something that educational researchers and practitioners should promote as a priority in our times.

In the spirit of such a project for educational praxis, we would invite critique of the broad position and, of course, debate about strategy and the way forward. As with the contemporary debate about environmental change and its causes, however, we argue that at some point discussion needs to move beyond questions about whether or not capitalism is in crisis, and/or whether it could (or should) be reformed, and instead concentrate on the enormous task of imagining, outlining, and creating the structures for, a better replacement system (see for example, Wallerstein: 2002b).

In drawing this broad conclusion, we argue also that on the question of scale, an anti-metanarrative critique of Wallerstein and Mészáros is likely to reveal a misreading of their work, and a wider misreading of what many argue is a non-debate in contemporary times—the idea that we can neatly divide work and ideas into binaries like global-local, structure-agency, reform-revolution, etc. Here, too, we explicitly endorse calls to draw a line under at least some debates, such as that made by de Sousa Santos (2008), and in the words of Wallerstein (1997a, 1255): "Stop fighting about nonissues, and the foremost of these nonissues is determinism versus free will, or structure versus agency, or global versus local, or macro versus micro...these antinomies are not a matter of correctness, or even of preference, but of timing and depth of perspective."

The attempt to provide an account of the world in its totality, in contexts of global crises and trends, requires us to surpass these sorts of debates about how to interpret or characterize what we are examining, and instead compels us to prioritize our efforts and energies in alternative, normative directions.

On the question of educational research, and particularly work under the broad banner of critical research, we conclude that there is limited engagement with these two scholars generally, at the very time that their work is most pertinent.[1] There is no need to rehash the case here about interest in the processes of globalization and neoliberalism, within and through supra-national agencies and organizations, on national and local education systems. Similarly, as has been consistently expressed in scholarship and international conferences in recent years, the phenomena of international comparisons of national education systems—via PISA and TIMSS primarily—and other regional systems, has pushed more and more educational researchers into the broad comparative and international education field. Why then the relative absence of these scholars' work from the comparative education field, particularly given the breadth of work in this field from across the social sciences?

Here we put forward two conclusions. The first is that we would expect much scholarship within the broad field of CIE to be dismissive of the conclusions of scholars like Mészáros and Wallerstein simply for political reasons. Their reading of systemic crisis and transition is not likely to be attractive for many whose efforts remain concentrated solely on reforming systems, or their pedagogical, organizational and curricular practices, for improved equity. As we have argued in the text, our intent here is not to dismiss this work as unimportant. Indeed, to do so would be to fall into the very binaries that we suggest should be overcome, whereas such reform projects are arguably part of the same process of building a broad movement for deeper systemic change. However, we can be fairly secure in our assumption that many would see the work of Mészáros and Wallerstein as too radical, too abstract, too impractical, too (neo)Marxist for contemporary research seeking to have an impact on practice. The tendency to categorize Wallerstein's work as an important part of the historical development of sociological and political theorizing, and particularly the critique of modernization theory, but also something which has since been surpassed (Griffiths and Knezevic: 2009), also accounts for its limited use.

Similarly, Mészáros' continued focus on structural Marxism positions him as an outsider, in relation to both contemporary (post) Marxists as well as liberals rejecting Marxism of any kind. Like Sartre in Paris, Mészáros in a global world is rejected by a number of camps that, we argue, would do well to engage with his work and would benefit from returning to these views of change. As we have noted, in recent times his work has been promoted by political radicals such as Venezuela's former President Hugo Chávez, which has presumably raised his profile amongst the broad political left internationally. Such actions risk entrenching differences rather than highlighting commonalities, however, in the need to resist capitalism's hegemony. Efforts that focus on the latter, which leaders like Chávez arguably advanced in his often-eclectic use of political theorists, are clearly required.

Our second conclusion relates to the take up/use of these scholars within the field of critical pedagogy. Here we might locate the lack of engagement within a general resistance to structural Marxist perspectives amongst critical pedagogy scholars, particularly as it "mutated under the influence of liberal/deconstructive/post-Marxist approaches to social change over the past two turbulent decades" (Martin: 2007, 340). In addition, the focus of neo-Marxist theories generally on critiquing the functional role of schooling for capitalist society, and elaborating the mechanisms by which this is achieved, was seen by many critical pedagogy adherents as a major shortcoming for failing to devote any, or sufficient, attention to the articulation of viable alternatives (Cho: 2013, 22).

It seems reasonable to assume that Wallerstein and Mészáros have been similarly viewed, or indeed overlooked, within the critical pedagogy camp, in contrast to the work of Freire in which the "language of possibility" and "language of hope" (Cho: 2013, 23) was found to be at the forefront. The perceived economic determinism of Wallerstein and Mészáros, linked to their neo-Marxist analyses

(Wallerstein's critique of orthodox Marxism notwithstanding), leaves little apparent space for their work and ideas.

Our presentation of Wallerstein's and Mészáros' work, however, demonstrates not just a misreading of their scholarship, as noted above, but highlights again the need for volumes like this that elaborate the actual and potential contributions of these meta-critiques of capitalism to the creation of alternatives, to the language of possibility and hope. We have emphasized this aspect of Wallerstein's work, manifest as the moral task of imagining better futures, and the political task of enacting what Freire describes as visions of a better future, these being two of the three pillars of his world-systems perspective. It is clear, we hope, that Wallerstein's world-systems analysis is all about praxis, whether reconstructing epistemological boundaries (Wallerstein: 2004a), or setting out a provisional program of political strategy, in the short, medium, and longer terms, to move toward a better future (Wallerstein: 2003b; 2003c).

Mészáros' form of praxis has always maintained two main aspects of his analysis: first, that alienation remains the crux of the social problem, and second that the hegemony of capital remains the crux of the political-economic problem in the contemporary world. The two taken together deliver the established structure in which societies find themselves in the late capitalist stage of historical development. Mészáros' view of pedagogical praxis is to reveal the workings, in true structural Marxist fashion, and to attempt to reformulate our everyday lives.

The current state of comparative and international educational research in the area of globalization studies finds world culture theorists debating those arguing for local diversity/difference, despite recognition on both sides that multiple levels of influence apply at all times, in all cases (see Griffiths and Arnove: 2014). This work builds on a substantial critique of methodological nationalism, which has normalized the need to consider supra-national influences over educational policies and practices (e.g., Dale: 2005). This broad and substantial area of study attracts ever more contributors under processes of neoliberal globalization that push policy makers and practitioners everywhere to engage in some level of international comparison. However, much of the work remains bogged down in development/modernist assumptions whereby education, following a level of policy reform, is presented as being able to play an ameliorative and redemptive function, offering more meritocratic upward social mobility for some. This may involve the language of (small) possibility within globalized neoliberal capitalism, but it is well short of the language of hope and possibility for the transformation of society, of the historical capitalist world-system, that these times require. The theoretical lenses of Immanuel Wallerstein and István Mészáros can illuminate, and help us to move toward, such possibilities, and to harness the power of mass education to this end.

Notes

Series Editor's Preface

1. See Bernstein, Basil (1990) for a detailed elaboration of re-contextualization in the institutional context of education where it refers to mediation between the *generative* field of production/creation (originating practices in science and art, etc.) and the *pedagogic context of reproduction* as curriculum and pedagogy.
2. See Barthes (1973; 1975), on the theme of open and closed textualities, 'writerly'and 'readerly' texts. In academic capitalism, however, we may suggest that the social dialectic in mass society forms of *reading* are consumption practices with *texts as commodities* and is distinguished from readerly texts which are self-revealingly open and thus *for the reader to write*; this is, in fact, transcended to some extent in higher education, and thus has the potentially critically realist relational form of knowledge- making practices contra commodification. Academic textbooks, while clearly commercial products with limited shelf life, are invitations to dialogue and to write, and thus are potentially very *productive* as creative sources of initiation. This has many ramifications at several levels of critical practices, not least for this text.
3. See: Small (2005) *Marx and Education*, Ashgate Publishing; also https://www.marxists.org/subject/education/index.htm.
4. See, for valuable illustration of dialogical possibilities the string at http://libcom.org/forums/theory/context-marxs-i-am-not-marxist-quote-09062009.
5. For an excellent exposition of Marx's dialectical methods, see: Olman (2003), especially Chapter 4, accessible at http://www.nyu.edu/projects/ollman/docs/ssr_ch04.php. Also on Marxism, Historical Materialism and Critical Realism: Sayer (1979); Bhaskar (1979); Bhaskar (1991, appendix two); Bhaskar and Callinicos (2003); Bhaskar (2008a).
6. "Andragogy" refers to post-secondary education, the on-going "education" of adults.

7. For situationist practices, see: Debord, G (1967) with illustrations at Google Images' "Eat the bankers."
8. "Social phenomenology" refers to the domain of conscious awareness in experienced active life, the focus of ethnographic inquiry.
9. *Immanent critique*: demonstrating both that system outcomes are necessary under present structural conditions but dialectically have the possibility of generating alternative progressive outcomes, too. *Ideology critique*: demonstrating the relations between structural powers and cultural forms, the articulations of power/knowledge. In this context, pedagogy of critique refers to the dialectics of open-ended teaching and learning from/in activist practices of resistance and to opposition combining immanent and ideology critique.
10. US Immigration Reform Bill, 2013.
11. *Existentialism* is a realist and materialist philosophy of practice referring to the individual's emergent and incomplete recognition of facticity of *being in the world* as a condition of any practices (e.g., in the objectivity of cultural forms in a variety of modes for ongoing thinking and acting within the time and place of *now*). See: Sartre (2008).
12. Empiricism tends uncritically to identify facts and reliable knowledge with immediate experience. Idealism tends to frame understanding in relation to abstracted philosophies of perfection.
13. Realism: philosophy of practice designating the object of knowledge as being "prior to" and/or outside the knowing procedures. Ontology takes precedence over epistemology.
14. Critical realism, while agnostic on assigning finality as truth in focused inquiry, seeks to identify realities as mechanisms lying "behind" the appearance in experiences (the "empirical" as delivered in specific disciplined information collection procedures) and combines ontological realism in the emergent relational nature of social and material realities, including emergent articulations in their confluences for any specified time/place with epistemological throwness, in that all knowledge is transitive and constituted in remediable and provisional "critical" cultural forms. For an excellent summary, see: Hedlund de-Witt, N (2013) "Critical Realism: a Synoptic Overview and Resource Guide for Integral Scholars," Mets Integral Foundation, accessible at https://metaintegral.org/sites/default/files/Critical%20Realism_4-12-2013.pdf.
15. This theme can only be lightly touched upon here. On another note of art as *creativity in critique*, the methodological themes of *critical realist historical materialism* may be invoked for considering the possibilities of critically representing *complexity of/in uncertainty* as existential issues for "intellectuals." Here we might cite innumerable creations in world literatures for "critically realizing" transcendence

without the "transcendental," while maintaining attention to depth ontology. See Maxim Gorky's drama *Children of the Sun*, amongst many other specific items across innumerable representational genres, including Brechtian, pre- and non-Brechtian theatre, etc.
16. Thus "textbooks" may be vital resources for productive work in recontextualization, too.
17. Emergence refers to the critical methodological theme that the *whole is always more than the sum of its parts*. The dynamics in the whole are autonomous from any such "summing," or, indeed, "summary," so while the parts are *necessary* conditions of the existence of the emergent "thing," its properties are not reducible to that "summing" and are *its own*, conditions of its integrity in "it-ness." For detailed elaborations, see: Bhaskar (1998; 2008; 2009).
18. See footnote "v."
19. The term is associated in sociology with Giddens (1984) by which structure is both medium and outcome of action.
20. Rawls' *difference principle* argues that inequalities in social relations should only exist if they work to the benefit of the least well-off (Rawls: 1999).
21. In the work of Garcia-Marquez (1989; 2003) alienation and repression are complex historical moments *in/as solitude* and are constituted critically by depiction in depth ontology, with dialectical, multi-levelled, poly-scalar textuality, as "materialist" and "realist" in this relational critical form. See: Guardiola-Rivera, O (2010).
22. For "pink tide," see for discussion and recent literature: Kirby, P (2010) "Probing the significance of Latin America's 'Pink Tide,'" *European Review of Latin America and the Caribbean Studies, 89 (Oct), pp. 127–133*; and Prevost, G (et al) (2012) *Social Movements and Leftist Government in Latin America: Confrontation or Co-optation*. London: Zed Books.
23. See current information on developments related to the League for the Fifth International, accessible at: http://www.fifthinternational.org/about-us.

1 Wallerstein and Mészáros: Scholars for the Twenty-First Century

1. See for example: http://spanishrevolution11.wordpress.com/2013/06/09/the-free-republic-of-taksim/.
2. See for example: *Monthly Review Press*'s use of this characterization and endorsement by Chávez in its publication of Mézsáros' work Meszaros, I. (2008), "The Challenge and Burden of Historical Time," *Monthly Review Press*, NewYork; Meszaros, I. (2010), "Social Structure and Forms of Consciousness," *Monthly Review Press*, New York.

2 Wallerstein's World-Systems Analysis

1. Two key terms are at times used interchangeably within the broad field of world-systems analysis (WSA)—"the capitalist world-system" and "the capitalist world-economy." In this text, we use capitalist world-economy when addressing and highlighting economic dimensions of systems, and world-system when consciously invoking the multiple dimensions and operations of what are often the subject of separate disciplinary studies, i.e., the operation of a single capitalist world-economy across ostensibly sovereign nation-states; these states with diverse national polities operate within an elaborated interstate system.
2. These figures are derived from a 2009 curriculum vitae available publicly for download here: http://www.iwallerstein.com/about/
3. The other two mechanisms were identified as the military strength or dominant/hegemonic powers in the world-system, and the ideological commitments of key cadre and administrative staff to the system, seeing their personal well-being as dependent on the survival of the system Wallerstein, I. (1979), *The Capitalist World-Economy,* Cambridge University Press, Cambridge.

4 Educating Critical Citizens for an Alternative World-System

1. A notable and tangible example of such an attempt, beyond his extensive academic writing and lectures, was Wallerstein's endorsement as part of the "Group of Nineteen" intellectuals, of the *Porto Alegre Manifesto* as part of the 2005 World Social Forum, setting out 12 proposals to "give sense and direction to the construction of another, different world" (http://www.openspaceforum.net/twiki/tiki-read_article.php?articleId=276).
2. The emphasis on standardized assessments across much of the world, linked to countries' participation in international testing regimes of PISA and TIMSS and the comparisons that follow, has clearly worked against such practices with teachers and schools pressured to focus on basic and decontextualized literacy and numeracy skills, and rote practice for testing.

8 Conclusion

1. We have noted the promotion of Mészáros, and to a lesser extent Wallerstein, within contemporary Venezuela, and acknowledge the likelihood of there being varying levels of engagement in different parts of the world. Our claim here is based on our working knowledge of contemporary research literatures, in English, in the fields of comparative and international education and political science.

Bibliography

Adorno, T. W. (1973), *Negative Dialectics*, London: Routledge & Kegan Paul.
Aguirre Rojas, C. A. (2000), "Rethinking Current Social Sciences: The Case of Historical Discourses in the History of Modernity," *Journal of World-Systems Research*, VI, 3, 750–66.
Allman, P. (2010), *Critical Education Against Global Capitalism: Karl Marx and Revolutionary Education*, Rotterdam: Sense Publishers.
Álvarez, V. (2010), *Del Estado burocrático al Estado comunal*, Caracas: Centro Internacional Miranda.
Amin, S. (1976), *Unequal Development: An Essay on the Social Formations of Peripheral Capitalism*, New York: Monthly Review Press.
Anderson-Levitt, K. (ed.) (2003), *Local Meanings, Global Schooling: Anthropology and World Culture Theory*, New York: Palgrave Macmillan.
Andreotti, V. D. O. (2011), "The Political Economy of Global Citizenship Education," *Globalisation, Societies and Education*, 9, 3–4, 307–10.
Apple, M. (1979), *Ideology and Curriculum*, London: Routledge & Kegan Paul.
Arendt, H. (1951), *The Origins of Totalitarianism*, New York: Harcourt.
Aristotle. (1941), *The Basic Works of Aristotle*, (ed.) R. Mckeon, New York: Random House.
Arnove, R. F. (1980), "Comparative Education and World-Systems Analysis," *Comparative Education Review*, 24, 1, 48–62.
Babones, S. J. and Chase-Dunn, C. (eds.) (2012), *Routledge Handbook of World-Systems Analysis*, London: Routledge.
Bain, O. (2013), "The Comprehensive School and Egalitarianism: From Demystification and Discreditation to Global Ascendance?" Griffiths, T. G. and Millei, Z., *Logics of Socialist Education: Engaging with Crisis, Insecurity and Uncertainty*. Dordrecht: Springer, 173–97.
Baker, D. P., et al. (2005), "Symbiotic Institutions: Changing Global Dynamics Between Family and Schooling," edited by Baker, D. P. and Letendre, G. K., *National Differences, Global Similarities: World Culture and the Future of Schooling*. California: Stanford University Press, 36–53.

Barrett, W. (1962), *Irrational Man: A Study in Existential Philosophy*, New York: Anchor Books.
Barthes, R. (1973), *The Pleasure of the Text*, New York: Hill and Wang.
Barthes, R. (1975), *S/Z: An Essay*, New York: Hill and Wang.
Beane, J. A. (1995), "Curriculum Integration and the Disciplines of Knowledge," *Phi Delta Kappan*, April, 616–22.
Bellamy Foster, J. (2013), "James Hansen and the Climate-Change Exit Strategy," *Monthly Review*, 64, 9, 1–19.
Bellhierz, P. (1994), "Theories of History—Agnes Heller and R.G. Collingwood," edited by J. Burnhiem, *The Social Philosophy of Agnes Heller*. Amsterdam: Rodopi, 121–36.
Benahabib, S. (1980), "On Instincts," *Telos*, 44, 211–21.
Bernstein, B. (1990), "The Social Construction of Pedagogic Discourse," *Class, Codes and Control*. Vol IV. London: Routledge.
Best, S and Kellner, D. (1991), *Postmodern Theory: Critical Interrogations*, New York: Guilford Press.
Bhaskar, R. (1979), "Review of D. Sayer, 'Marx's Method,'" *Radical Philosophy*, 25.
Bhaskar, R. (1991), "Marxist Philosophy from Marx to Althusser," *Philosophy and the Idea of Freedom*. Oxford, UK and Cambridge, MA: Blackwell.
Bhaskar, R. (1998), *The Possibility of Naturalism: A Philosophical Critique of the Contemporary Human Sciences*, 3rd edn. London & New York: Routledge.
Bhaskar, R. (2008a), *Dialectic the Pulse of Freedom*, 2nd edn. London: Routledge.
Bhaskar, R. (2008b), *A Realist Theory of Science*, 4th edn. London: Routledge.
Bhaskar, R. (2009), *Scientific Realism and Human Emancipation*, 2nd edn. London: Routledge.
Bhaskar, R. and Callinicos, A. (2003), "Marxism and Critical Realism: A Debate," *Journal of Critical Realism*, 1, 2, 89–114.
Boli, J., et al. (1985), "Explaining the Origins and Expansion of Mass Education," *Comparative Education Review*, 29, 2, 145–70.
Boswell, T. and Chase-Dunn, C. (2000), *The Spiral of Capitalism and Socialism: Toward Global Democracy*, Boulder, London: Lynne Rienner Publishers.
Bowles, S. and Gintis, H. (1976), *Schooling in Capitalist America*, London: Routledge & Kegan Paul.
Brown, D. M. (1988), *Towards a Radical Democracy: Political Economy of the Budapest School*, London: Unwin & Hyman.
Burbach, R., et al. (2013a), "Bolivia's Communitarian Socialism," edited by Burbach, R., Fox, M. and Fuentes, F., *Latin America's Turbulent Transitions: The Future of Twenty-First-Century Socialism*. London: Zed Books, 79–96.
Burbach, R., et al. (2013b), *Latin America's Turbulent Transitions: The Future of Twenty-First-Century Socialism*, London: Zed Books.

Camicia, S. P. and Franklin, B. M. (2011), "What Type of Global Community and Citizenship? Tangled Discourses of Neoliberalism and Critical Democracy in Curriculum and its Reform," *Globalisation, Societies and Education*, 9, 3–4, 311–22.
Camus, A. (1955), *The Myth of Sisyphus and Other Essays*, New York: Alfred A. Knopf.
Camus, A. (1956), *The Rebel: An Essay on Man in Revolt*, New York: Alfred A. Knopf.
Carnoy, M., et al. (2007), *Cuba's Academic Advantage: Why Students in Cuba Do Better in School*, California: Stanford University Press.
Chase-Dunn, C. (ed.) (1982), *Socialist States in the World System*, Beverly Hills: Sage Publications.
Chase-Dunn, C. and Grimes, P. (1995), "World-Systems Analysis," *Annual Review of Sociology*, 21, 387–17.
Cho, S. (2013), *Critical Pedagogy and Social Change: Critical Analysis on the Language of Possibility*, New York: Routledge.
Clayton, T. (2004), "'Competing Conceptions of Globalization' Revisited: Relocating the Tension between World-Systems Analysis and Globalization Analysis," *Comparative Education Review* 48, 3, 274–94.
Cohen, M. (1986), *A Theory of Human Needs*, Sussex: Harvester Press.
Connell, W. F. (1980), *A History of Education in the Twentieth Century World*, Canberra: Curriculum Development Centre.
Dale, R. (2005), "Globalisation, Knowledge Economy and Comparative Education," *Comparative Education*, 41, 2, 117–49.
Dale, R. and Robertson, S. (eds.) (2009), *Globalisation & Europeanisation in Education*, Oxford: Symposium.
Darder, A. (2011), *A Dissident Voice: Essays on Culture, Pedagogy and Power*, New York: Peter Lang.
Darder, A., et al. (eds.) (2008), *The Critical Pedagogy Reader: Second Edition*, New York: Routledge.
De Sousa Santos, B. (2008), "Depolarised Pluralities. A Left with a Future," edited by Barrett, P., Chavez, D., and Rodríguez-Garavito, C., *The New Latin American Left: Utopia Reborn*. Amsterdam: Pluto Press, 255–72.
Debord, Guy (1967), *The Society of the Spectacle*, Detroit: Black & Red.
Derrida, J. (1978), *Writing and Difference*, Great Britain: Routledge & Kegan Paul.
Duncan-Andrade, J. and Morrell, E. (2007), "Critical Pedagogy and Popular Culture in an Urban Secondary English Classroom," edited by Mclaren, P. and Kincheloe, J. L., *Critical Pedagogy: Where are We Now?* New York: Peter Lang, 183–99.
Egilda Castellano, M. (2004), "Entrevista a la fundadora y ex-rectora de la Universidad Bolivariana de Venezuela, Doña María Egilda Castellano," *Laberinto*, 16, 51–55.
Fiala, R. and Lanford, A. G. (1987), "Educational Ideology and the World Educational Revolution, 1950–1970," *Comparative Education Review*, 31, 3, 315–32.

Fields, G. S. (1982), "Educational Progress and Economic Development," edited by Anderson, L. and Windham, D. M., *Education and Development: Issues in the Analysis and Planning of Postcolonial Societies.* Massachusetts, Toronto: Lexington Books, 47–72.

Foucault, M. (1980), *Power/Knowledge: Selected Interviews and Other Writings -1972–1977,* New York: Pantheon Books.

Frank, A. G. (1966), "The Development of Underdevelopment," *Monthly Review,* 18, 7, 17–31.

Freire, P. (1970a), *Cultural Action for Freedom,* Great Britain: Penguin Books.

Freire, P. (1970b), *Pedagogy of the Oppressed,* Great Britain: Penguin Books.

Freire, P. (2007), *Daring to Dream; Toward a Pedagogy of the Unfinished,* Boulder, London: Paradigm Publishers.

Freire, P. (2012), "On the Right and the Duty to Change the World," Nikolakaki, M., *Critical Pedagogy in the New Dark Ages: Challenges and Possibilities.* New York: Peter Lang, 45–52.

Garcia-Marquez, G. (1989), *Love in the Time of Cholera,* London: Penguin Books.

Garcia-Marquez, G. (2003), *One Hundred Years of Solitude,* New York: Harper Collins.

Giddens, A. (1984), *The Constitution of Society: Outline of the Theory of Structuration,* Berkeley, CA: University of California Press.

Giroux, H. A. (2007), "Introduction: Democracy, Education, and the Politics of Critical Pedagogy," edited by Mclaren, P. and Kincheloe, J. L., *Critical Pedagogy: Where Are We Now?* New York: Peter Lange, 1–5.

Gore, J. M., et al. (2004), "Towards Better Teaching: Productive Pedagogy as a Framework for Teacher Education," *Teaching and Teacher Education,* 20, 375–87.

Griffiths, T. G. (2005), "Learning 'To Be Somebody'. Cuban Youth in the Special Period," *International Journal of Learning,* 11, 1267–74.

Griffiths, T. G. (2009a), "50 Years of Socialist Education in Revolutionary Cuba: A World-Systems Perspective," *Journal of Iberian and Latin American Research,* 15, 2, 45–64.

Griffiths, T. G. (2009b), "Social Justice, Equity, Schools and the Curriculum," *Curriculum Perspectives,* 29, 1, 76–82.

Griffiths, T. G. (2010a), "Las reformas curriculares y la educación Bolivariana: Una perspectiva del análisis sistema-mundo," *Ensayo y Error,* XIX, 38, 117–39.

Griffiths, T. G. (2010b), "Schooling for Twenty-First century Socialism: Venezuela's Bolivarian Project," *Compare: A Journal of Comparative and International Education,* 40, 5, 607–22.

Griffiths, T. G. (2011a), "El análisis sistema-mundo y el estudio educativo: Investigación para un mundo incierto," *Diálogo de Saberes,* 2, 5 & 6, 105–21.

Griffiths, T. G. (2011b), "World-Systems Analysis and Comparative Education for an Uncertain Future," *The International Education Journal: Comparative Perspectives*, 10, 1, 20–33.

Griffiths, T. G. (2013), "Higher Education for Socialism in Venezuela: Massification, Development and Transformation," edited by Griffiths, T. G. and Millei, Z., *Logics of Socialist Education: Engaging with Crisis, Insecurity and Uncertainty*. Dordrecht: Springer, 91–109.

Griffiths, T. G. and Arnove, R. F. (2014), "World Culture in the Capitalist World-System in Transition," *Globalisation, Societies and Education*, 12, 2, In Press.

Griffiths, T. G. and Knezevic, L. (2009), "World-Systems Analysis in Comparative Education: An Alternative to Cosmopolitanism," *Current Issues in Comparative Education*, 12, 1, 66–75.

Griffiths, T. G. and Knezevic, L. (2010), "Wallerstein's World-Systems Analysis in Comparative Education: A Case Study," *Prospects*, 40, 4, 447–63.

Griffiths, T. G. and Ladwig, J. G. (2003), "Meritocracy and the Competitive Individual: The Australian Case," edited by Rinne, R., Aro, M., Kivirauma, J., and Simola, H., *Adolescent Facing the Educational Politics of the 21st Century: Comparative Survey on Five National Cases and Three Welfare Models*. Finnish Educational Research Association, Turku, 235–66.

Griffiths, T. G. and Millei, Z. (2013a), "Education in/for Socialism: Historical, Current and Future Perspectives," *Globalisation, Societies and Education*, 11, 2, 161–69.

Griffiths, T. G. and Millei, Z. (2013b), "Introduction: Discovering and Negotiating Socialist Educational Logics Under Post-Socialist Conditions," edited by Griffiths, T. G. and Millei, Z., *Logics of Socialist Education: Engaging with Crisis, Insecurity and Uncertainty*. Springer, Dordrecht, 1–18.

Griffiths, T. G. and Millei, Z. (eds.) (2013c), *Logics of Socialist Education: Engaging with Crisis, Insecurity and Uncertainty*, Dordrecht: Springer.

Griffiths, T. G. and Williams, J. (2009), "Mass Schooling for Socialist Transformation in Cuba and Venezuela," *Journal of Critical Education Policy Studies*, 7, 2, 31–50.

Guardiola-Rivera, O. (2010), *What If Latin America Ruled the World?: How the South will take the North into the 21st Century*, London: Bloomsbury.

Haraszti, M. (1977), *Worker in a Worker's State*, Harmondsworth: Penguin.

Hayes, D., et al. (2006), *Teachers and Schooling Making a Difference; Productive Pedagogies, Assessment and Performance*, Crows Nest: Allen & Unwin.

Heidegger, M. (1962 [1927]), *Being and Time*, trans J. Macquarrie and E. Robinson, Oxford: Basil Blackwell.

Heller, A. (1964) *The Sociology of Morals or the Morals of Sociology*, Budapest, Akadémia Kiadó.
Heller, A. (1966), *Az aristotelési etika és az antik ethos*, Budapest, Akadémia Kiadó.
Heller, A. (1973), *Towards a Marxist Theory of Value*, Carbondale: University of Southern Illinois: Telos Books.
Heller, A. (1974), "Theory and Practice: Their Relation to Human Needs," *Social Praxis*, 1, 4, 359–373.
Heller, A. (1975), *Individuum and Praxis*, Frankfurt: Suhrkamp Verlag.
Heller, A. (1976), *The Theory of Need in Marx*, London: Allison and Busby.
Heller, A. (1977), "On the New Adventures of the Dialectic," *Telos*, 31, 134–142.
Heller, A. (1978a), *Renaissance Man*, trans. Richard E. Allen, Boston: Routledge and Kegan Paul.
Heller, A. (1978b), "Past, Present and Future of Democracy," *Social Research*, 45, 4, 866–86.
Heller, A. (1979a), *On Instincts*, trans. Mario Fenyo, Assen: Van Gorcum.
Heller, A. (1979b), *A Theory of Feelings*. Assen: Van Gorcum.
Heller A. (1979c), "Towards and Anthropology of Feeling," *Dialectical Anthropology*, 4, 1, 1–20.
Heller, A. (1980a), "Kurt Wolff's Existential Sociology," *Philosophical Forum*, 12, 1, 82–94.
Heller, A. (1980b), "Historicity and its Forms of Consciousness," *Philosophy and Social Criticism*, 7, 1–17.
Heller, A. (1980c), "Is Radical Philosophy Possible?," *Thesis Eleven*, 1, 19–28.
Heller, A. (1981), "The Power of Knowledge," *International Review of Sociology*, 17, 1, 3–21.
Heller, A. (1982a), *A Theory of History*, Boston: Routledge & Kegan Paul.
Heller, A. (1982b), "Marx and the Liberation of Humankind," *Philosophy and Social Criticism*. 9(3–4): 354–70.
Heller, A. (1983), "The Dissatisfied Society," *Praxis International*. 2(4): 359–70.
Heller, A. (1984a), *Everyday Life*. London: Routledge.
Heller, A. (1984b), *Lukács Revalued*, Oxford: Basil Blackwell.
Heller, A. (1985a), "The Great Republic," *Praxis International*, 5,1, 23–34.
Heller, A. (1985b), *The Power of Shame (A Rationalist Perspective)*, London: Routledge and Kegan Paul.
Heller, A. (1987), "The Human Condition," *Thesis Eleven*, 16, 4–12.
Heller, A. (1988), *Beyond Justice*, Oxford, Boston: Basil Blackwell.
Heller, A. (1989), *General Ethics*, Oxford, Boston: Basil Blackwell.
Heller, A. (1990a), *A Philosophy of Morals*, Oxford, Boston: Basil Blackwell.
Heller, A. (1990b), *Can Modernity Survive?* Cambridge: Polity Press and University of California Press.

Heller, A. (1996), *An Ethics of Personality*, Cambridge: Basil Blackwell.
Heller, A. (1999), *A Theory of Modernity*, Cambridge: Blackwell Publishers.
Heller, A. (2000), *The Time is Out of Joint: Shakespeare as Philosopher of History*, Cambridge: Blackwell Publishers.
Heller, A. (2004), *The Insolubility of the "Jewish Question," or Why Was I born Hebrew, and Why Not Negro?* Budapest: Múlt és Jövő Kiadó.
Heller, A. (2005), *Immortal Comedy: The Comic Phenomenon in Art, Literature, and Life*, Rowman and Littlefield Publishers, Inc.
Heller, A., and Feher, F. (1977), "Forms of Equality," *Telos*, 32, Summer, 6–26.
Heller, A., and Feher, F. (1986), *Eastern Left Western Left*, Cambridge: Polity Press.
Heller, A., and Feher, F. (1990), *From Yalta to Glasnost*, Oxford: Blackwell.
Heller, A., et al. (1983), *Dictatorship Over Needs*, Oxford: Blackwell
Hill, D. (2006), "Neoliberal Global Capital, Education and Resistance," *Social Change*, 36, 3, 47–76.
Huxley, J. (1947), *UNESCO: Its Purpose and Its Philosophy*, Washington DC: Public Affairs Press.
Imre, R. (2010), "Badiou and the Philosophy of Social Work: A Reply to Stephen Webb," *International Journal of Social Welfare*, 19, 2, 253–58.
Johnston, K. (2000), "Educational Equality: Meritocracy, Markets and...," *Education Links*, 60, 20–24.
Kahn, M. (1989), "Educational Reform and the Dependency Paradigm: Some Considerations from Botswana," *Compare: A Journal of Comparative Education*, 19, 2, 83–93.
Kiely, R. (2005), *Empire in the Age of Globalisation: U.S. Hegemony and Neo-Liberal Disorder*, London: Pluto Press.
Kierkegaard, S. (1973), *A Kierkegaard Anthology*, trans. Bretall, Princeton: Princeton University Press.
Kincheloe, J. L. (2007), "The Theoretical Dimensions of Critical Pedagogy," edited by Mclaren, P. and Kincheloe, J. L., *Critical Pedagogy : Where are We Now?* New York: Peter Lang, 9–42.
Klees, S. J. (2008a), "Neoliberalism and Education Revisited," *Globalisation, Societies and Education*, 6, 4, 409–14.
Klees, S. J. (2008b), "Presidential Address: Reflections on Theory, Method, and Practice in Comparative and International Education," *Comparative Education Review*, 52, 3, 301–28.
Klees, S. J. (2008c), "A Quarter Century of Neoliberal Thinking in Education: Misleading Analyses and Failed Policies," *Globalisation, Societies and Education*, 6, 4, 311–48.
Klees, S. J., et al. (eds.) (2012), *The World Bank and Education: Critiques and Alternatives*, Rotterdam: Sense Publishers.
Klein, N. (2007), *The Shock Doctrine: The Rise of Disaster Capitalism*, Canada: Knopf.

Kolakowski, L. (1978a), *Main Currents of Marxism: Its Rise, Growth and Dissolution, Volume 1: The Founders*, Oxford: Clarendon Press.
Kolakowski, L. (1978b), *Main Currents of Marxism: Its Rise, Growth and Dissolution, Volume 2: The Golden Age*, Oxford: Clarendon Press.
Kolakowski, L. (1978c), *Main Currents of Marxism: Its Rise, Growth and Dissolution, Volume 3: The Breakdown*, Oxford: Clarendon Press.
Li, M. (2008), *The Rise of China and the Demise of the Capitalist World-Economy*, New York: Monthly Review Press.
Lukács, G. (1971), *History and Class Consciousness: Studies in Marxist Dialectics*, trans. R. Livingstone, Great Britain: Merlin Press.
Lyotard, J. F. (1984), *The Postmodern Condition: A Report on Knowledge*, Minneapolis: University of Minnesota Press.
Lyotard, J-F. (1988), *The Differend: Phrases in Dispute*, Minneapolis: University of Minnesota Press.
Marković, M. and Petrović, G. (eds) (1979), *Praxis: Yugoslav Essays in the Philosophy and Methodology of the Social Sciences*, Dordrecht: Reidel.
Markus, G. (1982), *Language and Production*, Boston: Reidel.
Marr, D. and Wilkinson, M. (2003), *Dark Victory*, Crows Nest: Allen & Unwin.
Martin, G. (2005), "You Can't Be Neutral on a Moving Bus: Critical Pedagogy as Community Praxis," *Journal for Critical Education Policy Studies*, 3, 2, 1–29.
Martin, G. (2007), "The Poverty of Critical Pedagogy: Toward a Politics of Engagement," edited by Mclaren, P. and Kincheloe, J. L., *Critical Pedagogy: Where are we Now?* New York: Peter Lang, 337–53.
Marx, K (1845), *Theses on Fuerbach*. [Online] http://www.marxists.org/archive/marx/works/1845/theses/theses.htm.
Marx, K. (1852), *The Eighteenth Brumaire of Louis Bonaparte*. [Online] http://www.marxists.org/archive/marx/works/1852/18th-brumaire/ch01.htm.
Marx, K. (1867), *Capital*, I, 72–73; London: Penguin (1976), 163–64.
Marx, K. (1967), *Karl Marx, Frederick Engels, Collected Works*, Baltimore: Penguin Books.
Marx, K. and Engels, F. (1879), *Strategy and Tactics of the Class Struggle*. [Online] http://www.marxists.org/archive/marx/works/1879/09/17.htm.
Mclaren, P. and Kincheloe, J. L. (eds.) (2007), *Critical Pedagogy: Where Are We Now?*, New York: Peter Lang.
Mészáros, I. (1970), *Marx's Theory of Alienation*, London: Merlin Press.
Mészáros, I. (1971a), *The Necessity of Social Control: Isaac Deutscher Memorial Lecture*, London: Merlin Press.
Mészáros, I. (ed.) (1971b), *Aspects of History and Class Consciousness*, London: Routledge & Kegan Paul.
Mészáros, I. (1972), *Lukacs' Concept of Dialectic*, London: Merlin Press.

Mészáros, I. (1975) "From 'The Legend of Truth' to a 'True Legend': Phases of Sartre's Development," *Telos* 25, New York: Telos Press.
Mészáros, I. (1978), *Neo-Colonial Identity and Counter-Consciousness: Essays in Cultural Decolonisation*, London: Merlin Press.
Mészáros, I. (1986), *Philosophy, Ideology and Social Science: Essays in Negation and Affirmation*, Brighton: Harvester Wheatsheaf.
Mészáros, I. (1989), *The Power of Ideology*, Brighton: Harvester Wheatsheaf.
Mészáros, I. (1995), *Beyond Capital: Towards a Theory of Transition*, New York: New York University Press.
Mészáros, I. (2001), *Socialism or Barbarism: Alternative to Capital's Social Order: From The American Century to the Crossroads*, New York: Monthly Review Press.
Mészáros, I. (2008), *The Challenge and Burden of Historical Time*, New York: Monthly Review Press.
Mészáros, I. (2009), *Historical Actuality of the Socialist Offensive*, United Kingdom: Bookmarks.
Mészáros, I. (2010a), *Social Structure and Forms of Consciousness, Volume 1: The Social Determination of Method*, New York: Monthly Review Press.
Mészáros, I. (2010b), *The Structural Crisis of Capital*, New York: Monthly Review Press.
Mészáros, I. (2011), *Social Structure and Forms of Consciousness, Volume II: The Dialectic of Structure and History*, New York: Monthly Review Press.
Mészáros, I. (2012), *The Work of Sartre: Search for Freedom and the Challenge of History*, New York: Monthly Review Press.
Meyer, J. W. and Hannan, M. T. (eds.) (1979), *National Development and the World System: Educational, Economic, and Political Change, 1950–1970.*, Chicago and London: The University of Chicago Press.
Meyer, J. W., et al. (1997), "World Society and the Nation State," *American Journal of Sociology*, 103, 1, 144–81.
Mielants, E. (2012), "The Great Transition Debate," edited by Babones, S. J. and Chase-Dunn, C., *Routledge Handbook of World-Systems Analysis*. London: Routledge, 56–62.
Mills, C. (2007), "Transforming the Capital That Counts: Making a Difference for Students with Cultural Capital in the 'Wrong' Currency," *Curriculum Perspectives*, 27, 3, 11–21.
Moon, R. J. and Koo, J.-W. (2011), "Global Citizenship and Human Rights: A Longitudinal Analysis of Social Studies and Ethics Textbooks in the Republic of Korea," *Comparative Education Review*, 55, 4, 574–99.
Muhr, T. (2010), "Counter-Hegemonic Regionalism and Higher Education for All: Venezuela and the ALBA," *Globalisation, Societies and Education*, 8, 1, 39–57.
Muhr, T. and Verger, A. (2006), "Venezuela: Higher Education For All," *Journal of Critical Education Policy Studies*, 4, 1, 13.

Newmann, F. M., et al. (1995), *A Guide to Authentic Instruction and Assessment: Vision, Standards and Scoring*, Wisconsin: Wisconsin Center for Educational Research.

Niens, U. and Reilly, J. (2012), "Education for Global Citizenship in a Divided Society? Young People's Views and Experiences," *Comparative Education*, 48, 1, 103–18.

Nikolakaki, M. (2012a), "Critical Pedagogy in the New Dark Ages: Challenges and Possibilities: An Introduction," edited by Nikolakaki, M., *Critical Pedagogy in the New Dark Ages: Challenges and Possibilities*. New York, 3–31.

Nikolakaki, M. (2012b), "Preface," edited by Nikolakaki, M., *Critical Pedagogy in the New Dark Ages: Challenges and Possibilities*. New York: Peter Lang, xi–xii.

OECD (ed.) (2010), *PISA 2009 Results: Overcoming Social Background—Equity in Learning Opportunities and Outcomes (Volume II)*.

Ollman, B. (2003), *Dance of the Dialectic: Steps in Marx's Method*, Chicago, IL: University of Illinois Press.

Panitch, L., et al. (eds.) (2010), *Socialist Register 2011: The Crisis This Time*, Pontypool, Wales: Merlin Press.

Petras, J. (2009), "Latin America's Twenty-First Century Socialism in Historical Perspective." *Centre for Research on Globalization* [Online]. Available: http://www.globalresearch.ca/PrintArticle.php?articleId=15634 (Accessed May 24, 2010).

Petras, J. (2010), "Latin America: Roads to 21st Century Capitalist Development." *Venezuelanalysis* [Online]. Available: http://venezue-lanalysis.com/analysis/5726.

Plato. (1945), *The Republic*, trans. F. M. Cornford, New York: Oxford University Press.

Polanyi, K. (1957), *The Great Transformation: The Political and Economic Origins of Our Time*, Boston: Beacon Press.

Postman, N. and Weingartner, C. (1969), *Teaching as a Subjective Activity*, Great Britain: Penguin Books.

Ramirez, F. O. (2003), "Toward a Cultural Anthropology of the World?" edited by Anderson-Levitt, K. M., *Local Meanings, Global Schooling: Anthropology and World Culture Theory*. New York: Palgrave Macmillan, 239–54.

Ramirez, F. O. (2006), "Beyond Achievement and Attainment Studiesre—Vitalizing a Comparative Sociology of Education," *Comparative Education*, 42, 3, 431–49.

Ramirez, F. O. and Boli, J. (1987), "Global Patterns of Educational Institutionalization," *Institutional Structure: Constituting State, Society, and the Individual*. Newbury Park, California: Sage Publications, 150–72.

Ramirez, F. O. and Rubinson, R. (1979), "Creating Members: The Political Incorporation and Expansion of Public Education," edited by Meyer,

J. W. and Hannan, M. T., *National Development and the World System: Educational, Economic, and Political Change, 1950-1970*. Chicago: University of Chicago Press, 72–82.
Rawls, J. (1999), *A Theory of Justice*, Cambridge, MA: Harvard University Press.
Rodríguez-Garavito, C., et al. (2008), "Utopia Reborn? Introduction to the Study of the New Latin American Left," edited by Barrett, P., Chavez, D., and Rodríguez-Garavito, C., *The New Latin American Left: Utopia Reborn*. Amsterdam: Pluto Press, 1–41.
Rorty, R. (1989), *Contigency, Irony and Solidarty*, Cambridge: Cambridge University Press.
Sartre, J. P. (1956), *Being and Nothingness*, Northhampton: John Dickens & Co.
Sartre, J-P. (2008), *Between Existentialism and Marxism*, 2nd edn. London: Verso.
Sayer, D. (1979), *Marx's Method: Ideology, Critique in Capital*, Sussex: Harvester.
Schutz, A. (1972), *The Phenomenology of the Social World*, trans George Walsh and Frederick Lehnert, London: Heinemann Educational.
Schutz, A. and Luckman, T. (1973), *The Structures of the Life-World* (Strukturen der Lebenswelt.) edited by Alfred Schütz and Thomas Luckmann, trans Richard M. Zaner and H. Tristram Engelhardt, Jr. Evanston, IL: Northwestern University Press.
Skocpol, T. (1977), "Wallerstein's World Capitalist System: A Theoretical and Historical Critique," *American Journal of Sociology*, 82, 5, 1075–90.
Steinberg, S. R. (2007), "Preface: Where Are we Now?" edited by Mclaren, P. and Kincheloe, J. L., *Critical Pedagogy: Where are we Now?* New York: Peter Lang, ix–x.
Stiglitz, J. (2010), *Freefall: America, Free Markets, and the Sinking of the World Economy*, W. W. Norton: New York.
Symes, C. and Preston, N. (1997), *Schools and Classrooms: A Cultural Studies Analysis of Education: Second Edition*, South Melbourne: Addison Wesley Longman Australia Pvt Limited.
Szelenyi, I. (1991), "Classes and parties in post-communist transition: the case of Hungary, 1989-1990," (With Szonja Szelenyi), Lemke, C., *Crisis of Socialism, Eastern and Western Europe*, Durham: Duke University Press.
Tabulawa, R. (2003), "International Aid Agencies, Learner-Centred Pedagogy and Political Democratisation: A Critique," *Comparative Education*, 39, 1, 7–26.
Tomasevski, K. (2003), *Education Denied: Costs and Remedies*, London & New York: Zed Books.
UNESCO (1971), *World Survey of Education: Educational policy, legislation and administration*, Paris: UNESCO.

UNESCO (2013), *Education for All Global Monitoring Report Policy Paper 06: Education for All Is Affordable by 2015 and Beyond*. Paris: UNESCO.
United Nations (1948), "The Universal Declaration of Human Rights."
United Nations (2012), *The Millenium Development Goals Report 2012*. New York: United Nations.
Vajda, M. (1981), *The State and Socialism: Political Essays*, London: Alison and Busby.
Vally, S. and Spreen, C. A. (2012), "Human Rights in World Bank Education Strategy," edited by Klees, S. J., Samoff, J. and Stromquist, N. P., *The World Bank and Education: Critiques and Alternatives*. Rotterdam: Sense Publishers, 173–87.
Wallerstein, I. (1974a), *The Modern World-System I: Capitalist Agriculture and the Origins of the European World-Economy in the Sixteenth Century*, New York: Academic Press.
Wallerstein, I. (1974b), "The Rise and Future Demise of the World Capitalist System: Concepts for Comparative Analysis," *Comparative Studies in Society and History*, 16, 4, 387–415.
Wallerstein, I. (1979), *The Capitalist World-Economy*, Cambridge: Cambridge University Press.
Wallerstein, I. (1980), *The Modern World-System II: Mercantilism and the Consolidation of the European World-Economy, 1600–1750*, New York: Academic Press.
Wallerstein, I. (1983), *Historical Capitalism*, London: Verso.
Wallerstein, I. (1984), *The Politics of the World-Economy: The States, the Movements and the Civilizations*, Cambridge: Cambridge University Press.
Wallerstein, I. (1989), *The Modern World-System III: The Second Era of Great Expansion of the Capitalist World-Economy, 1730–1840s*, San Diego, California: Academic Press, Inc.
Wallerstein, I. (1990), "Culture as the Ideological Battleground of the Modern World-System," *Theory, Culture & Society*, 7, 31–55.
Wallerstein, I. (1991a), "The Ideological Tensions of Capitalism: Universalism versus Racism and Sexism," edited by Balibar, E. and Wallerstein, I., *Race, Nation, Class: Ambiguous Identities*. New York: Verso, 29–36.
Wallerstein, I. (1991b), *Unthinking Social Science—The Limits of Nineteenth Century Paradigms*, London: Polity Press.
Wallerstein, I. (1994), "The Agonies of Liberalism: What Hope Progress?" *New Left Review*, 204, 3–17.
Wallerstein, I. (1995a), *After Liberalism*, New York: The New Press.
Wallerstein, I. (1995b), "The Concept of National Development, 1917–1989: Elegy and Requiem," *After Liberalism*. New York: The New Press, 108–22.
Wallerstein, I. (1996), *Open the Social Sciences: Report of the Gulbenkian Commission on the Restructuring of the Social Sciences*, Stanford, California: Stanford University Press.

Wallerstein, I. (1997a), "Social Science and the Quest for a Just Society," *American Journal of Sociology*, 102, 5, 1241–57.
Wallerstein, I. (1997b), "SpaceTime as the Basis of Knowledge," *World Congress of Convergence* [Online]. http://www2.binghamton.edu/fbc/archive/iwsptm.htm (Accessed October 27, 2012).
Wallerstein, I. (1998a), *Historical Capitalism with Capitalist Civilization*, London: Verso.
Wallerstein, I. (1998b), "The Time of Space and the Space of Time: The Future of Social Science," *Political Geography*, 17, 1, 71–82.
Wallerstein, I. (1998c), *Utopistics: Or, Historical Choices of the Twenty-first Century*, New York: The New Press.
Wallerstein, I. (1999a), "Ecology and Capitalist Costs of Production," edited by Wallerstein, I., *The End of the World as we Know it: Social Science for the Twenty-First Century*. Minneapolis: University of Minnesota Press, 76–86.
Wallerstein, I. (1999b), "The Heritage of Sociology, The Promise of Sociology," *Current Sociology*, 47, 1, 1–37.
Wallerstein, I. (1999c), "The Rise and Future Demise of World-Systems Analysis," *The End of the World as We know it: Social Science for the Twenty-First Century*, 192–201.
Wallerstein, I. (1999d), "The Structures of Knowledge, or How Many Ways May We Know?" edited by Wallerstein, I., *The End of the World as we Know it: Social Science for the Twenty-First Century*. Minneapolis: University of Minnesota Press, 185–91.
Wallerstein, I. (2000a), "Globalization or the Age of Transition?: A Long-Term View of the Trajectory of the World-System," *International Sociology*, 15, 2, 249–65.
Wallerstein, I. (2000b), "Hold the Tiller Firm: On Method and the Unit of Analysis," *The Essential Wallerstein*. New York: The New Press, 149–59.
Wallerstein, I. (2001a), "Marx and Underdevelopment," edited by Wallerstein, I., *Unthinking Social Science: The Limits of Nineteenth-Century Paradigms*. Philadelphia: Temple University Press, 151–69.
Wallerstein, I. (2001b), "Marxisms as Utopias: Evolving Ideologies," edited by Wallerstein, I., *Unthinking Social Science: The Limits of Nineteenth-Century Paradigms*. Philadelphia: Temply University Press, 170–84.
Wallerstein, I. (2002a), "Citizens All? Citizens Some! The Making of the Citizen," *Comparative Studies in Society and History*, 45, 4, 650–79.
Wallerstein, I. (2002b), "New Revolts Against the System," *New Left Review*, 18, 29–39.
Wallerstein, I. (2003a), "Anthropology, Sociology, and Other Dubious Disciplines," *Current Anthropology*, 44, 4, 453–65.
Wallerstein, I. (2003b), "The Left I: Theory and Praxis Once Again," edited by Wallerstein, I., *The Decline of American Power: The U.S. in a Chaotic World*. New York: The New Press, 219–58.

Wallerstein, I. (2003c), "The Left II: An Age of Transition," edited by Wallerstein, I., *The Decline of American Power: The U.S. in a Chaotic World*. New York: The New Press, 249–58.
Wallerstein, I. (2003d), "The Others: Who Are We? Who Are The Others?," *The Decline of American Power*. New York: The New Press, 124–47.
Wallerstein, I. (2004a), *The Uncertainties of Knowledge*, Philadelphia: Temple University Press.
Wallerstein, I. (2004b), "World-Systems Analysis," edited by Modelski, G. and Denemark, R. A., *World System History*. Oxford: EOLSS Publishers, 13–26.
Wallerstein, I. (2004c), *World-Systems Analysis: An Introduction*, London: Duke University Press.
Wallerstein, I. (2005), "After Developmentalism and Globalization, What?" *Social Forces*, 83, 3, 321–36.
Wallerstein, I. (2006), *European Universalism: The Rhetoric of Power*, New York: The New Press.
Wallerstein, I. (2007), *La decadencia del imperio: Estados Unidos en un mundo caótico*, Caracas: Monte Ávila Editores Latinoamericana C.A.
Wallerstein, I. (2008), *Un mundo incierto*, Caracas: Monte Ávila Editores Latinoamericana.
Wallerstein, I. (2010), "Structural Crises," *New Left Review*, 62, 133–42.
Wallerstein, I. (2011a), *The Modern World System I: Capitalist Agriculture and the Origins of the European World-Economy in the Sixteenth Century*, Berkeley: University of California Press.
Wallerstein, I. (2011b), *The Modern World-System IV: Centrist Liberalism Triumphant, 1789–1914*, Berkeley: University of California Press.
Wallerstein, I. (2011c), "Structural Crisis in the World-System: Where Do We Go from Here?" *Monthly Review*, 62, 10, 31–39.
World Bank (1980), *Education Sector Policy Paper*, Washington, DC: World Bank.
Young, M. F. D. (ed.) (1971), *Knowledge and Control: New Directions for the Sociology of Education*, London: Collier-Macmillan.
Zinn, H. and Macedo, D. (2012), "Schools and the Manufacture of Mass Deception: A Dialogue," edited by Nikolakaki, M., *Critical Pedagogy in the new dark ages: Challenges and Possibilities*. Peter Lang, New York, 120–43.
Žižek, S. (2010), "A Permanent Economic Emergency," *New Left Review*, 64, 85–95.

Index

absolute limits, 28–32
absolute relativism, rejected, 98
abundance, 150
academics and educators
   critical pedagogy and, 70–3, 75
   curricular design, 87
   exploring alternatives, 37–8
   political engagement, 76, 78–9
   role of, 37–8
   world-systems analysis and, 37, 39
accumulation of capital, 31, 48–9.
   See also surplus value
activist work, 37–8
Adorno, T.W., 106–7, 140–1
adult and lifelong education, 82, 84
aesthetics. *See* art
agency and action
   broad principles for, 77
   critical pedagogy and, 71–2, 74–5
   structure versus, 38, 46
   see also praxis
alienation. *See* Marxist view of human alienation
alternative dependency theory, 20
alternative pedagogy, 8, 70–2
alternative world-system, 32, 76–7, 80, 160, 164
   educating critical citizens for, 67–98, 161
   transition to an uncertain, 47
   See also critical world-systems education

American empirical sociological inquiry, 117
Amsterdam, rise of, 18, 24
anthropology. *See* philosophical anthropology; social anthropology
"anti-statism," 36
anti-systemic movement, 2–3
   anti-capitalist regimes, 15, 128
   development of Marxism by, 68–9
   equity goals, 46
   multiple polities and, 15
   operation within the capitalist world-economy, 79
   socialism and, 16
   world-system in transition and, 31–2, 36
Arendt, H., 114
Aristotle, 102, 108, 116, 130, 138, 154
art, 135, 140, 150, 153
asylum seekers and refugees, 60, 96
asymptotes/absolute limits, 29
attitudes, change in, 139
Austro-Marxists, 112–13
authentic life, 137, 140–1
authoritarian political systems, 126–8
auto-domestication, 152

Badiou's interpretations of socialism, 116
"banking concept of education," 70

INDEX

"best price/best value" for produced goods, 119
bias. *See* prejudices
binaries, 162
Bolivarian Revolution, 4, 68, 84
Bolivia, 68–9
bourgeois society, 124–5, 129
Budapest School, 105–6, 119–33
   analysis of capitalism by, 121–2
   development of Marxism by, 3, 100
   moral maxims, 130
   radical democracy and. *See* radical democracy
   social theory and, 112

capital
   accumulation of, 16–17, 31, 48–9
   decision-making and, 123
   historical development of, 125
   needs and, 144–5, 150
   power of, 131–3, 164
   relocation of, 29–30, 36
   transitions in capital seeking, 29–30
   See also global capital/ism; surplus value
capitalism, 78–9, 159–60
   analysis of, 121–3
   contemporary, 119
   contradictions of, 5–6
   in East-Central Europe, 121
   human capital theory and. *See* human capital theory
   inductive approach to classifying, 48
   production under, 126, 129–32
   role in educational policy, 163
   "sense of blasphemy" in challenge to, 39
   social inequalities of, 124–5
   transitions in, 28–30
   See also non-capitalist alternatives
capitalist world-economy
   alternatives to. (*see* alternative world-system; critical world-systems education)
   commodity chains in, 21–3, 48–9
   critical pedagogy and, 75, 78–9
   cycles in, 28–30, 94
   division of labor in. (*see* division of labor)
   equilibrium in, 28–9
   expansion of, 13–14
   externalization of costs, 30
   geoculture of liberalism and. (*see* geoculture of liberalism)
   globalization theorizing, 35–7
   hegemonic states in, 19, 24–5
   interstate system. (*see* interstate system)
   labor control and, 16–17. (*see also* work)
   mass education in. (*see* mass education)
   meritocracy in. (*see* meritocracy)
   multiple polities in, 13–17, 23–5
   nation-states in. (*see* nation-states)
   socialist states as part of, 15–16. (*see also* socialism)
   strain from emerging economies, 49–50
   structural requirements for, 11–12, 49–50, 60–1
   thought-system of, 75–6
   "underdevelopment" as part of, 20–2, 59–60
   unequal exchange in, 21–3, 37, 65
   work in, 47–50. (*see also* work)
capitalist world-system
   citizenship, approach to, 95–7
   collapse of. (*see* global transition and crises)
   human capital in. (*see* human capital theory)
   knowledge and skills to understand, 47
   mass education in. (*see* mass education)
   transformation of. (*see* transformation of the world)

See also capitalist world-economy; geoculture/world cultural framework; nation-states
categorical imperative of human emancipation. *See* emancipation (freedom)
centrist liberalism, 24–8, 31–2
chaotic struggle, 92
Chávez, Hugo, 163
China, 29–30, 49–50
citizens, critical world-systems education and, 95–7
civil society. *See* bourgeois society
class interests
 class-based educational and occupational tracks, 45
 collective action and, 99
 historical evolution, 120–2, 127–8
 needs and values and, 145–7, 150–1, 157–8
coercion, 156
collectivity. *See* community and collectivity
commodity chains, 21–3, 48–9
commons, destruction of the, 143
community and collectivity, 99, 108, 113, 116, 118, 128, 136
 alternative models of schooling based on, 8
 "natural propensity" for, 8, 99
comparative and international education (CIE), 42
 education for global citizenship, 95
 meritocracy and, 45
 world-systems analysis, 35–6, 52–4, 159, 162, 164
conflict theories, mass education, 53–4
consciousness, 78–9, 90–1, 105
 critical pedagogy, 70–2
conservatism, French Revolution and, 26–7
"continental categorical system," 138
contingency, 102–4, 137
core zones
 accumulation of capital in, 21–2
 economic cycles and, 28–30
 education in, 94
 hegemonic status and, 19, 24–5
 proletarianized labor, 49–50
 transnational commodity chains and, 21–3
costs, externalization of, 30
creativity, 8, 37
credentials. *See* educational credentials
crises. *See* global transition and crises
critical citizens, 67–98
critical Marxism, 100–1, 157–8
critical pedagogy, 163–4
 action as intended outcome of, 71–2, 77–8
 heritage of, 69–72
 identity construction and, 76
 unidisciplinary curriculum and, 91
 Wallerstein used within field of, 72–6
 what could and ought to be, 92–3
 world-systems analysis and, 72–80
critical realism. *See* immanent critique
critical research, 162
critical theory, 126, 142, 158
critical world-systems education, 33, 80–1
 chaotic struggle, 92
 citizenry and, 95–7
 defined, 80
 human capital formation, 93–5
 mass education, 60–5
 organizational structure, 81–5
 pedagogical praxis, 91–3
 provisional certainty, 98
 triuimph of, 62–3
 unidisciplinary curriculum, 85–91
 See also alternative world-system; world-systems analysis

cross or interdisciplinary
    approach, 86
Cuba, 15–16
    education in, 44, 82
cultural capital, 46–7
cultural differences
    cultural modernity, 135–6
    in historical evolution, 120
    inequalities and, 87–8
    value systems, 117–18
    See also geoculture/world
        cultural framework; world
        culture theory
curriculum, 88–90
    unidisciplinary, 85–91
cyclico-ideological timespace, 64

daily activity of change, 107–8. See
    also everyday life
decision-making, 132
    power over, in capitalism, 123–4
    stratified, 125
deficit discourses, 47, 56, 58
democracy, 121
    democratization of production,
        126, 129
    public life, 116
    radical. (see radical democracy)
    role of State, 123
    within socialism, 101, 112
dependency theory critiques, 44
despair, 107–8, 137
"destruction of the commons," 143
development. See economic
    development; national
    development
developmentalism, 27
dialectics, 104–8
disadvantaged individuals and
    groups, 46–7, 56, 58
    "relevant" or "meaningful"
        curriculum for, 47
    unidisciplinary knowledge
        and, 88
    See also inequalities
disciplines, 28–33, 161

conceptualization of, 60–5
    "multi," "pluri," "trans," or
        "inter" disciplinarity, 35
    subject-based classes in schools, 85
    unidisciplinary view, 5, 62–4, 74,
        85–91, 159
    "the West and the rest," 63
    See also idiographic epistemology;
        nomothetic epistemology;
        science; social sciences
discrimination, 58. See also
    inequalities; racism-sexism
diversity. See cultural differences
division of labor, 48–9
    discrimination and, 58
    transnational, in commodity
        chains, 21–3
    in world-economy, 13–14
    world-system in transition, 29–30
    see also workforce
dominant groups. See hegemony
dreams, critical pedagogy and, 73,
    79, 90–2
dualism (Mészáros), 100
Dutch hegemony, 18–20

East Germany, 101
East-Central Europe, 101–2,
    105–7, 109–10, 112–13,
    117–18, 148, 157
    capitalism in, 121
    class interests in, 121–2
    Western Left analysis of, 126–9
    see also Budapest School
economic determinism, 163–4
economic development, 27
    benefits of expansion of
        education, 42–4
    capitalist. (see capitalist world-
        economy)
    education for, 51, 54, 94
    human capital theory and, 94
    linear. (see linear
        developmentalism)
    mixed economies, 121–2, 129.
        (see also radical democracy)

INDEX

national. (*see* national development)
pragmatic policies of Szelenyi, 121
pursuit of, 51–2
stage theory perspective, 53–4
structural causes of, 44
"two-step strategy," 28
economic sphere, 126–7
Polanyi on, 143
in radical democracy, 130–1, 133
stratified power structure in, 123
economistic method, 122, 126–7
education
as a basic human right, 42–3
critical. (*see* critical pedagogy)
expansion of, 42
formal, 62–3, 85, 89
for global citizenship, 95
international. (*see* comparative and international education)
investment in, 43–4
mass. (*see* mass education)
Millennium Development Goals (EFA), 42, 81, 85
role in capitalist society, 163–4
social good from, 83
social inequality and, 6–7
for understanding of society, 69–71, 93
for work preparation, 5–6, 50–65, 119
world-systems analysis and, 38–9
see also critical world-systems education
educational credentials, 44–6, 55–60, 78, 82
educational policy and practice
educational praxis, 161
expansive conceptualization of education, 93
global dimensions of, 7, 52–4
human capital theory role in, 43–4
normative outcomes, 50–1
reforms for economic growth, 94

research, 162
"unthinking social sciences" and, 33
Education for All (EFA) Millennium Development Goals, 42, 81, 85
educators. *See* academics and educators
efficiency, 119
ego system, 154–5
emancipation (freedom), 105–8, 112–15, 118–19, 128, 140, 152–3, 156
bourgeois society and, 124–5
categorical imperative of human emancipation, 120, 139–41, 144
contingency and, 103, 105
freedom of the spirit (Hegel), 105
freedom-unto-death, 106
instincts and feelings and, 153–8
needs and values and, 146–50
in orthodox Marxism, 111–12, 126–7
philosophical anthropology and, 134–5, 137–8, 142
self-knowing freedom, 105
see also Budapest School
emerging economies (RIC countries), 49–50
emotions (feelings), 151–8
empiricism, humanizing empiricism, 117–18
"enclosure" phenomenon, 143
end to suffering, maxim of Budapest School, 130
England, 19–20. *see also* Industrial Revolution
Enlightenment philosophy, 124
environmental cleanup and control, externalization of costs, 30
epistemologies
alternative epistemologies, 64
dominant, WSA as protest against, 32–3
"epistemological revolution," 33–4

epistemologies—*Continued*
  epistemology of Marxism, 113
  formalized structure of knowledge into disciplines, 61–2
  problem of freedom, 113
equality, 16
  citizenship and inclusion, 96–7
  equal self-determination, 125, 130
  see also inequalities; meritocracy; unequal exchange and development
equilibrium, period of heightened free will when far from, 38
equity agenda, 162–3
  cultural capital and, 46–7
  equity or disadvantaged groups. (*see* disadvantaged individuals and groups)
  meritocracy and, 45–6
  more radical, transformative goals replaced by, 46
  recognizing cultural difference/diversity, 88
  workforce development and, 59
essence of the species. *See* species-essential individual
essentialized social groups, 58
established disciplines, WSA as protest against, 28–32
"eternal timespace," 63–4
ethics. *See* moral philosophy
Euro-communist social theorists, 127–8, 132
Europe, emergence of the European world-economy, 13
European dominance. *See* hegemony
European Renaissance, 120, 135–6
everyday life, 134–42, 160
  emancipation and, 147–8, 150
  history subordinate to, 108
  instincts and feelings and, 156
  needs and values and, 143–4
  philosophy and, 149
  see also daily activity of change
existentialism, 103–5, 107, 115–16, 133, 141
externalization of costs, capital seeking and, 30

feelings (emotions), 151–8
feudalism, 13
Feuerbach, Marx's eleventh thesis on, 108
finite nature of human beings, 136, 147–8
finitude, 104–5
formal democracy, 122, 124
formal education
  change of status of disciplines in, 62–3
  schooling, 85
forms of labor control, 15–17. *see also* multiple polities
France, 19
Frankfurt School, 126, 148
free market economies, 125, 129
  analysis of capitalism in, 121–4
  collapse of geoculture of liberalism, 31
  see also neoliberalism
freedom. *See* emancipation
Freire, Paulo, 69–71, 79, 86, 90, 92
French Revolution, 25–6

generational sacrifice, 110, 113–15
geoculture of development, 51
geoculture of liberalism, 24–8, 55
  alternatives to, 67–9
  centrist liberalism, 24–8, 31–2
  collapse of, 31–2
  taxation and, 31
  see also human capital theory; liberalism
geoculture/world cultural framework, 51–2
  alternative approaches to, 67–8
  economics linked to culture, 56
  expansion of education and, 42–3
  French Revolution as, 25–6

new, 67–9
see also geoculture of liberalism; world polity
geographical division of disciplines, 63–4
German Idealism, 101, 111. see also Hegel; Kant
global capital/ism, 2, 6, 161. see also capital; capitalist world-system
global citizenship, 95, 97
global financial crisis (GFC), 60, 94, 161
global transition and crises, 28–32, 49–51, 77–8, 160–2
  absolute limits and asymptotes, 28–32
  collapse of capitalist world-system, 77
  ecological, 80
  economic, 1, 60, 93–4, 161
  holistic view/unidisciplinary, 5
  nation-states response to, 93–4
  period of heightened free will, 38–9
  responses to, 1–3, 7
global warming, 3, 30, 65, 69, 161
globalization, 35–7. see also neoliberalism
"good citizens," 130, 138
good, searching for, 76, 88–9, 113–16, 138
Gramscian view of hegemony, 8, 99
Great Britain. See United Kingdom

Habermas, 100, 119, 141–2
happiness, 116
Hegel, 105, 108–9, 113, 138–9. see also objectivation
hegemony
  in capitalist world-economy, 19, 24–5, 164
  cultural resistance and, 59
  European, 88
  in geoculture of liberalism, 67–8
  Gramscian view of, 8, 99

mass education and, 53–4, 58, 72
Heidegger, M., 103, 124, 137–41
Heller, Agnes, 101–4, 106–7, 109–10, 113–16, 120, 125, 132–40, 144–52
  departure from, and return to, teaching, 116–17
  on emancipation. (see emancipation)
  on everyday life. (see everyday life)
  move away from Marxism, 133–4
  philosophical anthropology and. (see philosophical anthropology)
historical capitalism. See capitalism
historical change, 145–6
historical communism, 31
historical determinism, 120
historical development of societies, 4
historical materialism, 106, 128
historical social sciences, 4–5, 34–5, 73
historical socialism, 79
  alternative interpretation of, 15–16
  collapse of geoculture of liberalism, 31
  human capital theory and, 44
  interstate system and, 25
  school education, 82
  see also socialism
historical variability, 139
historicity, 103–4, 156
history, 33
  accidentality of, 120
  laws of the process of, 104
  role of, 105
homeostasis, 154–5
hope, 16, 163–4
Horthy, Admiral, 109
human agency. See agency and action; community and collectivity
human beings. See individuals

human capital theory, 5–6, 52, 93–5
  mass education, 39, 54, 65
  role in educational policy, 43–4, 52
  workforce skills and, 43–4
human experience/activity. See everyday life
human nature, 100
  "first nature" and "second nature," 152
  innate human propensities, 150–6
  science of the human condition, 135–6
  see also philosophical anthropology; species-essential individual
human rights and education, 42–3, 82–3, 87
humanism
  emancipation and, 113–15
  see also Budapest School
humanity's relationship to the world, 101–5, 107, 111. see also contingency; dialectics; everyday life; praxis
humanization, 115, 117–18
  of everyday life, 135, 137
Hungarian Communists, 109–10, 113, 116, 122

ideal forms (Plato), 102–3
ideal polis (Aristotle), 116, 138
identity construction, 76
ideologies, struggle between, 26–7
idiographic epistemology, 45, 61–4
  "historical social sciences," 35
  reintegrating, 89
imagining the future, 37, 72–3, 76, 79, 164
immanent critique, 144–8, 158
inclusion. See equality
independent thinking, 115
individuals
  autonomy of, 115
  bourgeois society and, 124–5
  constraints on, 124–5
  in contrast to "particularist person," 139–40
  focus of analysis, 158
  free development of, 115–16, 125–6, 147–8. (see also emancipation)
  instincts and feelings of. (see instincts and feelings)
  needs and values of. (see needs and values)
  problem of, 132–3
  realization of capabilities/potential, 115–16, 135, 140, 142, 145, 150, 152–3, 155–7
  reproduction of the person, 137–8
  sociological inquiry, 118
  see also human nature; self.; social conditioning; species-essential individual
inductive approach to classifying capitalism, 48–9
industrial revolution, 2, 9, 99, 143
inequalities, 58
  in capitalist world-economy, 18–19, 127
  citizenship and, 96–7
  cultural status and, 87–8
  freedom versus, 124–5
  legitimized by dominant group, 58
  meritocracy within the capitalist world-economy, 46
  power over decision-making, 123
  rules and norms and, 130
  social inequalities, 6–7, 45–6
  unequal exchange and development, 21–3, 37, 65
  universalism and, 55–6, 59
  see also disadvantaged individuals and groups; discrimination; equality
innate human propensities, 150–1
instincts and feelings, 151–3

integrated curriculum, 86
intellectual work, 37–8, 87. *see also* academics and educators
interests. *See* class interests
international agencies and agreements, 68
citizenship rhetoric, 97
international capitalism. *See* global capital/ism
international crises. *See* global transition and crises
international education. *See* comparative and international education
international trade. *See* trade
interstate system
  in capitalist world-economy, 23–5
  defined, 23–4
  world polity and, 67
  see also nation-states
investment. *See* return on investment for education

justice, 130

Kant, 109, 112–13, 115, 125
Kierkegaard, 102–3
knowledge
  disciplines. (*see* disciplines)
  universal. (*see* universal knowledge)
  WSA as a knowledge movement, 32–7
Kun, Béla, 109

labor, 131
  labor control, 16–17
  see also division of labor; mass labor; workforce
"language of possibility and hope," 163–5
Latin America, 68, 81
liberalism, 61, 64–5, 69
  centrist liberalism, 24–8, 31–2
  extreme liberalism, 84
  see also geoculture of liberalism; neoliberalism
liberation, 96–7, 113, 130, 140
"life world," 141
lifelong education. *See* adult and lifelong education
linear developmentalism, 27, 51–2, 54, 59, 61
local relevance in curriculum content, 86–7, 92–3
Lukács, Georg, 100, 104–6, 109, 111, 113, 120, 125, 140, 150. *see also* Budapest School

market economies. *See* free market economies
Marxism-Leninism
  Budapest School. (*see* Budapest School)
  capitalist world-economy and, 15, 17, 19–20
  collapse of geoculture of liberalism and, 32
  critical Marxism, 100–1
  critical pedagogy, 71
  existentialism and, 116
  French Revolution and, 26–7
  historical determinism, 120
  human capital theory and, 44
  international division of labor and, 23
  interstate system and, 24
  lack of freedom in, 111–12
  modernization theories and, 33
  moral Marxism, 111–17
  organizing categories, 114–15, 120
  orthodox. (*see* orthodox Marxism)
  phenomenon of mass schooling, 53
  philosophy, 109
  practical implications, 107. (*see also* praxis)
  proletarianized labor, 48–9
  renaissance of, 112, 118, 124, 133, 158

Marxism-Leninism—*Continued*
  social change and ethical questions, 113
  social theory. (*see* social theory)
  transition to an uncertain alternative world-system, 78
  unequal exchange and development and, 23
  world-systems analysis and, 28
  see also socialism
Marxist view of human alienation, 119, 121–2, 140, 146, 164
Marx's eleventh thesis on Feuerbach, 108
mass education, 42–7, 54, 56, 71
  in the capitalist world-system, 39–66
  citizens and, 95–7
  conclusions, 159, 161, 165
  contesting the dominant narratives, 91–2
  cultural framework for, 52–4
  directed to the dilemmas that confront the world, 90
  disciplinary divisions and, 60–4
  general support for, 61
  global dimensions of, 7, 52–3
  human capital theory, 54, 65
  loyal citizens, 95–7
  organization of, 81
  politicized pedagogical practice, 91
  purposes of, 50–4. (*see also* critical pedagogy)
  universal, free, and secular, 81–2
  "unthinking social sciences" and, 33
  work and, 60–5, 119
  see also critical world-systems education
mass labor, 99. *see also* community and collectivity
mass society, 119
material goods, 125–6. *see also* resources
mercantilist strategy, 20–1
meritocracy, 44–6, 56–9, 164
  educational credentials as a commodity, 44
  formation of workers and, 56–60
  see also equality
Mészáros, István
  approach and contributions of, 2–7, 133–4, 159–65
  departure from Hungary, 111
  "traditional" view of collective action, 99
  Wallerstein's work and, 99
meta-narratives, 160–1, 164
Millennium Development Goals (EFA), 42, 81, 85
"minority" groups, 57
mixed economies, 121–2, 129. *see also* radical democracy
modernity, 154
  Budapest School and, 100, 103, 118
  French Revolution and, 25–6
  "genealogy of cultural modernity," 135–6
  principles of equality, democracy, and justice, 98
  work in, 120
modernization theories, 20, 33, 78
moral Marxism, 111–17
moral philosophy
  development of, 111–13, 115
  moral sphere in radical democracy, 133
  morality not to be used for political ends, 116
  revolution and, 110
  right to participate and, 132
  searching for the good, 76, 88–9, 113–16, 138
  universalization of ethical norms, 115
  see also imagining the future; norms
multiple polities
  expansion and, 13–14
  forms of labor control and, 15–17

within an interstate system, 23–5
world-systems analysis and,
  13–17
multiple specific production
  activities. *See* commodity
  chains

Nagy, Imre, 110–12
narratives, 11, 98, 160–1
national development
  alternative approaches to,
    67–9, 79
  formal educational credentials,
    55–60
  particularist conceptions of
    culture and, 55–6
  stages of, 20–1
  unequal exchange and
    development, 21–3, 37, 65
  see also economic development;
    linear developmentalism
nation-states
  deficit discourses, 56, 58–60
  impact of world geoculture
    on, 52
  public education, 42–3, 95–7
  responses to global crises, 94
  see also interstate system
nature–nurture debate, 152, 156
needs and values, 132, 136,
  143–51, 156
  satisfaction of human needs,
    125–6
  social anthropology and, 151–2,
    157–8
  social inquiry and, 117–18
  universal and basic needs, 147–8
  see also norms; value systems
neoliberalism, 36, 46, 60, 93–4,
  159, 164–5
  citizenship and, 97
  dreams and, 73
  school education, 81–2
  universal education and, 84
  see also geoculture of liberalism;
    liberalism

neo-Marxism, 122, 134, 163–4
  critique of modernization
    theory, 74
  see also philosophical
    anthropology
nomothetic epistemology, 45, 61–4
  "historical social sciences," 35
  reintegrating, 89
non-capitalist alternatives, 6–7, 160
  see also alternative world-system
normative principles, 37–8
  calls for action, 159–60
  critical world-systems education,
    89–91
  educational policy outcome, 50–1
  political projects, 37–8, 77
  for unidisciplinary approach, 88
norms, 136
  inequalities and, 130
  social inquiry and, 117–18
  universal norms, 115–16

objectivation, 138–41, 153
organizational structure, 81–5
orthodox Marxism, 109–11, 158
  critique of developmentalism of,
    78–9
  reaction against, 101

pain and suffering, 140, 155
  end to, 130
particularism, 35, 139–40
  "minority" groups, 57
  workforce development and,
    55–9
particular knowledge, 55–7, 89
  critical world-systems education, 87
pedagogical praxis, 164
  bias and hidden curriculum of, 45
  critical world-systems education,
    91–3
  student decision-making power,
    92–3
  see also comparative and
    international education; critical
    pedagogy; education

perfectibility, 139–40
peripheral zones, 20–1
  alternative approaches to integration of, 79
  education in, 94
  surplus transfer away from, 22–3
  textile production and, 29
  world-systems analysis and, 17–21, 29–30, 49–50
philosophical anthropology, 99–100, 134–6, 139, 141, 143–4
  instincts and feelings and, 153–6
  needs and values and, 144–5, 157–8
  see also human nature; social anthropology
philosophy, 101, 149
"philosophy of essence," 107
Plato, 102, 154
Poland, 101
Polanyi, Karl, 123–4, 126
  on global capital, 143
  revision of Marxist economics, 122
  on "tragedy of the commons," 8–9, 143
political issues
  development of political parties, 3
  dismissal of work, 162
  French Revolution and political change, 25–6
  no coercion, 116
  normative political agenda, 76–7
  political place of economic activity, 143
  politically engaged work, 37–8, 78
  politicized pedagogical practice, 70, 91
  repolitisization of the economic sphere, 122
  WSI as a political project, 37
  see also public life
possibility, language of, 163–4
post-industrial world, work in, 119–40

postmodernism, 75–6, 103, 106, 136
post-school education, 81, 83–5
post-structuralism, 75–6
power of decision-making, 123. see also hegemony
practice. See praxis; theory and practice
Prague Spring, 31, 37, 101
praxis, 108–9
  changing social conditions and, 108
  social, 145–6, 156
  see also agency and action; pedagogical praxis; revolutionary praxis
prejudices, 117–18
primary (elementary) schooling, 84–6
  Millennium Development Goals, 42, 81–2, 85
primary resources. See renewable primary resources
private property, 121, 123, 129
problem-based learning, 86–7
productive capacity, 132
profit. See surplus value
project-based education, 86
proletarianization, 29–30, 48–9
property. See private property
protective response, 122–4
Prussia, 24
public education, 42–3
public life, 116
public spending priorities, 83

racism-sexism, 56–9, 88
radical democracy, 121–2, 124, 129–30, 132–3, 157
  moral maxims, 130
radical needs, 148–50
radical social praxis, 145–6
radical transformation, 114. see also revolution
radical universalism, 158
Rákosi, Mátyás, 110–11

rational principles, 98, 115, 157, 160. *see also* democracy; equality; justice
raw material-producing areas, 21
real-life learning (local relevance), 86–7, 92–3
reason. *See* rational principles
"reform Marxism," 3. *see also* Nagy, Imre
reform projects, 162–3
reformist politics, 110
refugees, 60, 96
relations of production, 132
relationship of humans to the world. *See* humanity's relationship to the world
relationships between states. *See* interstate system
remediation, 47
Renaissance. *See* European Renaissance; Marxism-Leninism: renaissance of
renewable primary resources, 30
reproduction of society and of the person, 137–8
resources
  abundance as requirement for freedom, 124–5
  distribution of, 129–31
  see also material goods
return on investment for education, 43–4
"reverse-racism," 59
revolution, 112
  moral position of, 113–15
  see also sacrifice of a generation
"revolutionary critical pedagogy," 76
revolutionary praxis, 76, 107–8
RIC countries (Brazil, Russia, India, China), 49–50
rules, inequalities and, 130
Russian Revolution, 15

sacrifice of a generation, 110, 113–15

Sartre, 103, 115–16, 120, 124, 133, 140–1
  compared to Adorno, 106
schooling. *See* education
science, 135–6
  belief in, 27
  "complexity studies," 35
  science of meritocracy, 45–6
  unequal distribution of power, 45–6
  in unidisciplinary curriculum, 88–9
scientific universalism, 33, 89, 160
secondary school education, 86
  Millennium Development Goals, 42, 81–2, 85
self-creation, 103–4, 136
self-determination, 27, 125
self-development. *See* individuals
self-differentiation, consciousness and, 105
self-knowing freedom, 105
self-realization, 135, 140, 142, 145, 150, 152–3, 155–7
  individuals as autonomous units in, 115–16
self-reflection, 106
self-reproduction of the person, 137–8
semi-peripheral zones
  in capitalist world-economy, 21
  commodity chains and, 22–3
  education in, 94
  unequal exchange and, 22–3
  world-system in transition, 29–30
  world-systems analysis and, 17–21, 49–50
semi-proletarianized workforces, 48–9
sensuality, 108
sexism, 56–9, 88
social and cultural diversity. *See* cultural differences
social anthropology, 134–5, 151–2
  use of term, 151–2
  see also philosophical anthropology

social change, 163
  critical pedagogy and, 70–2, 75–8
  everyday life and, 139, 156
  French Revolution and, 25–6
  needs and values and, 145–6, 149
  utopian dreams and, 72–3
social conditioning, 157–8
  instincts and feelings and, 151, 153–5
  needs and values and, 147–50
social conditions, 112, 137
  analysis of, 102
  praxis and, 108
  responses of social strata to, 120
  transformation of, 114
social construction
  nature of knowledge, 75
  rules and regulations, 120
social criticism, 100–1
social decision-making. *See* decision-making
social democracies, 101, 111–12, 129
social good from education, 83, 93
social groups, 148
social inequalities, 6–7
  of capitalism, 124–5
  educational attainment influenced by, 45–6
social inquiry, value systems and, 117–18
social justice agenda, 46
social life. *See* everyday life
social policy
  education for social organization, 95–7
  expansion of education, 42–3
  social place of economic activity, 143
social praxis, 145–6, 156
social reality, 159–60
  claims to truth, 75
  critical pedagogy and, 70–2, 74–6
  timespace and, 63–4

social relations, 53
social sciences
  construction of, 33–5, 61–4, 73
  Marxist, 109, 150, 159–65
  relationship between value systems and, 117–18
  timespace and, 63–4
  "unthinking social science," 33
  see also historical social sciences
social theory, 109, 112–13, 141, 157–8
  Budapest School and, 119, 121
  emancipatory. (*see* emancipation)
  moral philosophy. (*see* moral philosophy)
  social inequalities of capitalism and, 124
socialism
  alternative world-system, 32, 160
  anti-capitalism and, 128
  class interests in, 121–2
  contemporary circumstances, 117–18, 126
  democratic structures within, 101, 112
  French Revolution and, 26–7
  Latin America, 68, 81
  liberal-socialist variant of, 26–7
  productive capacity in, 132
  "reform" and "revolution," 3
  socialist phase of development, 128–9
  socialist transformation, 131–2
  within world-economy, 15
  see also historical socialism; Marxism-Leninism; radical democracy
"socialist realism," 109
sociography, 112
sociology
  humanizing empiricism, 117–18
  sociology of knowledge, 45
sovereign nation-states. *See* interstate system; nation-states
Soviet societies, 126–7, 129, 132
  class interests in, 121–2

Soviet Union
  collapse of geoculture of liberalism and, 31, 65
  Hungary and, 109–10
Spanish empire, 18–19, 24
species-essential individual, 124, 134–5, 137–8, 144–7, 149–52, 155, 157
Stalinism, 110
state structures
  equality and inclusion and, 96–7
  hegemonic status and, 25
  importance of in capitalist world-economy, 18–19, 36
  for producing surpluses, 19–20, 22
  role in capitalist society, 123, 129–30
  "two-step strategy" for State power, 28
  see also interstate system
structural crises of capitalism, 7
structural determinism, 38
structural timespace, 64
structure versus agency, 38, 46
structuring of knowledge. *See* disciplines
students. *See* education; pedagogical praxis
suffering. *See* pain and suffering
supranational citizenship. *See* global citizenship
surplus labor, alienation and, 122
surplus value
  in capitalist world-economy, 16–17, 19–20, 22–3, 30, 48–9
  economic crises and, 94
  emerging economies and, 50
  see also accumulation of capital; capitalist world-economy
Sweden, 24
"system-immanent" critique, 135
Szelenyi, Ivan, 121, 129

taxation, demands on the state and, 30–1
technical post-school education, 84
temporal division of disciplines, 63–4
textile production, 29
theory and practice, 108, 144, 156
"thing-in-itself," 106
Third-Worldism, 56
"thrownness," 137
timespaces, 63–4
trade
  in capitalist world-economy, 13–14
  commodity chains and. (*see* commodity chains)
  in essential goods, 13–14
  unequal exchange in hidden, 23
  universal desire to develop, 8, 99
"tragedy of the commons," 143
transformation of the world, 67, 165
  curriculum and, 38, 87, 90–1
transformational timespace, 64
transition. *See* global transition and crises
transnational commodity chains. *See* commodity chains
truth, claims to, 75, 88–9

underdevelopment, 20–1, 59–60
unequal exchange and development, 21–3, 37, 65
  hidden, 23
  world-systems analysis and, 21–3
  see also national development
unidisciplinary view, 5, 62–4, 74, 159
  curriculum and, 85–91
United Kingdom, 19–20, 24. *see also* Industrial Revolution
United Nations Universal Declaration of Human Rights, 82–3
United States, 24–5, 31, 36
unity (Badiou), 116
unity (Mészáros), 99–100
universal claims, responses of "minority" groups, 57

Universal Declaration of Human
    Rights, 82–3
universal education, 84
universal knowledge, 35, 55–9,
    62–3, 97, 160
  critical world-systems
    education, 87
  employed for the good, 157
  "eternal timespace," 63–4
  particularizing universal
    claims, 88
  radical universalism, 158
  workforce development
    and, 55–9
universal norms, 115–16
universal values and dispositions,
    148–9
  particular conception of, 57
  promoted by formal education
    systems, 55
universality (Mészáros),
    99–100, 104
university education, free, 83–4
"unthinking social science," 33
utility-maximizing thesis, 119
utopian (utopistic) dreams, 72–3
utopian projects, 16, 79
  critical pedagogy and, 90–2

value systems, 113
  plurality of values, 120
  relationship with the social
    sciences, 117–18
  social inquiry and, 117–18
  values of life and freedom, 112,
    114–15
  see also needs and values; norms
Venezuela, 4, 84, 163
vertical integration, 21, 49
vocation, 82
vocational post-school
    education, 84
Vygotsky's work, 70

wage labor. See labor
Wallerstein, Immanuel
  approach and contributions of,
    2–7, 38–9, 159–65
  Mészáros' work and, 99
  use in critical pedagogy, 72–6
  Wallerstein's world-systems
    analysis. (see world-systems
    analysis)
waste, externalization of costs, 30
welfare states, development of, 31
Western tradition of Marxism,
    106–7, 132, 148
  misunderstandings, 126–8
work
  capitalist world-economy, 47–50
  education as preparation for, 5–6
  link with schooling, 119
  in the post-industrial world,
    119–40
  radicalizing of democracy
    and, 121
  structural requirements for
    capitalism, 49–50
workforce
  class-based occupational
    tracks, 45
  education of workers, 50–5, 60–5
  human capital theory and, 43–4
  meritocracy and, 55–60
world. See humanity's relationship
    to the world
world crises. See global transition
    and crises
world culture theory, 50–4,
    164. see also comparative
    and international education;
    geoculture/world cultural
    framework; human capital
    theory
world polity
  interstate system and, 24, 67
  "myth of progress," 54
  see also geoculture/world cultural
    framework
world-economy, 13
  see also capitalist world-economy;
    socialism

world-empire, distinguished from world-economy, 13
world-systems, stages of development of, 20–1
world-systems analysis (WSA), 11–39, 56, 159
  1968 events, 31, 37, 101
  1989 events, 31, 37, 65
  alternatives assessed using, 76–7. (*see also* alternative world-system)
  broad principles for action, 77
  capitalist. (*see* capitalist world-system)
  centrist liberalism and, 25–8, 31–2
  claims to truth, 75, 88–9
  contemporary conditions, 2–5
  critical pedagogy and, 72–80
  culture and. (*see* geoculture/world cultural framework)
  cyclical trends within longer-term structures, 74
  education and, 38–9
  geoculture of liberalism. (*see* geoculture of liberalism)
  globalization theorizing, 36
  human capital theory and. (*see* human capital theory)
  international education. (*see* comparative and international education)
  institutionalist branch of, 24
  interstate system in, 23–5, 67
  as a knowledge movement, 32–7
  mass education, explanatory framework for the rise of, 52
  multiple polities and, 13–17
  narratives in, 11, 98, 160–1
  period of heightened free will, 38–9
  as politically engaged work, 37–8
  realist approach to citizenship, 95–7
  of socialist states, 15, 17
  transition and crises. (*see* global transition and crises)
  unequal exchange and development, 21–3
  unidisciplinary curriculum and. (*see* unidisciplinary view)
  Wallerstein and. (*see* Wallerstein, Immanuel)
  workers and, 48–55
  zones in. (*see* zones in capitalist world-economy)
world-systems education. See critical world-systems education
world-systems theory
  concept of rejected, 12
  Wallerstein's resistance to claims of, 32–3
WSA. See world-systems analysis

Zhdanov doctrine, 140
zones in capitalist world-economy, 17–21, 49–50
  core. (*see* core zones)
  early establishment of, 22
  economic cycles and, 28–30
  peripheral. (*see* peripheral zones)
  semi-peripheral. (*see* semi-peripheral zones)

GPSR Compliance
The European Union's (EU) General Product Safety Regulation (GPSR) is a set of rules that requires consumer products to be safe and our obligations to ensure this.

If you have any concerns about our products, you can contact us on

ProductSafety@springernature.com

In case Publisher is established outside the EU, the EU authorized representative is:

Springer Nature Customer Service Center GmbH
Europaplatz 3
69115 Heidelberg, Germany

www.ingramcontent.com/pod-product-compliance
Lightning Source LLC
LaVergne TN
LVHW011816060526
838200LV00053B/3809